The Calvin and Hobbes
LAZY SUNDAY BOOK

A Collection of Sunday Calvin and Hobbes Cartoons
by BILL WATTERSON

SPHERE BOOKS LTD

To Rich West

A SPHERE BOOK

First published in Great Britain by Sphere Books Ltd 1990
Reprinted 1990

All characters in this publication are fictitious and any resemblance to real persons, living or dead, is purely coincidental.

ISBN 0 7474 0768 1

Printed and bound in Great Britain by
BPCC Hazell Books
Aylesbury, Bucks, England
Member of BPCC Ltd.

Sphere Books Ltd
A Division of
Macdonald & Co (Publishers) Ltd
Orbit House
1 New Fetter Lane
London EC4A 1AR
A member of Maxwell Macmillan Pergamon Publishing Corporation

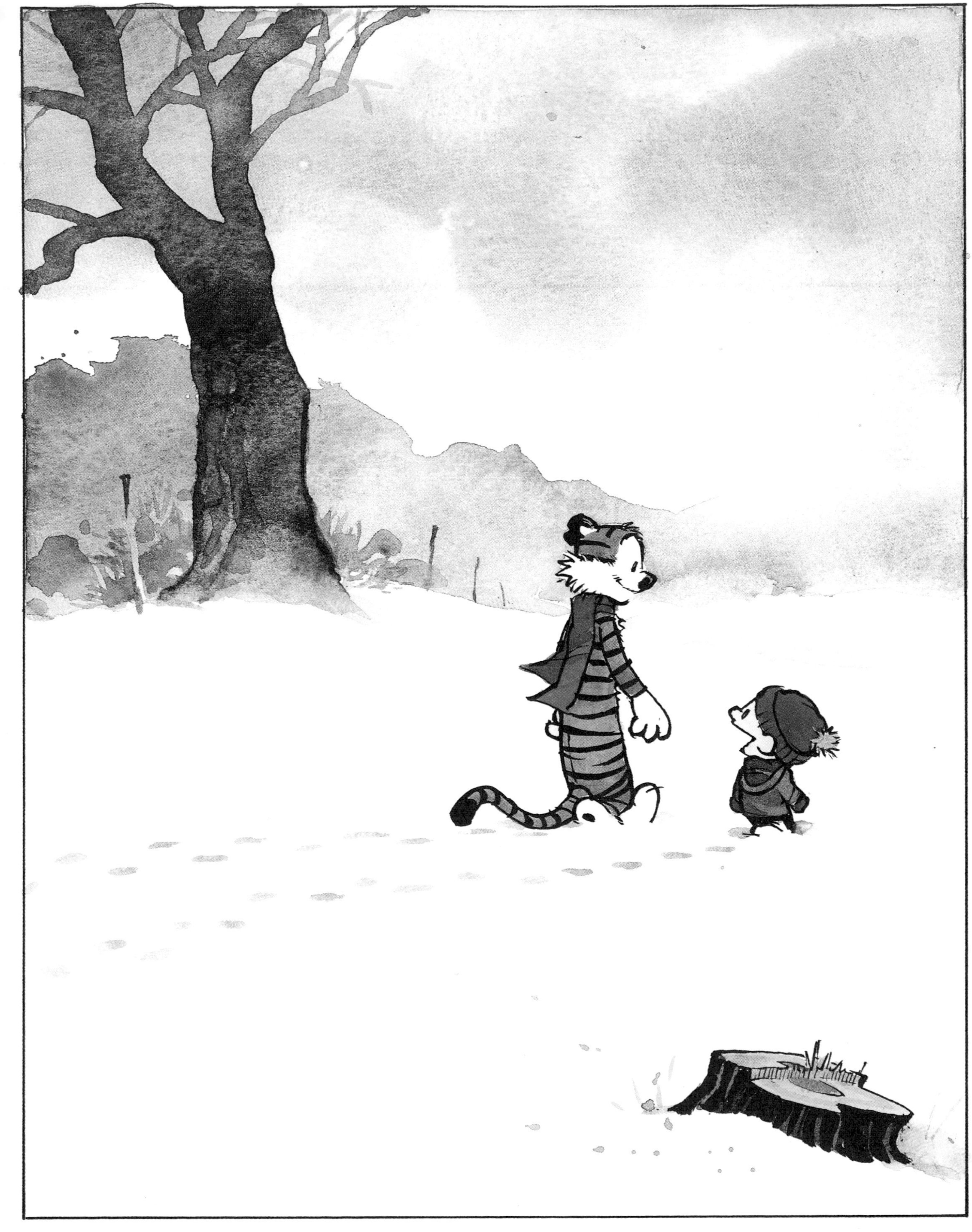

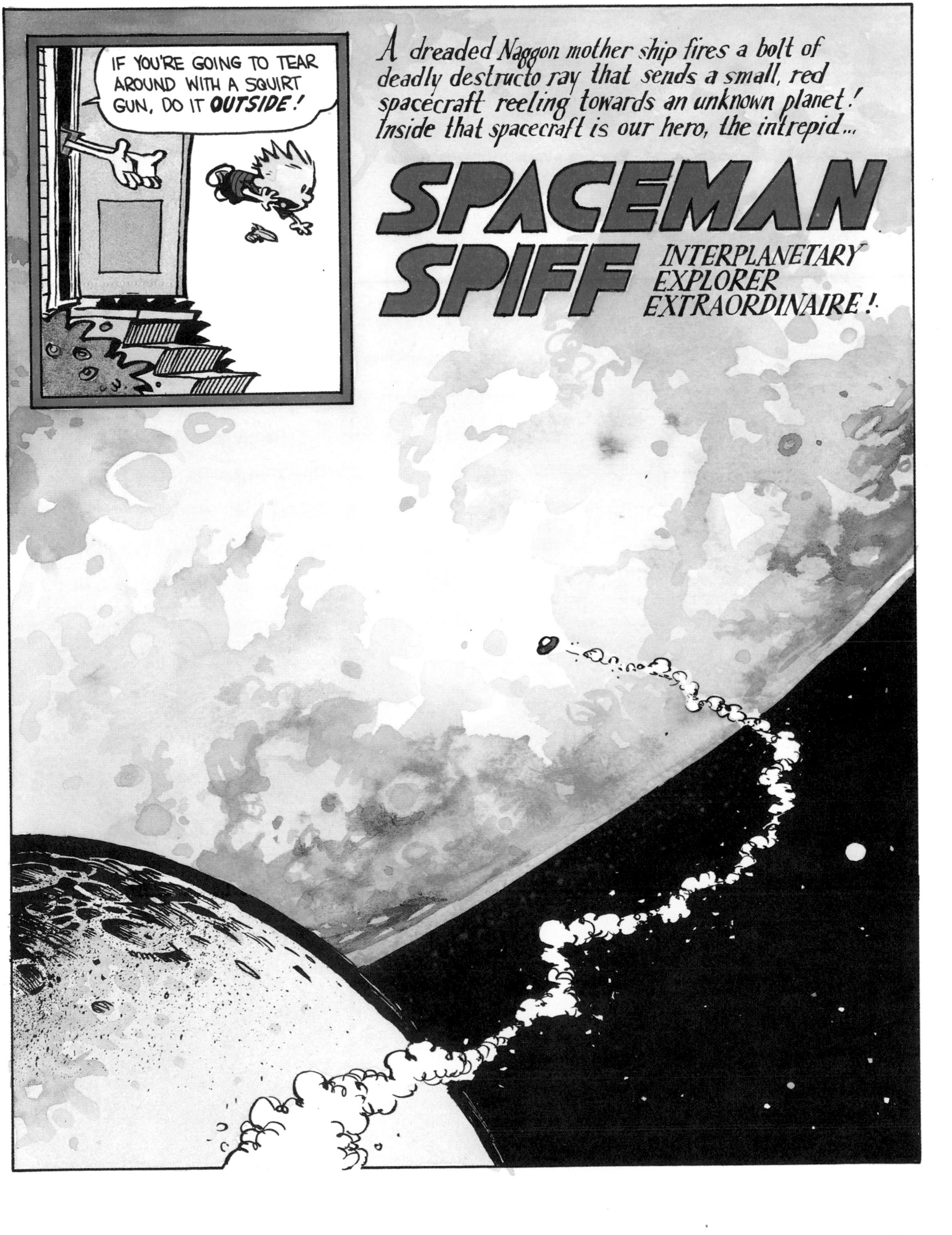
IF YOU'RE GOING TO TEAR AROUND WITH A SQUIRT GUN, DO IT OUTSIDE!
A dreaded Naggon mother ship fires a bolt of deadly destructo ray that sends a small, red spacecraft reeling towards an unknown planet! Inside that spacecraft is our hero, the intrepid...
SPACEMAN SPIFF
INTERPLANETARY EXPLORER EXTRAORDINAIRE!

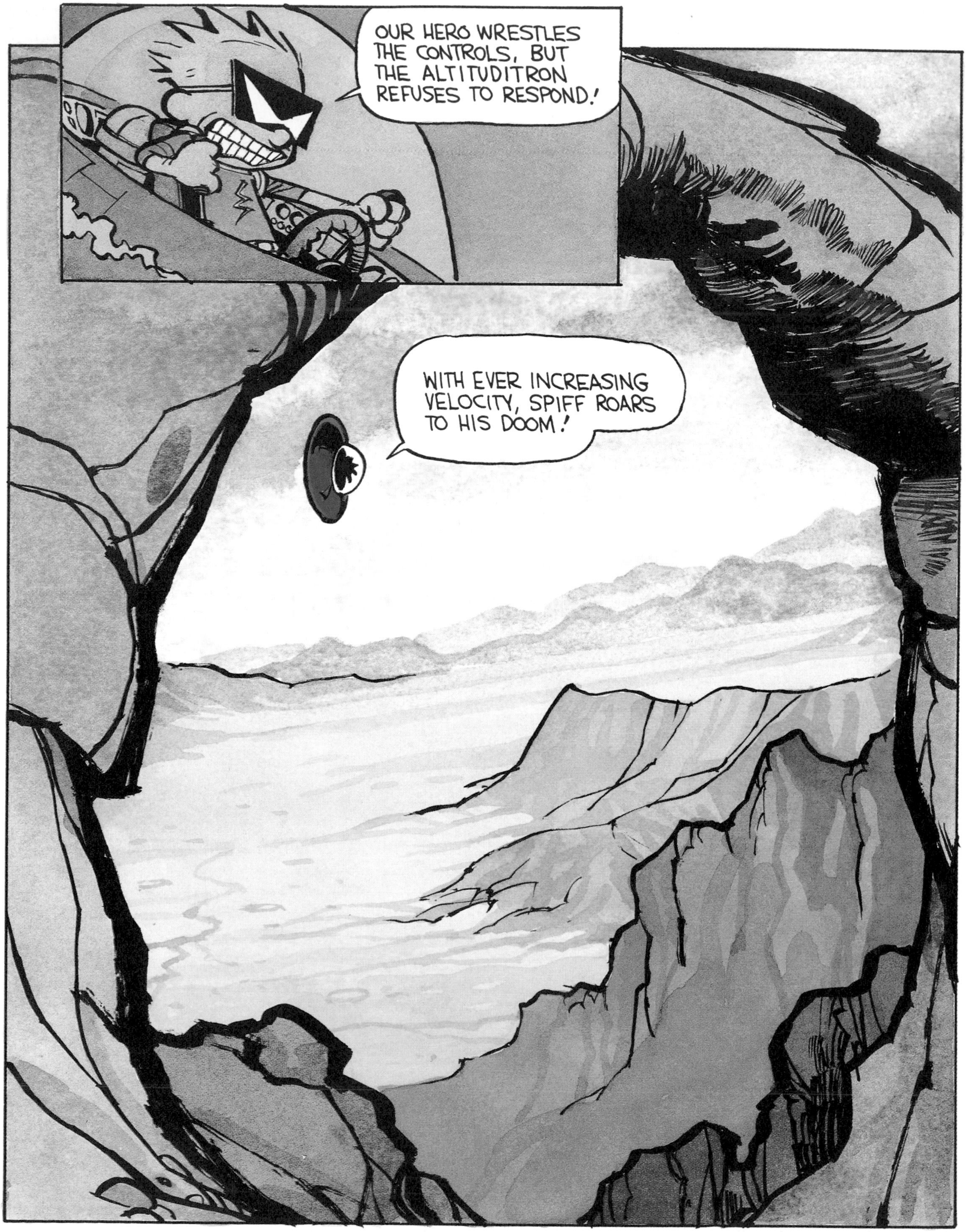
OUR HERO WRESTLES THE CONTROLS, BUT THE ALTITUDITRON REFUSES TO RESPOND!
WITH EVER INCREASING VELOCITY, SPIFF ROARS TO HIS DOOM!

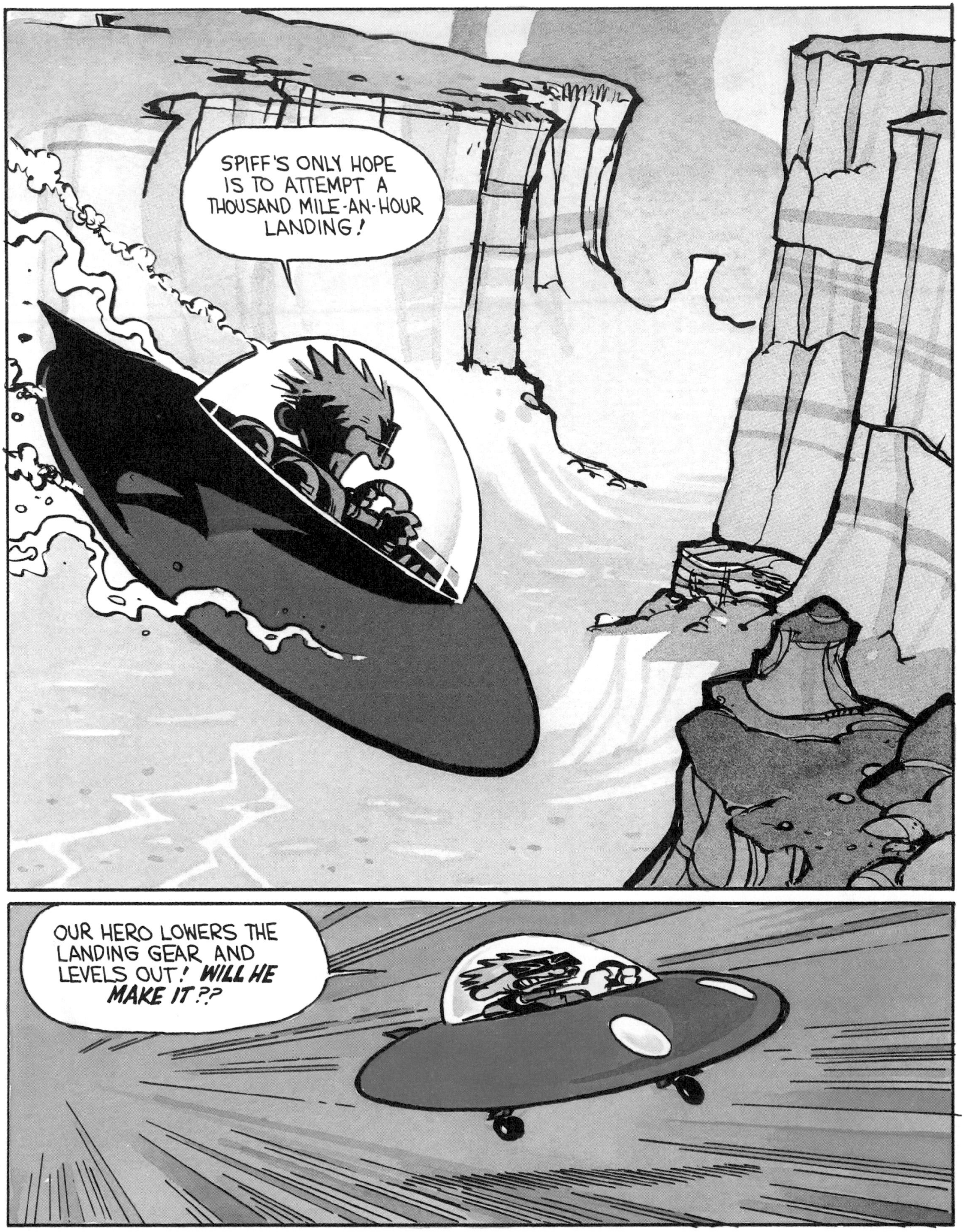
SPIFF'S ONLY HOPE IS TO ATTEMPT A THOUSAND MILE-AN-HOUR LANDING!
OUR HERO LOWERS THE LANDING GEAR AND LEVELS OUT! **WILL HE MAKE IT??**

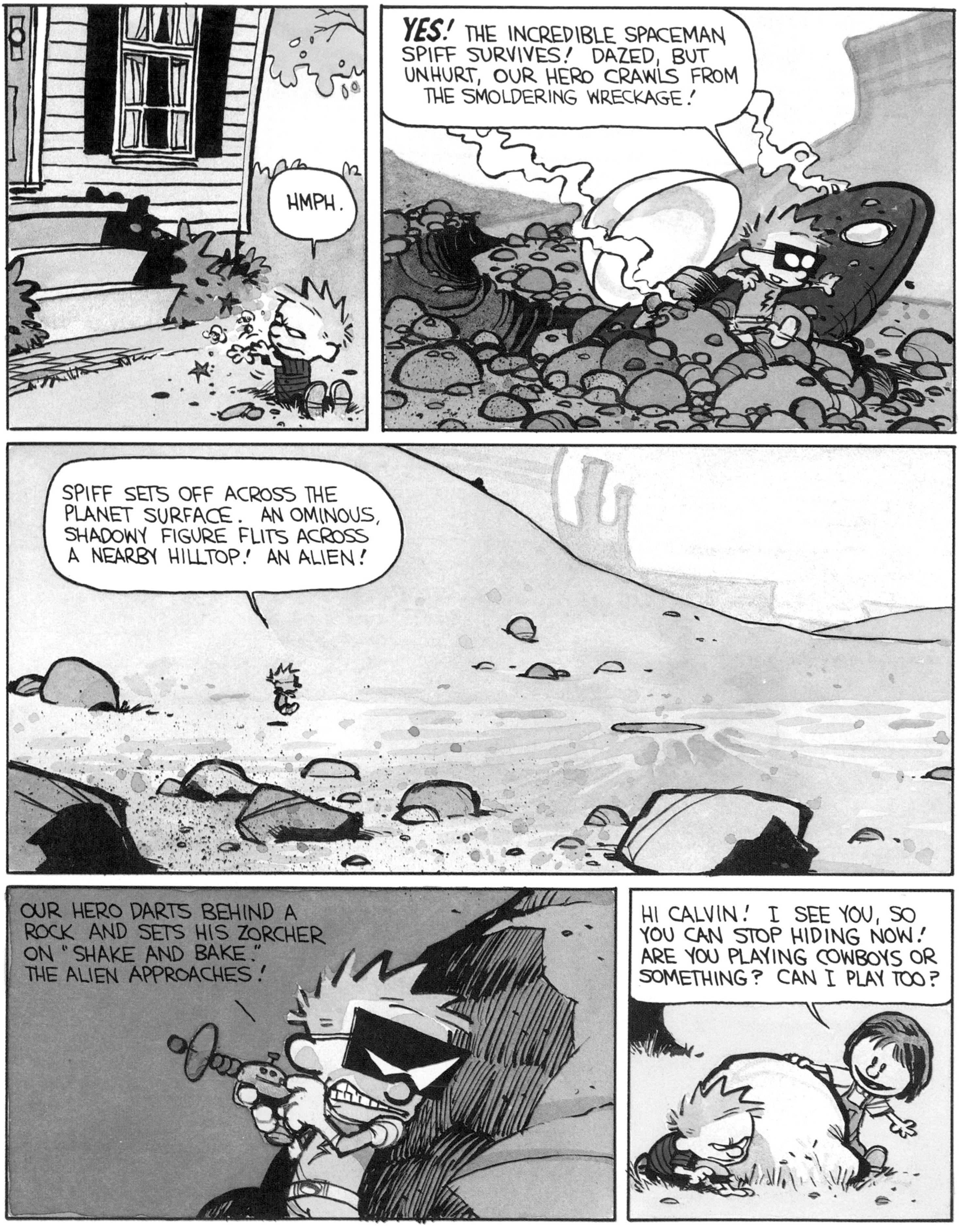
HMPH.
YES! THE INCREDIBLE SPACEMAN SPIFF SURVIVES! DAZED, BUT UNHURT, OUR HERO CRAWLS FROM THE SMOLDERING WRECKAGE!
SPIFF SETS OFF ACROSS THE PLANET SURFACE. AN OMINOUS, SHADOWY FIGURE FLITS ACROSS A NEARBY HILLTOP! AN ALIEN!
OUR HERO DARTS BEHIND A ROCK AND SETS HIS ZORCHER ON "SHAKE AND BAKE." THE ALIEN APPROACHES!
HI CALVIN! I SEE YOU, SO YOU CAN STOP HIDING NOW! ARE YOU PLAYING COWBOYS OR SOMETHING? CAN I PLAY TOO?

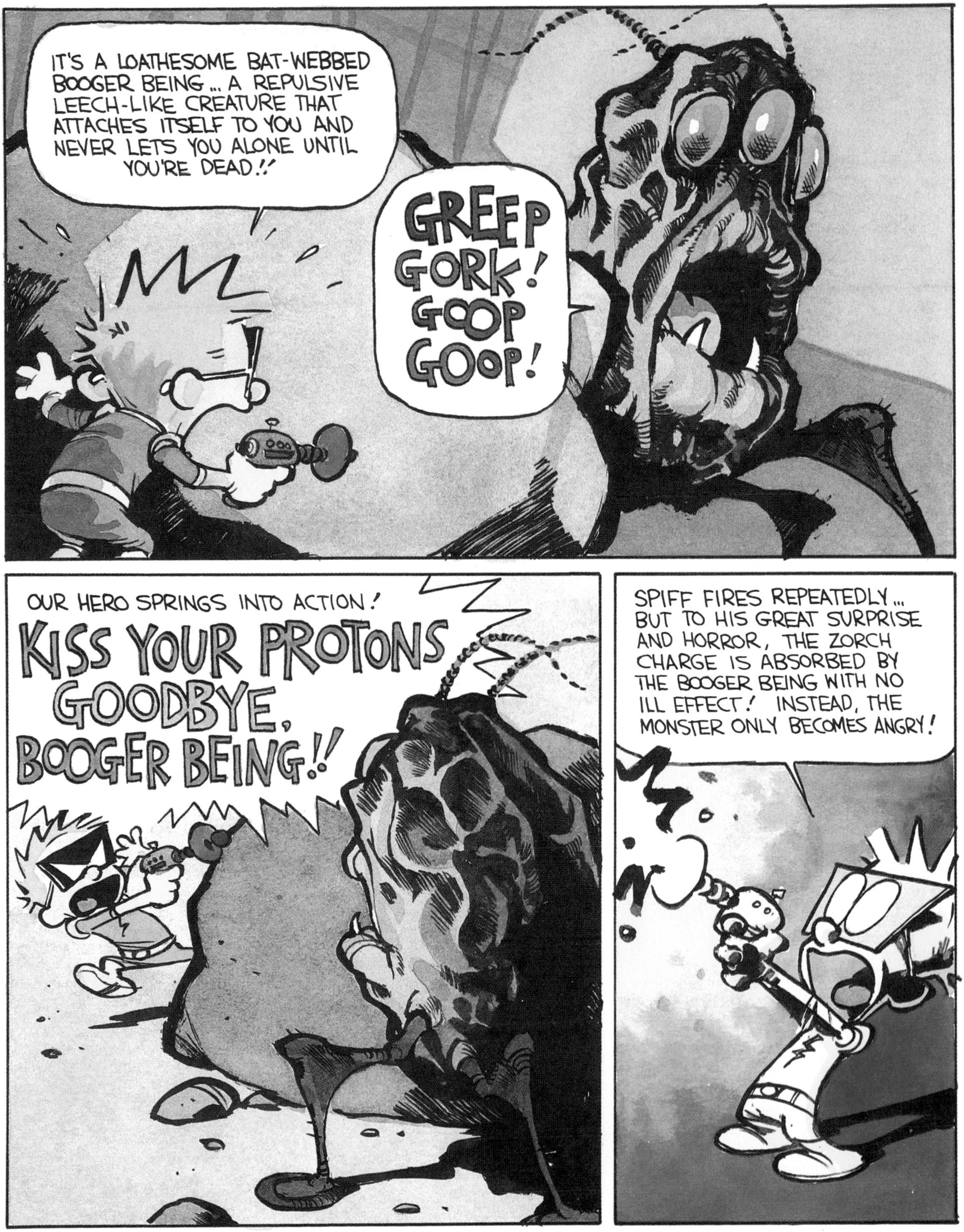

IT'S A LOATHESOME BAT-WEBBED BOOGER BEING ... A REPULSIVE LEECH-LIKE CREATURE THAT ATTACHES ITSELF TO YOU AND NEVER LETS YOU ALONE UNTIL YOU'RE DEAD!!
GREEP GORK! GOOP GOOP!
OUR HERO SPRINGS INTO ACTION!
KISS YOUR PROTONS GOODBYE, BOOGER BEING!!
SPIFF FIRES REPEATEDLY ... BUT TO HIS GREAT SURPRISE AND HORROR, THE ZORCH CHARGE IS ABSORBED BY THE BOOGER BEING WITH NO ILL EFFECT! INSTEAD, THE MONSTER ONLY BECOMES ANGRY!

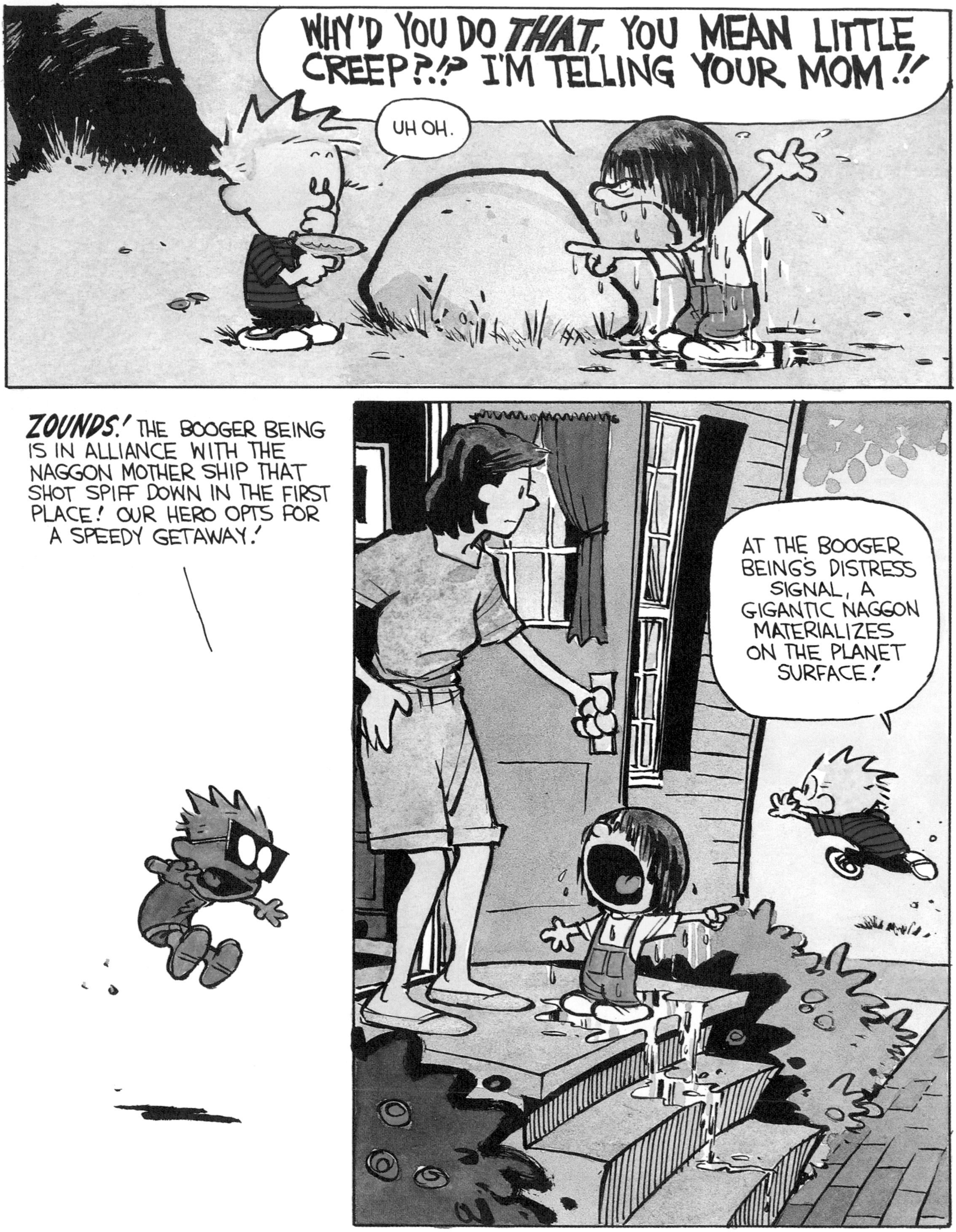
WHY'D YOU DO THAT, YOU MEAN LITTLE CREEP?!? I'M TELLING YOUR MOM!!
UH OH.
ZOUNDS! THE BOOGER BEING IS IN ALLIANCE WITH THE NAGGON MOTHER SHIP THAT SHOT SPIFF DOWN IN THE FIRST PLACE! OUR HERO OPTS FOR A SPEEDY GETAWAY!
AT THE BOOGER BEING'S DISTRESS SIGNAL, A GIGANTIC NAGGON MATERIALIZES ON THE PLANET SURFACE!

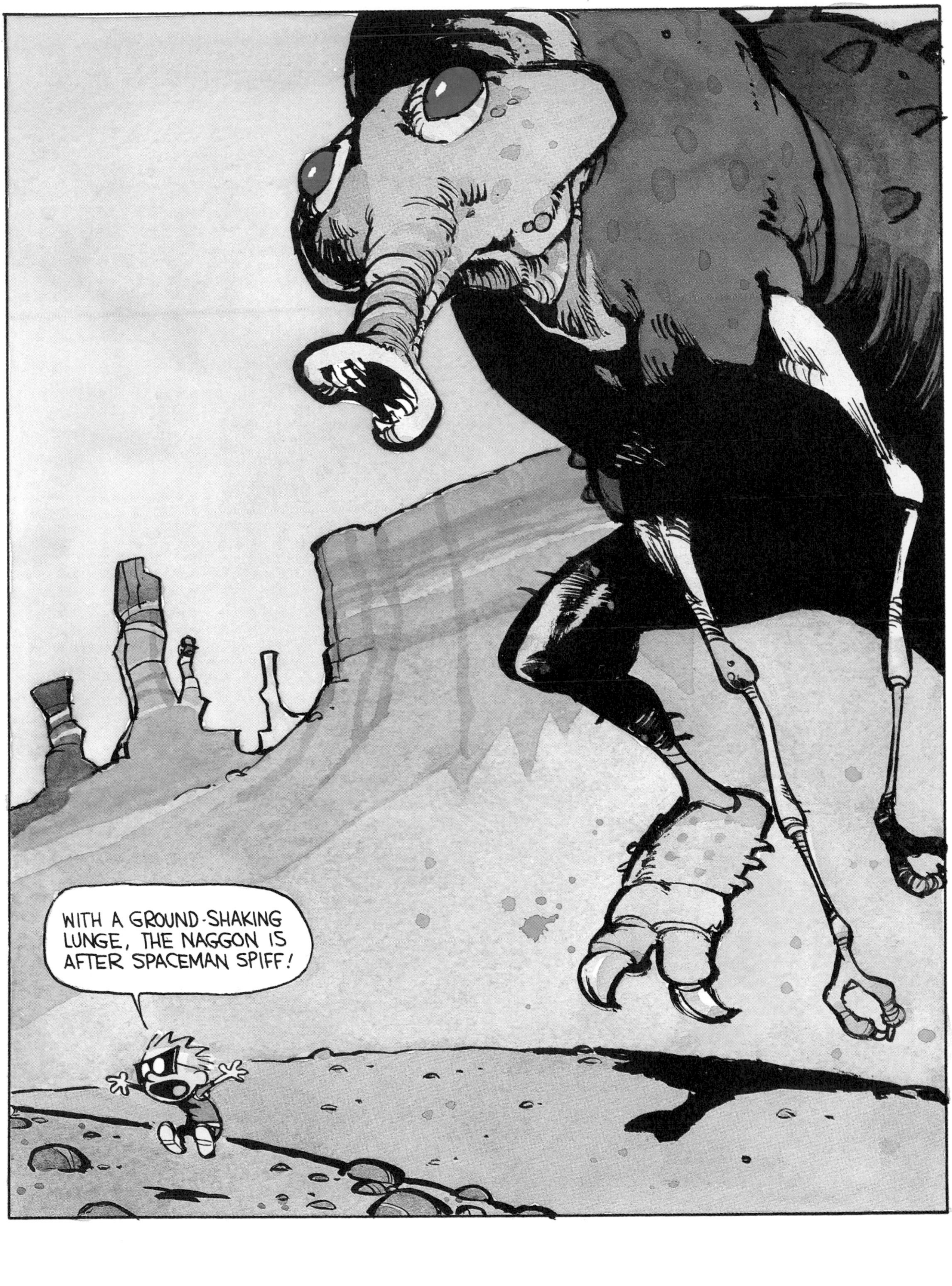
WITH A GROUND-SHAKING LUNGE, THE NAGGON IS AFTER SPACEMAN SPIFF!

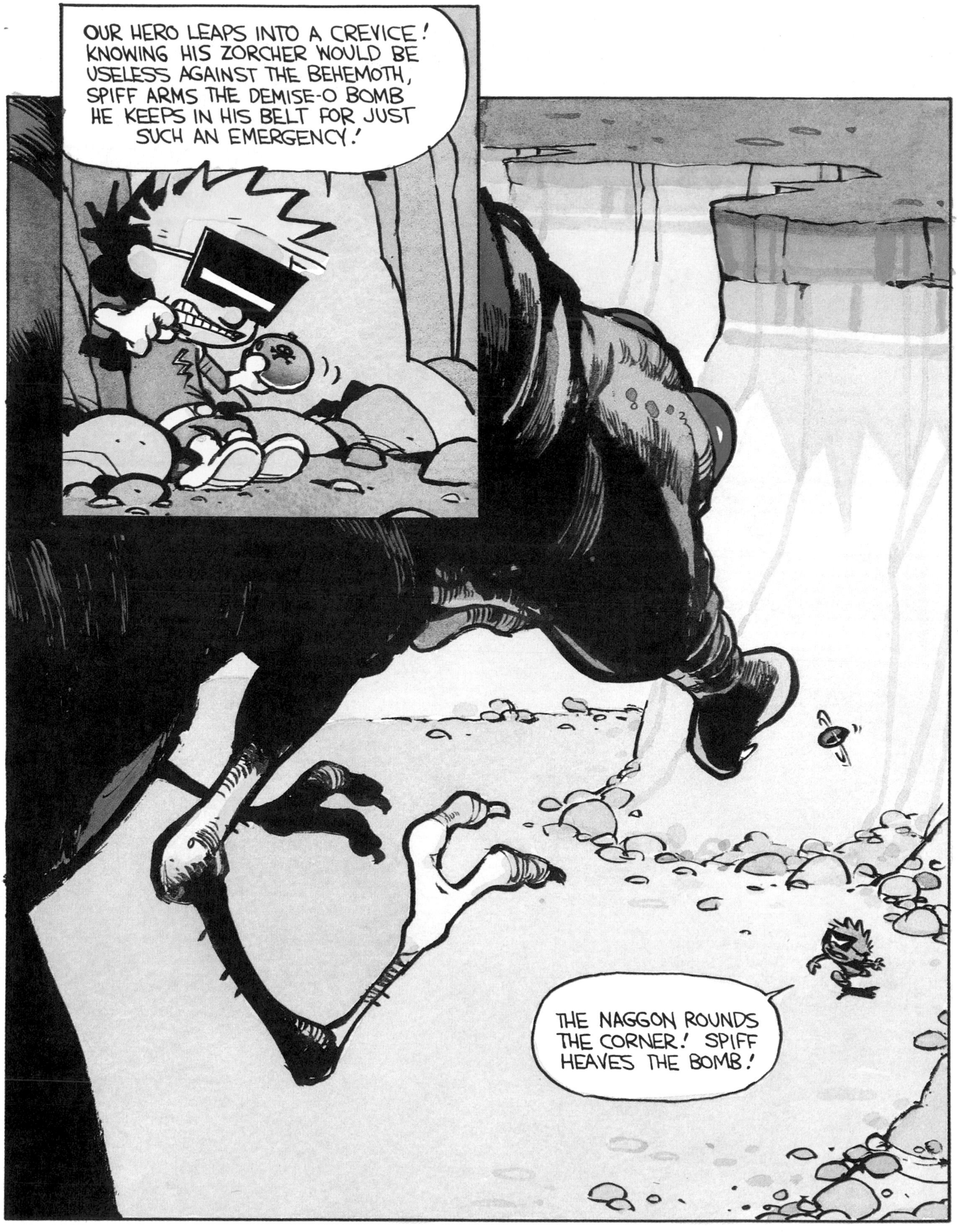
OUR HERO LEAPS INTO A CREVICE! KNOWING HIS ZORCHER WOULD BE USELESS AGAINST THE BEHEMOTH, SPIFF ARMS THE DEMISE-O BOMB HE KEEPS IN HIS BELT FOR JUST SUCH AN EMERGENCY!
THE NAGGON ROUNDS THE CORNER! SPIFF HEAVES THE BOMB!

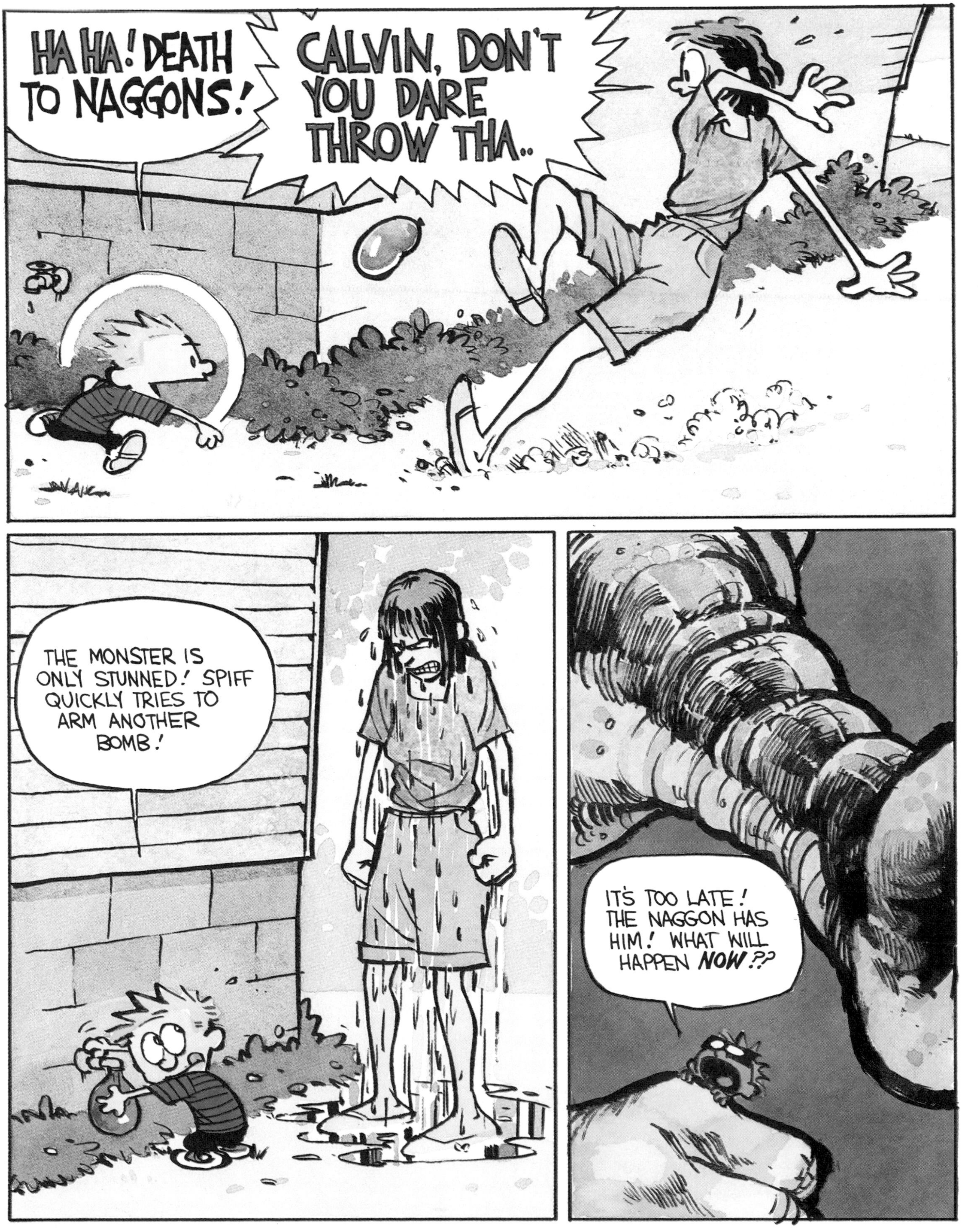
HA HA! DEATH TO NAGGONS!
CALVIN, DON'T YOU DARE THROW THA..
THE MONSTER IS ONLY STUNNED! SPIFF QUICKLY TRIES TO ARM ANOTHER BOMB!
IT'S TOO LATE! THE NAGGON HAS HIM! WHAT WILL HAPPEN NOW?!?

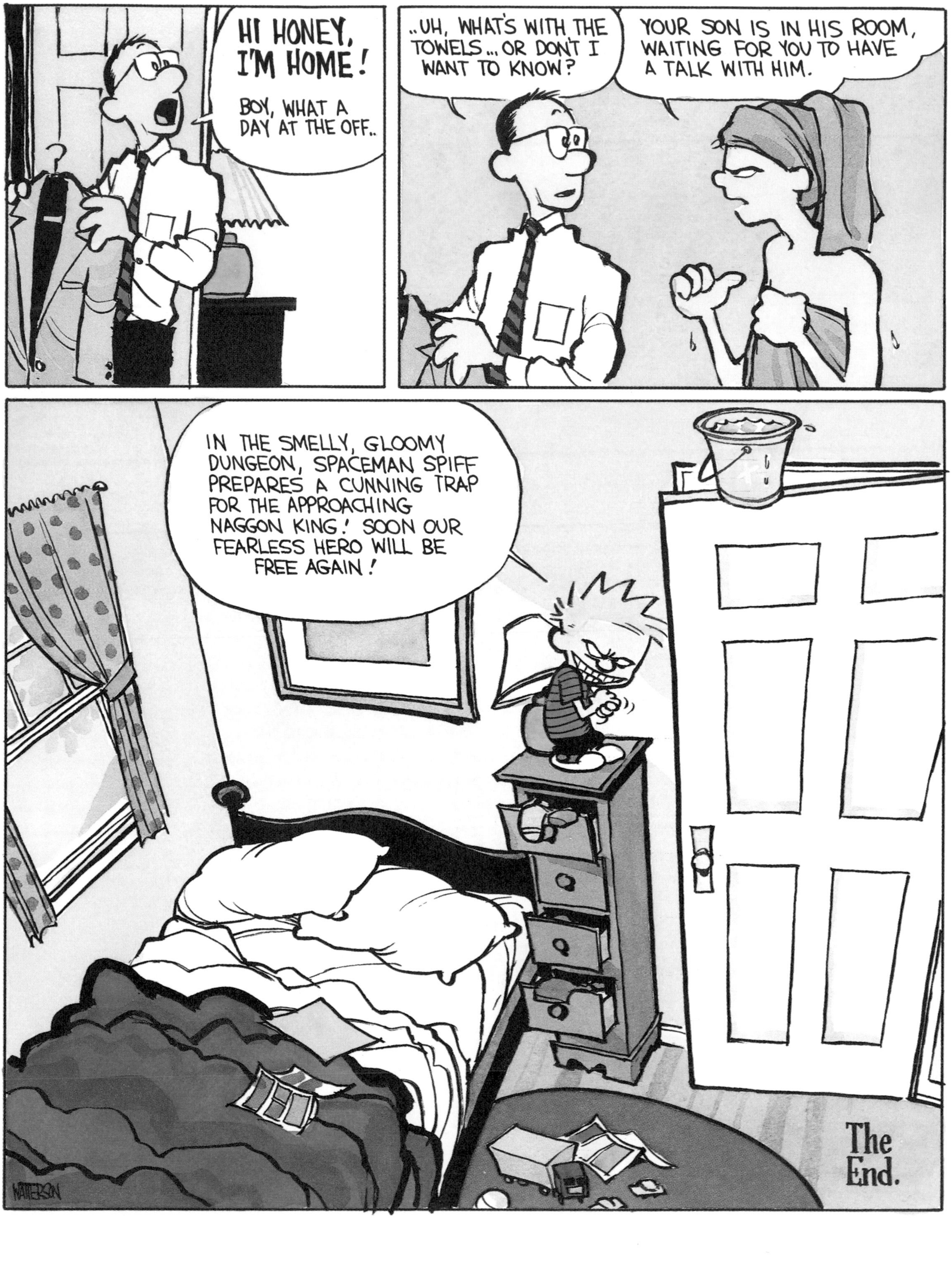
HI HONEY, I'M HOME!
BOY, WHAT A DAY AT THE OFF..
..UH, WHAT'S WITH THE TOWELS... OR DON'T I WANT TO KNOW?
YOUR SON IS IN HIS ROOM, WAITING FOR YOU TO HAVE A TALK WITH HIM.
IN THE SMELLY, GLOOMY DUNGEON, SPACEMAN SPIFF PREPARES A CUNNING TRAP FOR THE APPROACHING NAGGON KING! SOON OUR FEARLESS HERO WILL BE FREE AGAIN!
The End.
WATTERSON

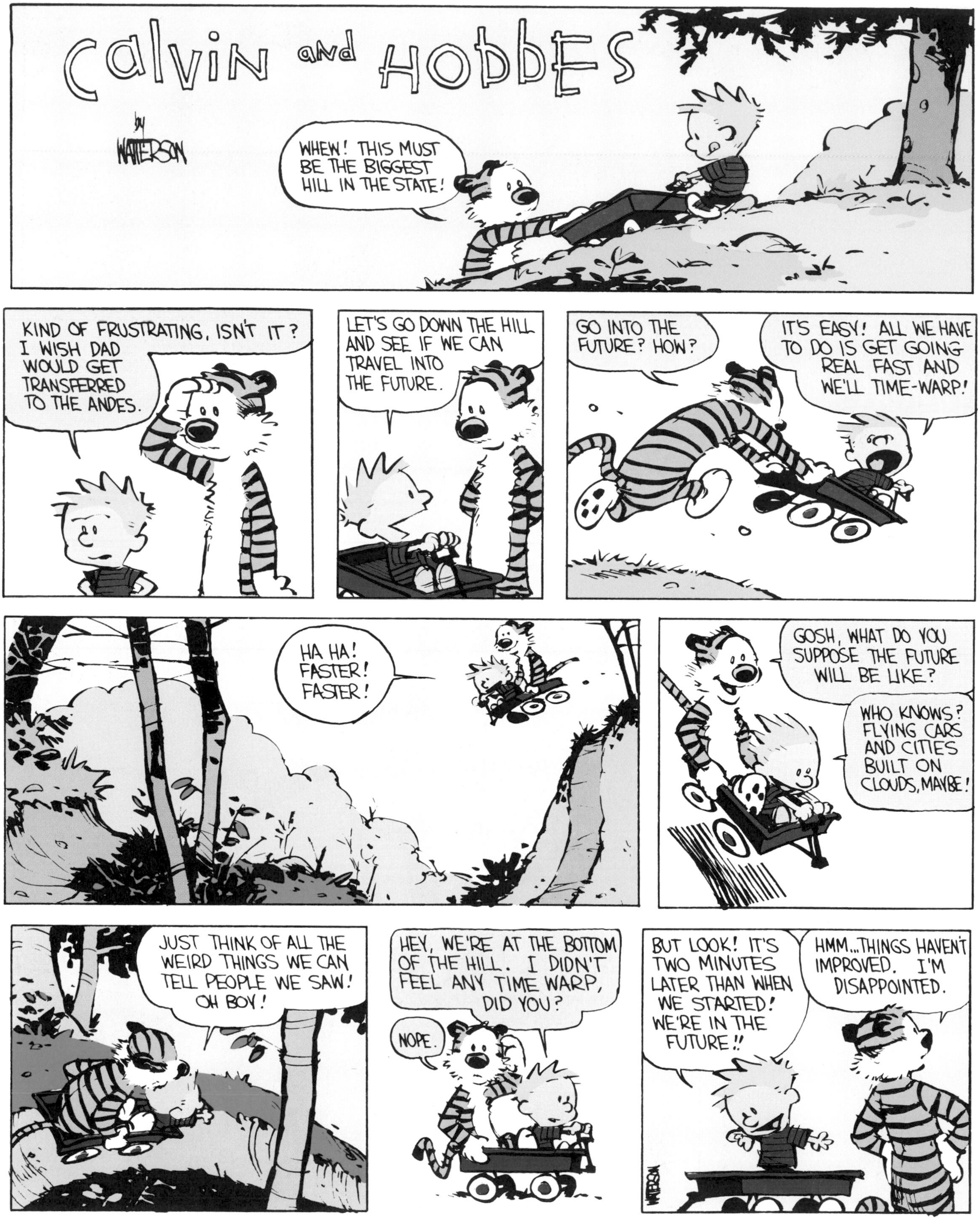
Calvin and HOBBES
by WATTERSON
WHEW! THIS MUST BE THE BIGGEST HILL IN THE STATE!
KIND OF FRUSTRATING, ISN'T IT? I WISH DAD WOULD GET TRANSFERRED TO THE ANDES.
LET'S GO DOWN THE HILL AND SEE IF WE CAN TRAVEL INTO THE FUTURE.
GO INTO THE FUTURE? HOW?
IT'S EASY! ALL WE HAVE TO DO IS GET GOING REAL FAST AND WE'LL TIME-WARP!
HA HA! FASTER! FASTER!
GOSH, WHAT DO YOU SUPPOSE THE FUTURE WILL BE LIKE?
WHO KNOWS? FLYING CARS AND CITIES BUILT ON CLOUDS, MAYBE!
JUST THINK OF ALL THE WEIRD THINGS WE CAN TELL PEOPLE WE SAW! OH BOY!
HEY, WE'RE AT THE BOTTOM OF THE HILL. I DIDN'T FEEL ANY TIME WARP, DID YOU?
NOPE.
BUT LOOK! IT'S TWO MINUTES LATER THAN WHEN WE STARTED! WE'RE IN THE FUTURE!!
HMM...THINGS HAVEN'T IMPROVED. I'M DISAPPOINTED.
WATTERSON

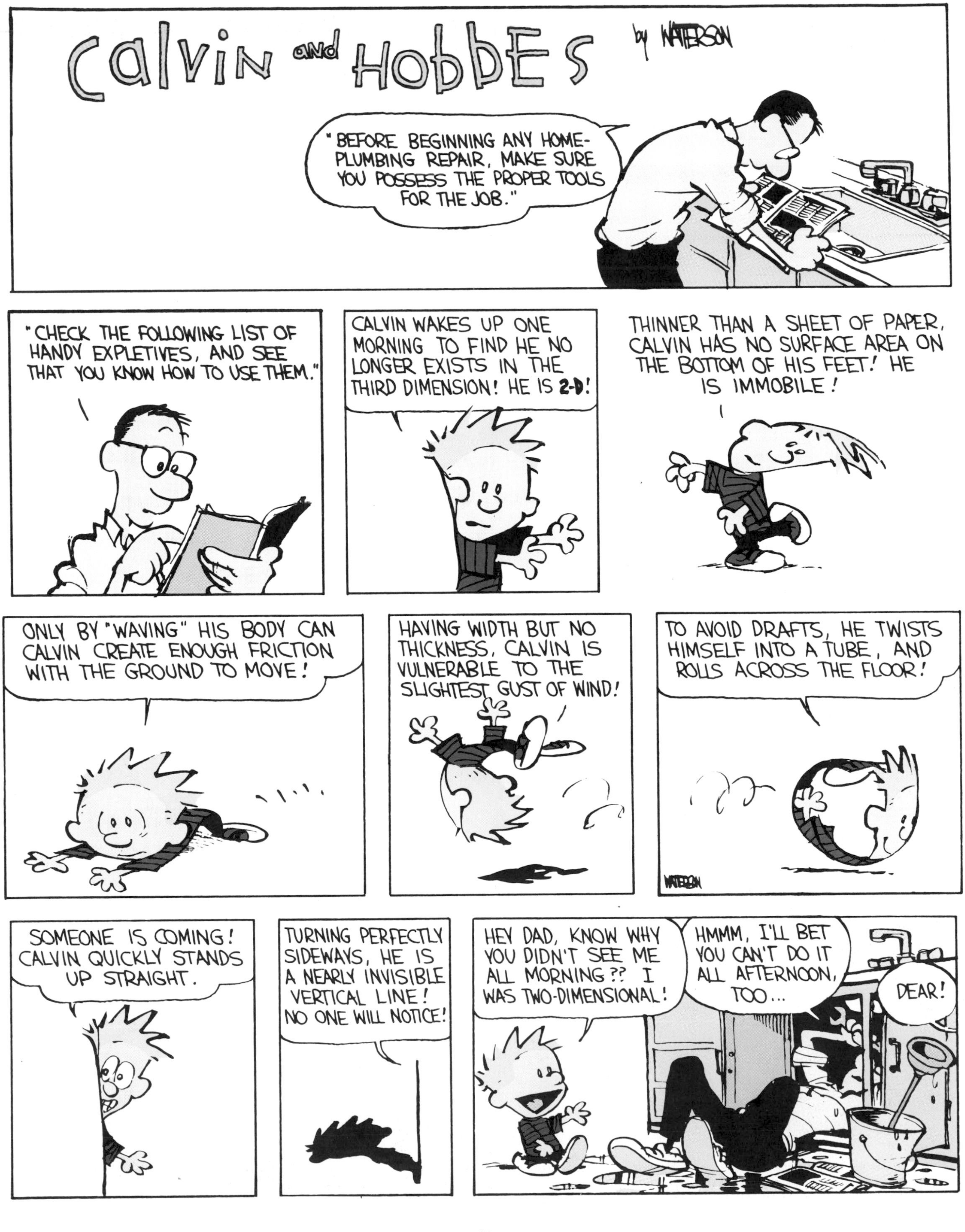
Calvin and HobbEs
by WATTERSON
"BEFORE BEGINNING ANY HOME-PLUMBING REPAIR, MAKE SURE YOU POSSESS THE PROPER TOOLS FOR THE JOB."
"CHECK THE FOLLOWING LIST OF HANDY EXPLETIVES, AND SEE THAT YOU KNOW HOW TO USE THEM."
CALVIN WAKES UP ONE MORNING TO FIND HE NO LONGER EXISTS IN THE THIRD DIMENSION! HE IS 2-D!
THINNER THAN A SHEET OF PAPER, CALVIN HAS NO SURFACE AREA ON THE BOTTOM OF HIS FEET! HE IS IMMOBILE!
ONLY BY "WAVING" HIS BODY CAN CALVIN CREATE ENOUGH FRICTION WITH THE GROUND TO MOVE!
HAVING WIDTH BUT NO THICKNESS, CALVIN IS VULNERABLE TO THE SLIGHTEST GUST OF WIND!
TO AVOID DRAFTS, HE TWISTS HIMSELF INTO A TUBE, AND ROLLS ACROSS THE FLOOR!
WATTERSON
SOMEONE IS COMING! CALVIN QUICKLY STANDS UP STRAIGHT.
TURNING PERFECTLY SIDEWAYS, HE IS A NEARLY INVISIBLE VERTICAL LINE! NO ONE WILL NOTICE!
HEY DAD, KNOW WHY YOU DIDN'T SEE ME ALL MORNING?? I WAS TWO-DIMENSIONAL!
HMMM, I'LL BET YOU CAN'T DO IT ALL AFTERNOON, TOO...
DEAR!

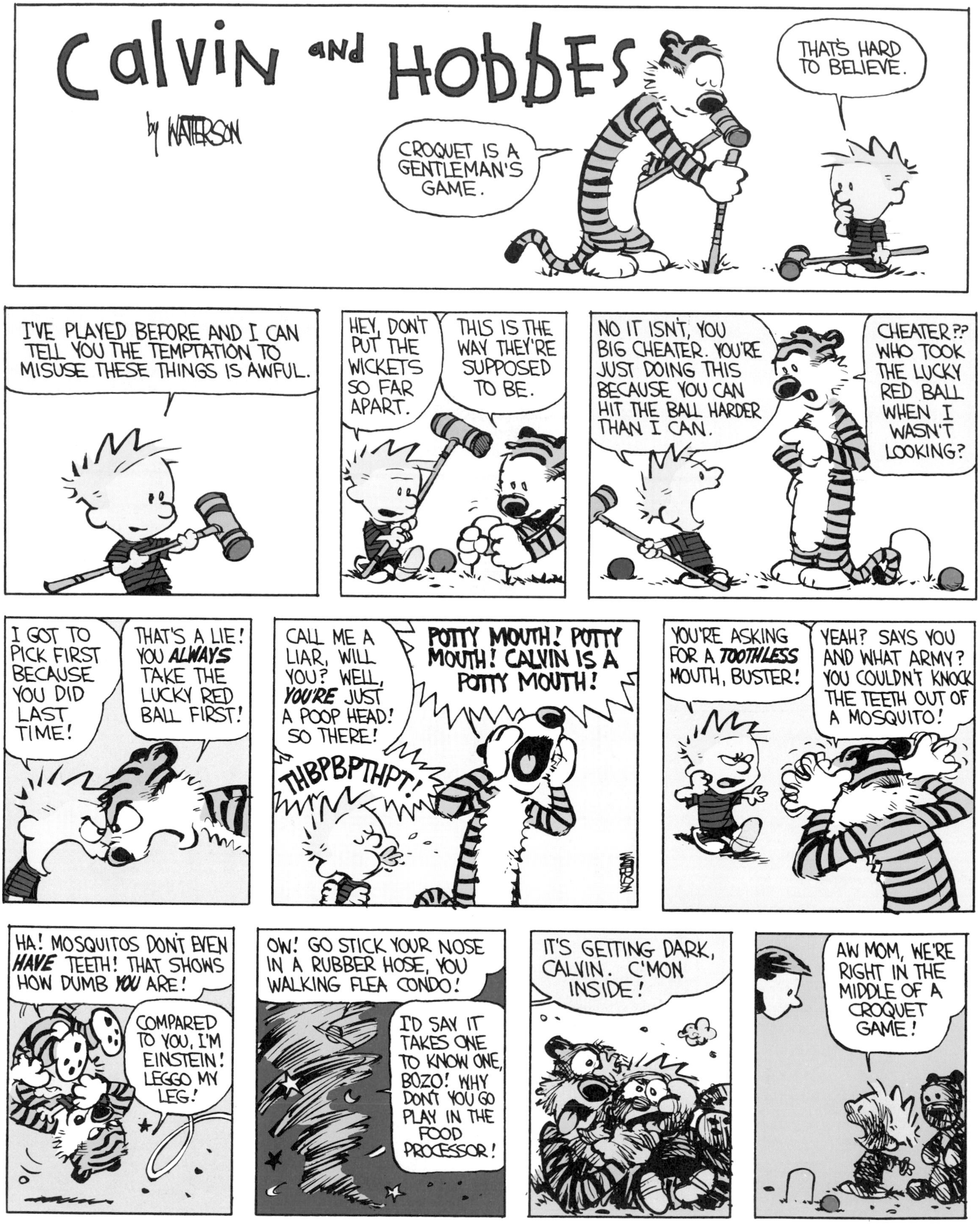
Calvin and HOBBES
by WATTERSON
CROQUET IS A GENTLEMAN'S GAME.
THAT'S HARD TO BELIEVE.
I'VE PLAYED BEFORE AND I CAN TELL YOU THE TEMPTATION TO MISUSE THESE THINGS IS AWFUL.
HEY, DON'T PUT THE WICKETS SO FAR APART.
THIS IS THE WAY THEY'RE SUPPOSED TO BE.
NO IT ISN'T, YOU BIG CHEATER. YOU'RE JUST DOING THIS BECAUSE YOU CAN HIT THE BALL HARDER THAN I CAN.
CHEATER?? WHO TOOK THE LUCKY RED BALL WHEN I WASN'T LOOKING?
I GOT TO PICK FIRST BECAUSE YOU DID LAST TIME!
THAT'S A LIE! YOU ALWAYS TAKE THE LUCKY RED BALL FIRST!
CALL ME A LIAR, WILL YOU? WELL, YOU'RE JUST A POOP HEAD! SO THERE!
POTTY MOUTH! POTTY MOUTH! CALVIN IS A POTTY MOUTH!
THBPBPTHPT!
WATTERSON
YOU'RE ASKING FOR A TOOTHLESS MOUTH, BUSTER!
YEAH? SAYS YOU AND WHAT ARMY? YOU COULDN'T KNOCK THE TEETH OUT OF A MOSQUITO!
HA! MOSQUITOS DON'T EVEN HAVE TEETH! THAT SHOWS HOW DUMB YOU ARE!
COMPARED TO YOU, I'M EINSTEIN! LEGGO MY LEG!
OW! GO STICK YOUR NOSE IN A RUBBER HOSE, YOU WALKING FLEA CONDO!
I'D SAY IT TAKES ONE TO KNOW ONE, BOZO! WHY DON'T YOU GO PLAY IN THE FOOD PROCESSOR!
IT'S GETTING DARK, CALVIN. C'MON INSIDE!
AW MOM, WE'RE RIGHT IN THE MIDDLE OF A CROQUET GAME!

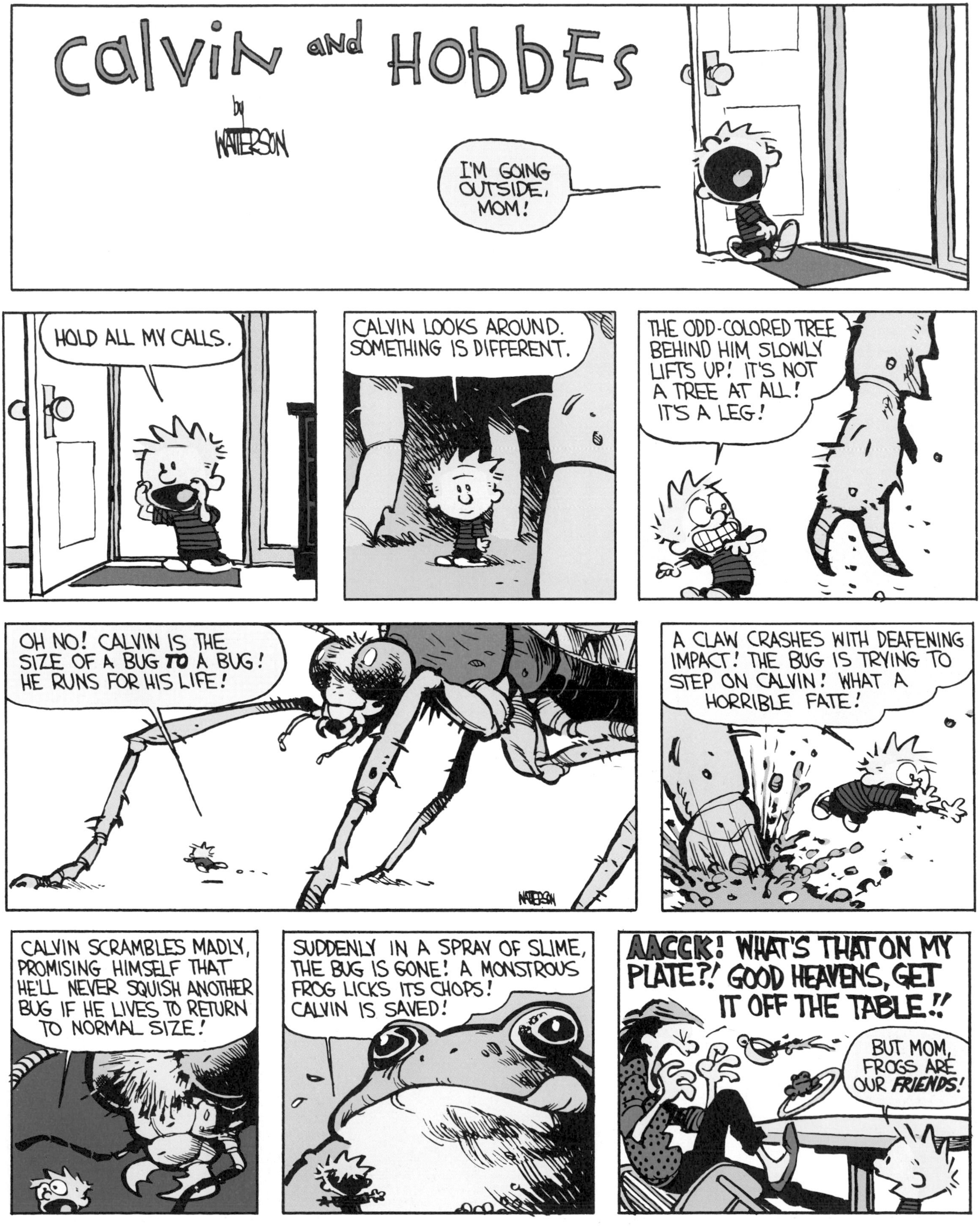
Calvin and HOBBES
by WATTERSON
I'M GOING OUTSIDE, MOM!
HOLD ALL MY CALLS.
CALVIN LOOKS AROUND. SOMETHING IS DIFFERENT.
THE ODD-COLORED TREE BEHIND HIM SLOWLY LIFTS UP! IT'S NOT A TREE AT ALL! IT'S A LEG!
OH NO! CALVIN IS THE SIZE OF A BUG TO A BUG! HE RUNS FOR HIS LIFE!
WATTERSON
A CLAW CRASHES WITH DEAFENING IMPACT! THE BUG IS TRYING TO STEP ON CALVIN! WHAT A HORRIBLE FATE!
CALVIN SCRAMBLES MADLY, PROMISING HIMSELF THAT HE'LL NEVER SQUISH ANOTHER BUG IF HE LIVES TO RETURN TO NORMAL SIZE!
SUDDENLY IN A SPRAY OF SLIME, THE BUG IS GONE! A MONSTROUS FROG LICKS ITS CHOPS! CALVIN IS SAVED!
AACCK! WHAT'S THAT ON MY PLATE?! GOOD HEAVENS, GET IT OFF THE TABLE!!
BUT MOM, FROGS ARE OUR FRIENDS!

CaLViN and HobbEs by WATTERSON

OY OH BOY OH BOY OH BOY OH BOY OH BOY OH BOY OH BOY OH BOY OH BOY

WAIT! WAIT! I'VE GOT TO SAVOR THIS MOMENT! THE BRILLIANCE OF IT ALL! I'M A GENIUS! A SHEER *GENIUS!*

SUSIE'S PLAYING ON THE SIDEWALK! NOW'S MY CHANCE TO USE THE SNOW-BALL I'VE BEEN SAVING IN THE FREEZER!

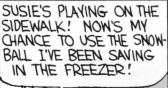

SHE'LL NEVER EXPECT A SNOW-BALL IN *JUNE!* BOY, WILL SHE BE MAD! HA HA HA!

THIS IS GOING TO BE GREAT! HERE IT COMES! OH BOY! OH BOY!

HEY SUSIE!!

PIFF

I *MISSED!* DARN IT DARN IT DARN IT!! OF ALL THE MISERABLE LUCK!

AAARRGHH!

THERE MUST'VE BEEN A CROSS BREEZE! I CAN'T BELIEVE IT! I SAVED THAT SNOWBALL FOR THREE WHOLE MONTHS! I...

SCOOP SCOOP

I.. I...UH...

POW

THE IRONY OF THIS IS JUST SICKENING.

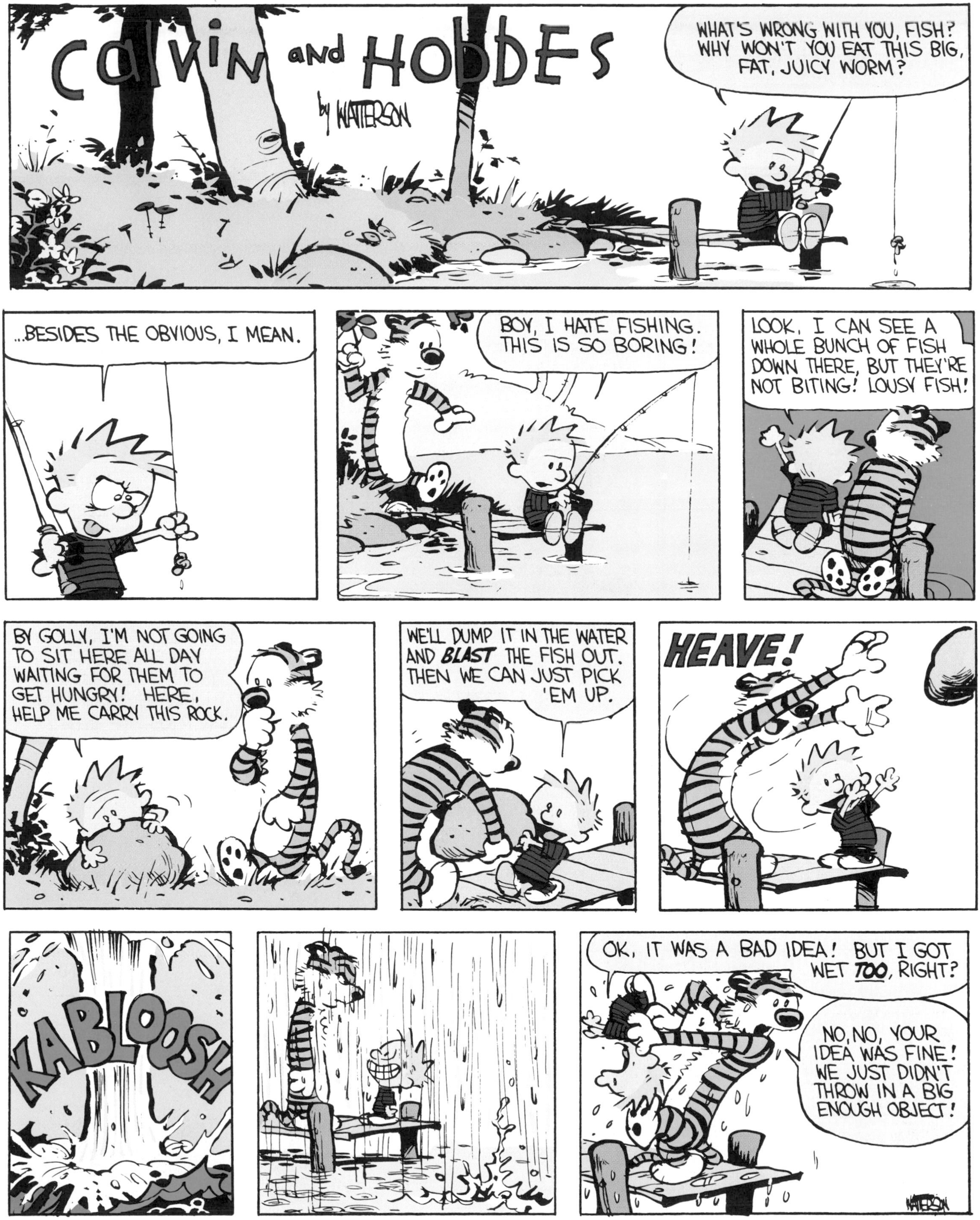

Calvin and Hobbes
by WATTERSON
WHAT'S WRONG WITH YOU, FISH? WHY WON'T YOU EAT THIS BIG, FAT, JUICY WORM?
...BESIDES THE OBVIOUS, I MEAN.
BOY, I HATE FISHING. THIS IS SO BORING!
LOOK, I CAN SEE A WHOLE BUNCH OF FISH DOWN THERE, BUT THEY'RE NOT BITING! LOUSY FISH!
BY GOLLY, I'M NOT GOING TO SIT HERE ALL DAY WAITING FOR THEM TO GET HUNGRY! HERE, HELP ME CARRY THIS ROCK.
WE'LL DUMP IT IN THE WATER AND BLAST THE FISH OUT. THEN WE CAN JUST PICK 'EM UP.
HEAVE!
KABLOOSH
OK, IT WAS A BAD IDEA! BUT I GOT WET TOO, RIGHT?
NO, NO, YOUR IDEA WAS FINE! WE JUST DIDN'T THROW IN A BIG ENOUGH OBJECT!
WATTERSON

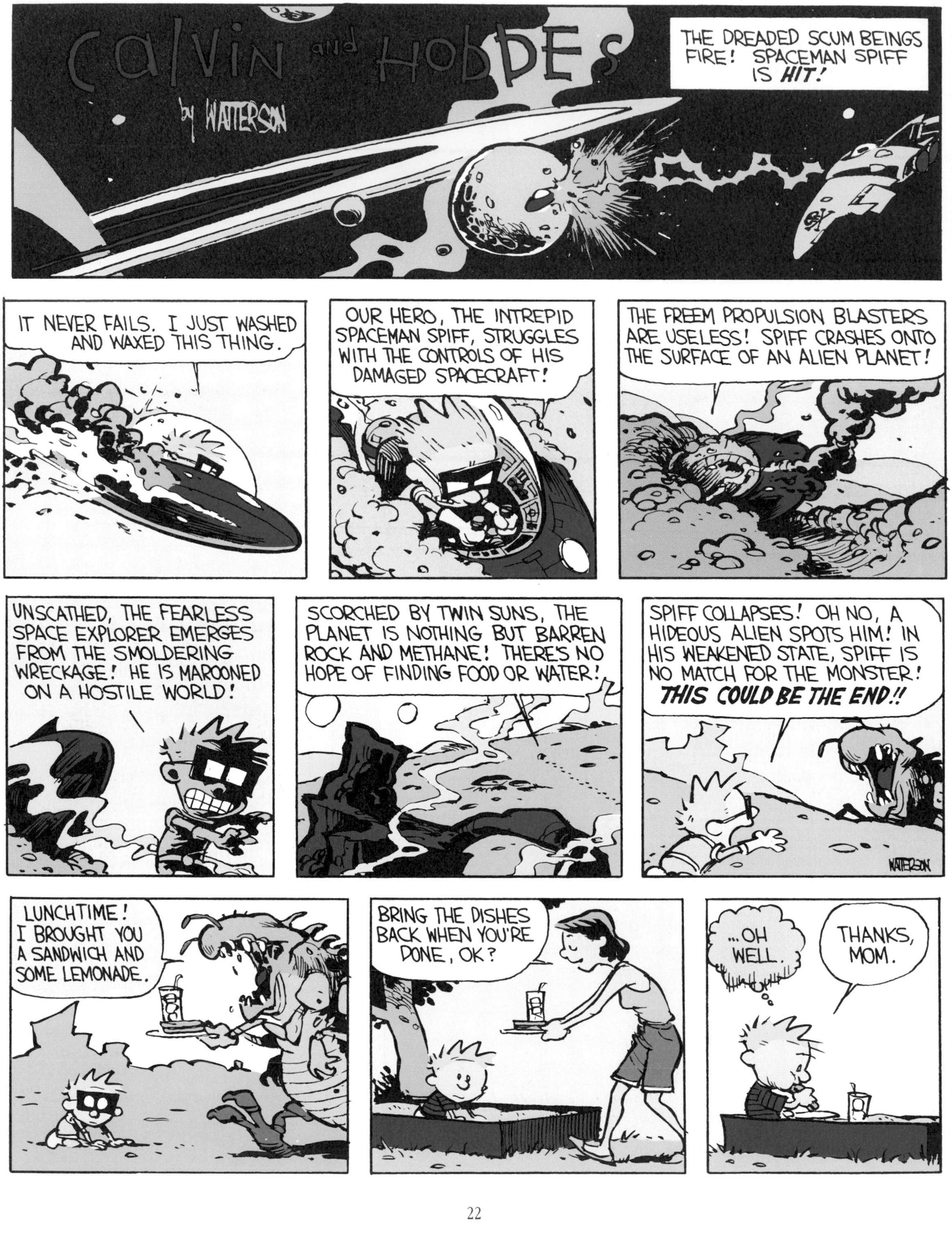
Calvin and Hobbes
by WATTERSON
THE DREADED SCUM BEINGS FIRE! SPACEMAN SPIFF IS *HIT!*
IT NEVER FAILS. I JUST WASHED AND WAXED THIS THING.
OUR HERO, THE INTREPID SPACEMAN SPIFF, STRUGGLES WITH THE CONTROLS OF HIS DAMAGED SPACECRAFT!
THE FREEM PROPULSION BLASTERS ARE USELESS! SPIFF CRASHES ONTO THE SURFACE OF AN ALIEN PLANET!
UNSCATHED, THE FEARLESS SPACE EXPLORER EMERGES FROM THE SMOLDERING WRECKAGE! HE IS MAROONED ON A HOSTILE WORLD!
SCORCHED BY TWIN SUNS, THE PLANET IS NOTHING BUT BARREN ROCK AND METHANE! THERE'S NO HOPE OF FINDING FOOD OR WATER!
SPIFF COLLAPSES! OH NO, A HIDEOUS ALIEN SPOTS HIM! IN HIS WEAKENED STATE, SPIFF IS NO MATCH FOR THE MONSTER! **THIS COULD BE THE END!!**
WATTERSON
LUNCHTIME! I BROUGHT YOU A SANDWICH AND SOME LEMONADE.
BRING THE DISHES BACK WHEN YOU'RE DONE, OK?
...OH WELL.
THANKS, MOM.

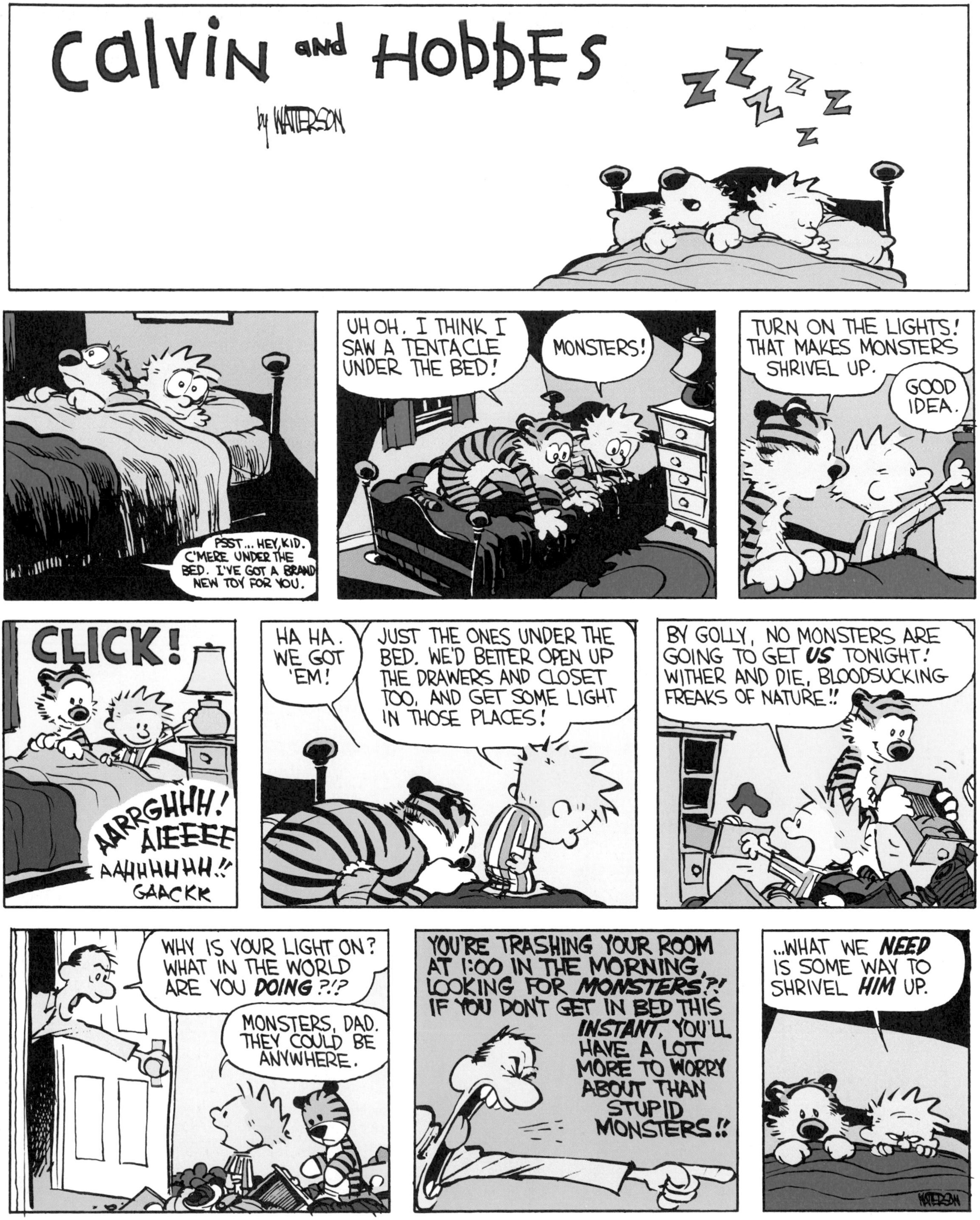
Calvin and Hobbes
by WATTERSON
ZZZZZZZ
PSST... HEY, KID. C'MERE UNDER THE BED. I'VE GOT A BRAND NEW TOY FOR YOU.
UH OH. I THINK I SAW A TENTACLE UNDER THE BED!
MONSTERS!
TURN ON THE LIGHTS! THAT MAKES MONSTERS SHRIVEL UP.
GOOD IDEA.
CLICK!
AARRGHHH! AIEEEE AAHHHHHH!! GAACKK
HA HA. WE GOT 'EM!
JUST THE ONES UNDER THE BED. WE'D BETTER OPEN UP THE DRAWERS AND CLOSET TOO, AND GET SOME LIGHT IN THOSE PLACES!
BY GOLLY, NO MONSTERS ARE GOING TO GET US TONIGHT! WITHER AND DIE, BLOODSUCKING FREAKS OF NATURE!!
WHY IS YOUR LIGHT ON? WHAT IN THE WORLD ARE YOU DOING?!?
MONSTERS, DAD. THEY COULD BE ANYWHERE.
YOU'RE TRASHING YOUR ROOM AT 1:00 IN THE MORNING, LOOKING FOR MONSTERS?! IF YOU DON'T GET IN BED THIS INSTANT, YOU'LL HAVE A LOT MORE TO WORRY ABOUT THAN STUPID MONSTERS!!
...WHAT WE NEED IS SOME WAY TO SHRIVEL HIM UP.
WATTERSON

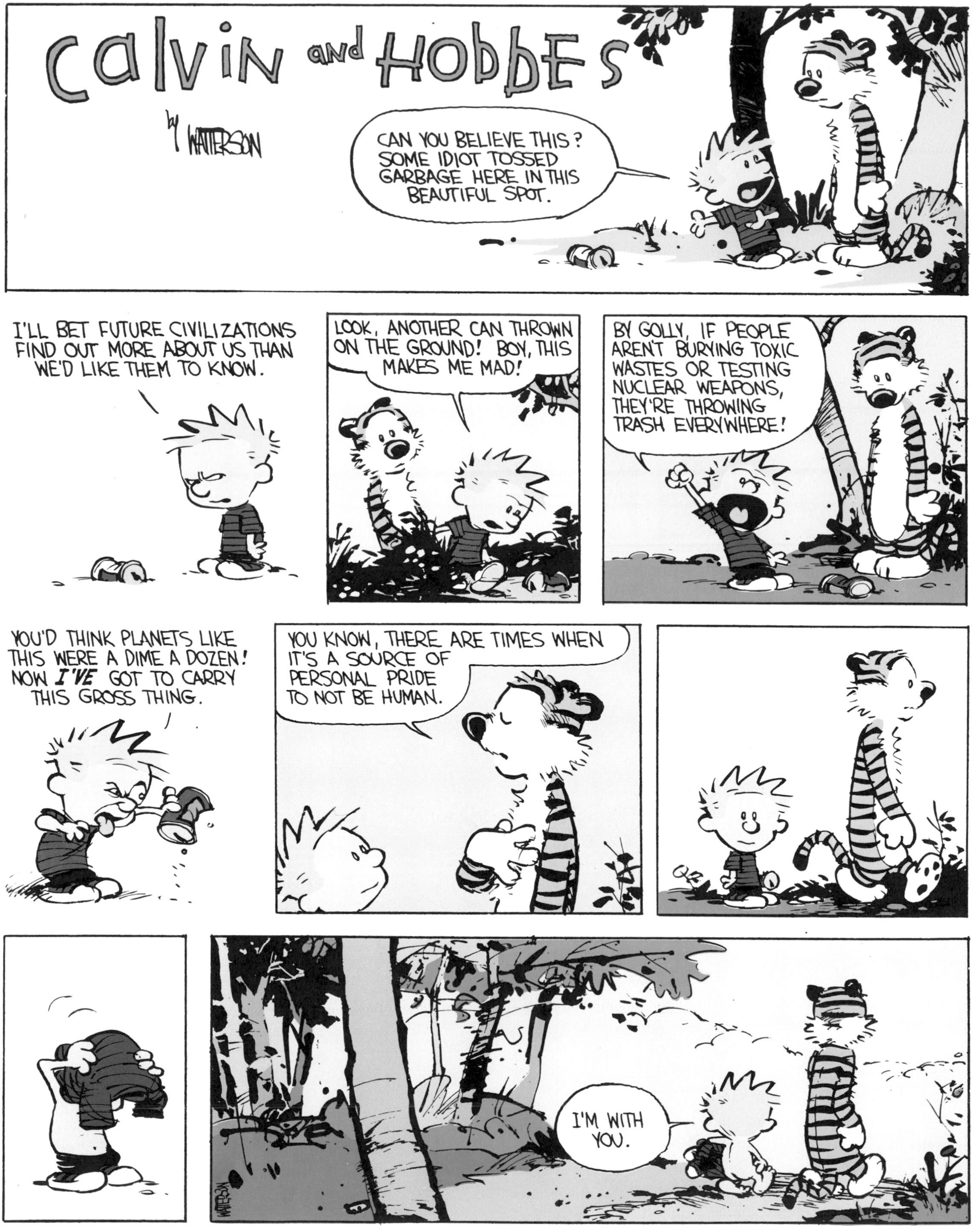
CALVIN and HOBBES
by WATTERSON
CAN YOU BELIEVE THIS? SOME IDIOT TOSSED GARBAGE HERE IN THIS BEAUTIFUL SPOT.
I'LL BET FUTURE CIVILIZATIONS FIND OUT MORE ABOUT US THAN WE'D LIKE THEM TO KNOW.
LOOK, ANOTHER CAN THROWN ON THE GROUND! BOY, THIS MAKES ME MAD!
BY GOLLY, IF PEOPLE AREN'T BURYING TOXIC WASTES OR TESTING NUCLEAR WEAPONS, THEY'RE THROWING TRASH EVERYWHERE!
YOU'D THINK PLANETS LIKE THIS WERE A DIME A DOZEN! NOW *I'VE* GOT TO CARRY THIS GROSS THING.
YOU KNOW, THERE ARE TIMES WHEN IT'S A SOURCE OF PERSONAL PRIDE TO NOT BE HUMAN.
I'M WITH YOU.
WATTERSON

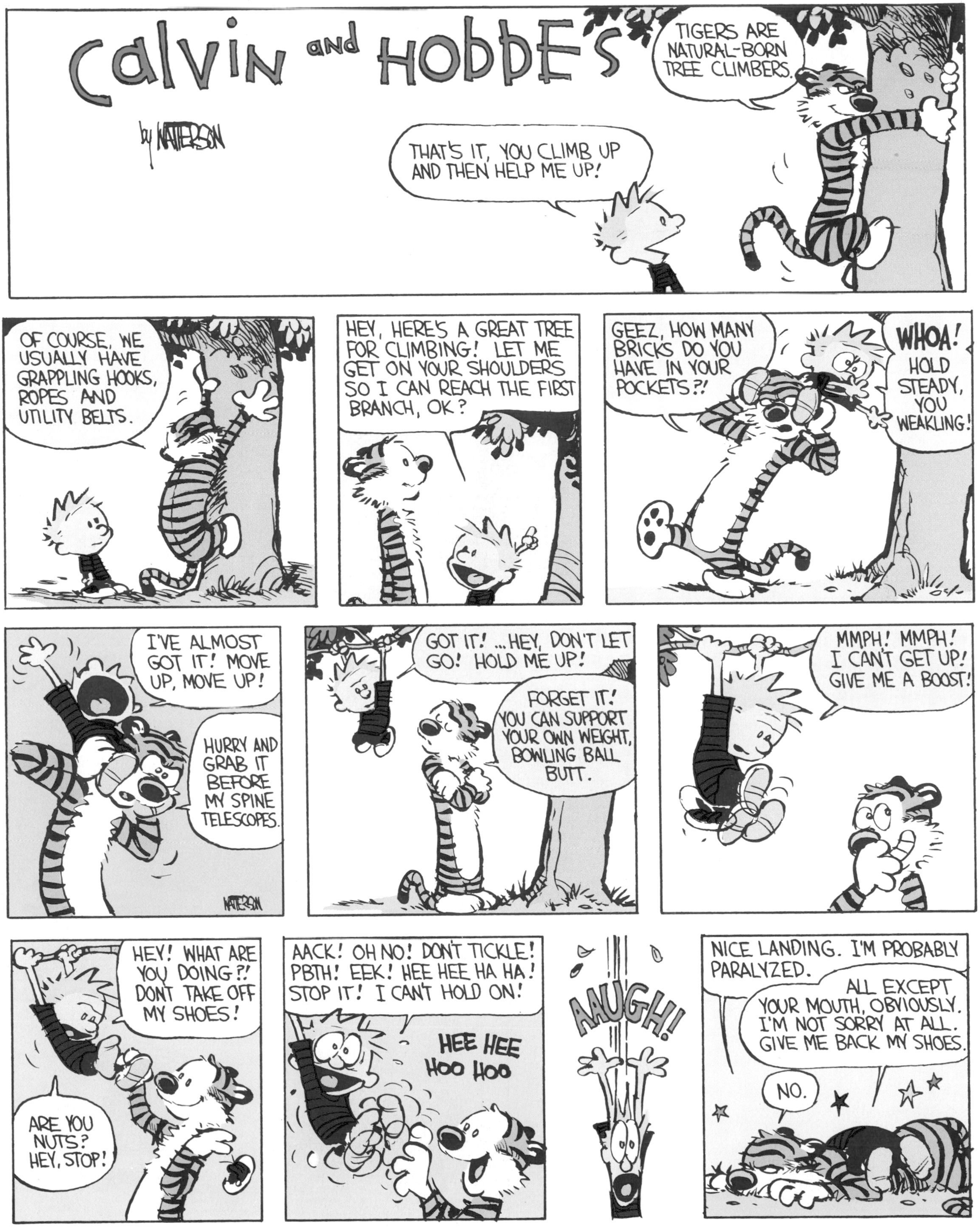
Calvin and HOBBES
by WATTERSON
TIGERS ARE NATURAL-BORN TREE CLIMBERS.
THAT'S IT, YOU CLIMB UP AND THEN HELP ME UP!
OF COURSE, WE USUALLY HAVE GRAPPLING HOOKS, ROPES AND UTILITY BELTS.
HEY, HERE'S A GREAT TREE FOR CLIMBING! LET ME GET ON YOUR SHOULDERS SO I CAN REACH THE FIRST BRANCH, OK?
GEEZ, HOW MANY BRICKS DO YOU HAVE IN YOUR POCKETS?!
WHOA! HOLD STEADY, YOU WEAKLING!
I'VE ALMOST GOT IT! MOVE UP, MOVE UP!
HURRY AND GRAB IT BEFORE MY SPINE TELESCOPES.
WATTERSON
GOT IT! ...HEY, DON'T LET GO! HOLD ME UP!
FORGET IT! YOU CAN SUPPORT YOUR OWN WEIGHT, BOWLING BALL BUTT.
MMPH! MMPH! I CAN'T GET UP! GIVE ME A BOOST!
HEY! WHAT ARE YOU DOING?! DONT TAKE OFF MY SHOES!
ARE YOU NUTS? HEY, STOP!
AACK! OH NO! DON'T TICKLE! PBTH! EEK! HEE HEE HA HA! STOP IT! I CAN'T HOLD ON!
HEE HEE HOO HOO
AAUGH!
NICE LANDING. I'M PROBABLY PARALYZED.
ALL EXCEPT YOUR MOUTH, OBVIOUSLY. I'M NOT SORRY AT ALL. GIVE ME BACK MY SHOES.
NO.

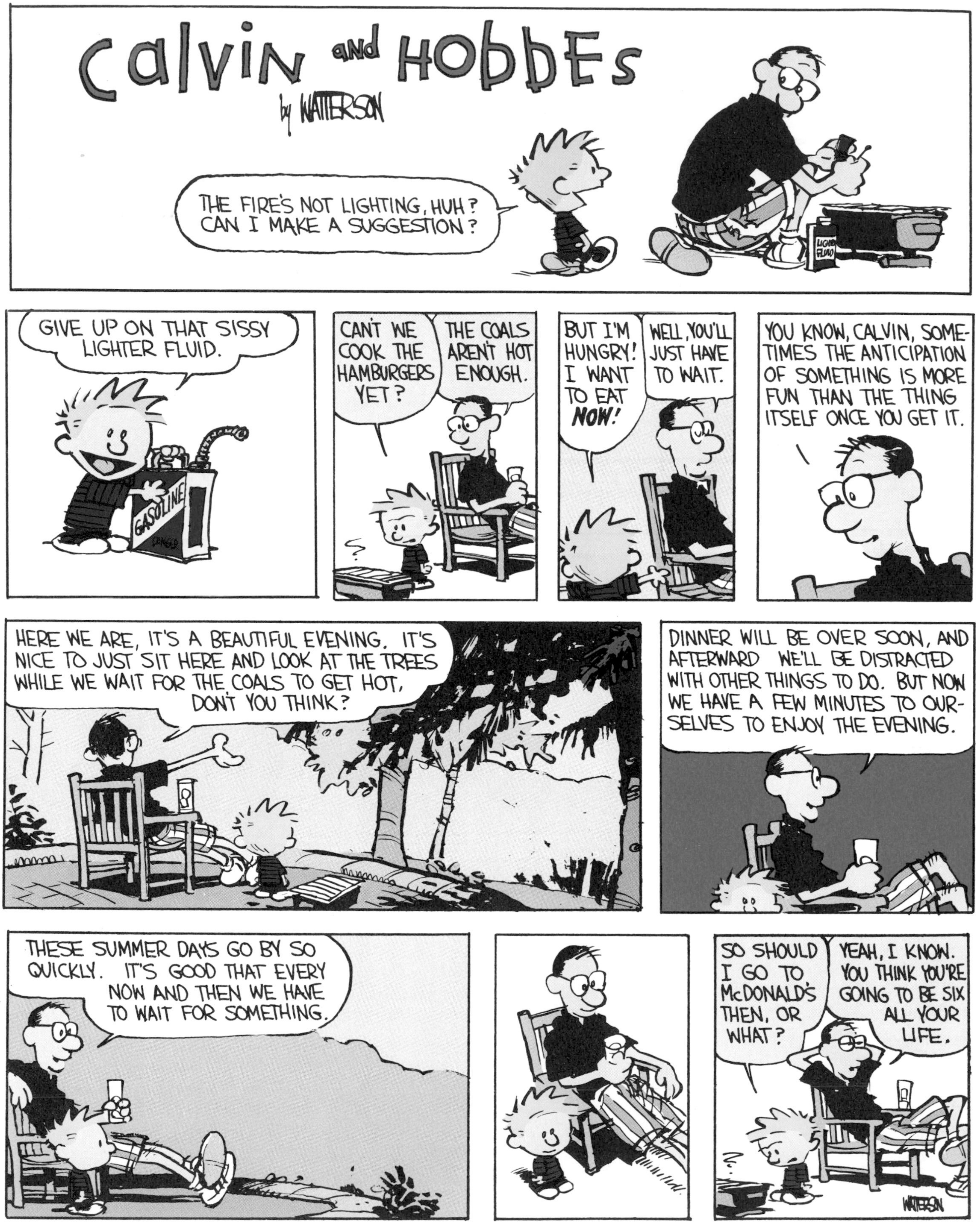
Calvin and HOBBES
by WATTERSON
THE FIRE'S NOT LIGHTING, HUH? CAN I MAKE A SUGGESTION?
LIGHTER FLUID
GIVE UP ON THAT SISSY LIGHTER FLUID.
GASOLINE
DANGER
CAN'T WE COOK THE HAMBURGERS YET?
THE COALS AREN'T HOT ENOUGH.
BUT I'M HUNGRY! I WANT TO EAT **NOW!**
WELL, YOU'LL JUST HAVE TO WAIT.
YOU KNOW, CALVIN, SOMETIMES THE ANTICIPATION OF SOMETHING IS MORE FUN THAN THE THING ITSELF ONCE YOU GET IT.
HERE WE ARE, IT'S A BEAUTIFUL EVENING. IT'S NICE TO JUST SIT HERE AND LOOK AT THE TREES WHILE WE WAIT FOR THE COALS TO GET HOT, DON'T YOU THINK?
DINNER WILL BE OVER SOON, AND AFTERWARD WE'LL BE DISTRACTED WITH OTHER THINGS TO DO. BUT NOW WE HAVE A FEW MINUTES TO OURSELVES TO ENJOY THE EVENING.
THESE SUMMER DAYS GO BY SO QUICKLY. IT'S GOOD THAT EVERY NOW AND THEN WE HAVE TO WAIT FOR SOMETHING.
SO SHOULD I GO TO McDONALD'S THEN, OR WHAT?
YEAH, I KNOW. YOU THINK YOU'RE GOING TO BE SIX ALL YOUR LIFE.
WATTERSON

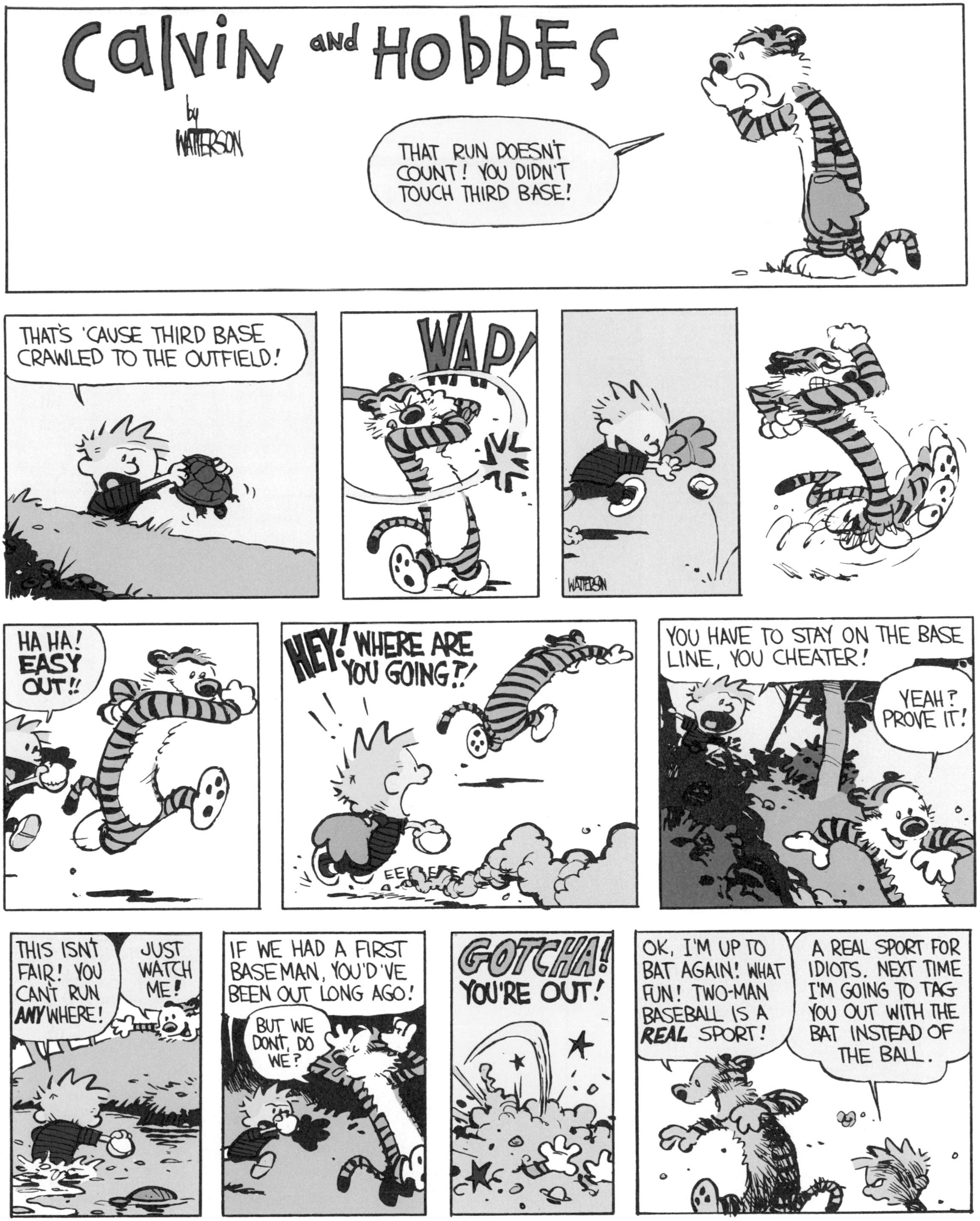
Calvin and Hobbes
by WATTERSON
THAT RUN DOESN'T COUNT! YOU DIDN'T TOUCH THIRD BASE!
THAT'S 'CAUSE THIRD BASE CRAWLED TO THE OUTFIELD!
WAP!
WATTERSON
HA HA! EASY OUT!!
HEY! WHERE ARE YOU GOING?!
EEK EEK
YOU HAVE TO STAY ON THE BASE LINE, YOU CHEATER!
YEAH? PROVE IT!
THIS ISN'T FAIR! YOU CAN'T RUN ANYWHERE!
JUST WATCH ME!
IF WE HAD A FIRST BASEMAN, YOU'D'VE BEEN OUT LONG AGO!
BUT WE DON'T, DO WE?
GOTCHA! YOU'RE OUT!
OK, I'M UP TO BAT AGAIN! WHAT FUN! TWO-MAN BASEBALL IS A REAL SPORT!
A REAL SPORT FOR IDIOTS. NEXT TIME I'M GOING TO TAG YOU OUT WITH THE BAT INSTEAD OF THE BALL.

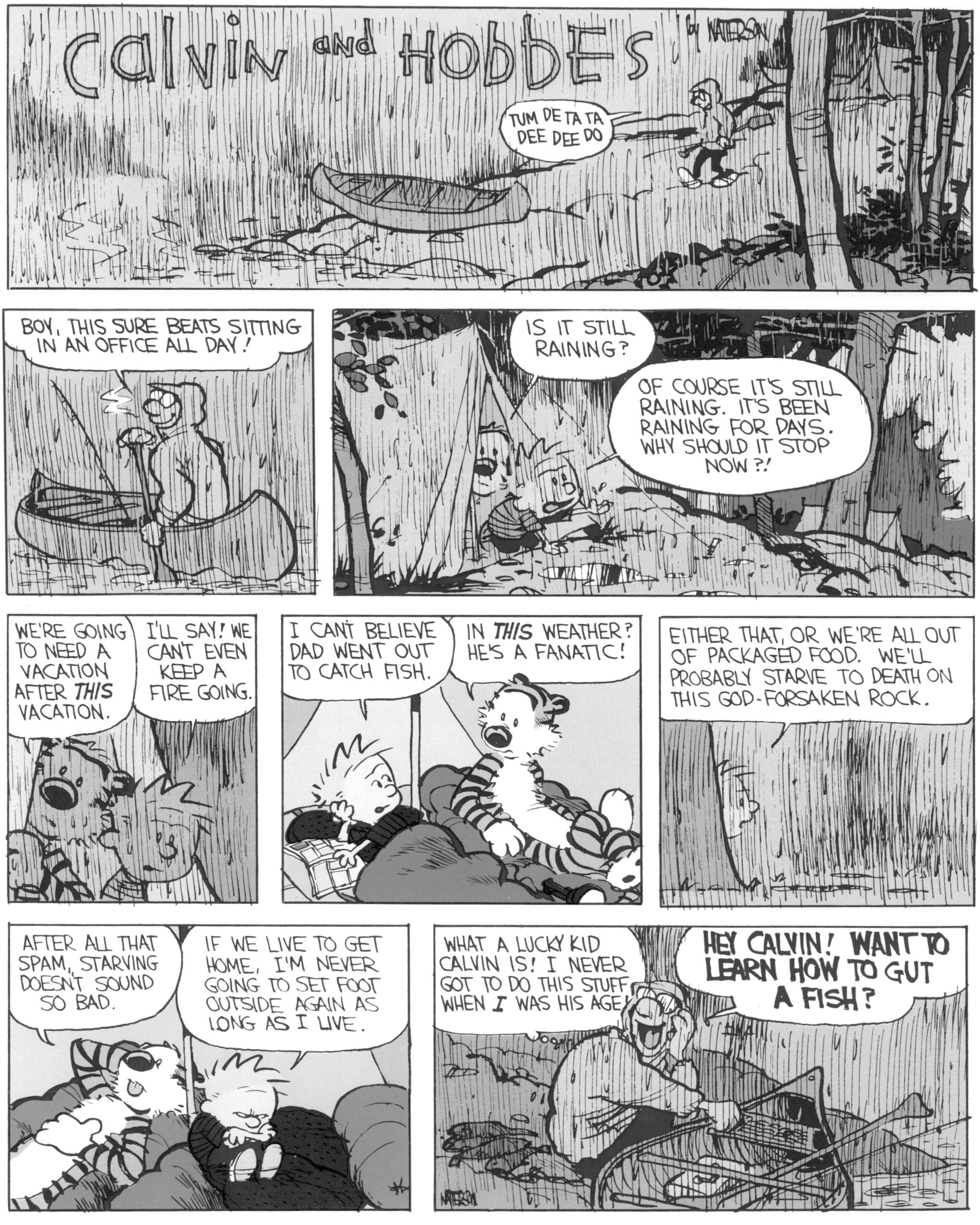
Calvin and HOBBES
by WATTERSON
TUM DE TA TA DEE DEE DO
BOY, THIS SURE BEATS SITTING IN AN OFFICE ALL DAY!
IS IT STILL RAINING?
OF COURSE IT'S STILL RAINING. IT'S BEEN RAINING FOR DAYS. WHY SHOULD IT STOP NOW?!
WE'RE GOING TO NEED A VACATION AFTER THIS VACATION.
I'LL SAY! WE CAN'T EVEN KEEP A FIRE GOING.
I CAN'T BELIEVE DAD WENT OUT TO CATCH FISH.
IN THIS WEATHER? HE'S A FANATIC!
EITHER THAT, OR WE'RE ALL OUT OF PACKAGED FOOD. WE'LL PROBABLY STARVE TO DEATH ON THIS GOD-FORSAKEN ROCK.
AFTER ALL THAT SPAM, STARVING DOESN'T SOUND SO BAD.
IF WE LIVE TO GET HOME, I'M NEVER GOING TO SET FOOT OUTSIDE AGAIN AS LONG AS I LIVE.
WHAT A LUCKY KID CALVIN IS! I NEVER GOT TO DO THIS STUFF WHEN I WAS HIS AGE!
HEY CALVIN! WANT TO LEARN HOW TO GUT A FISH?
WATTERSON

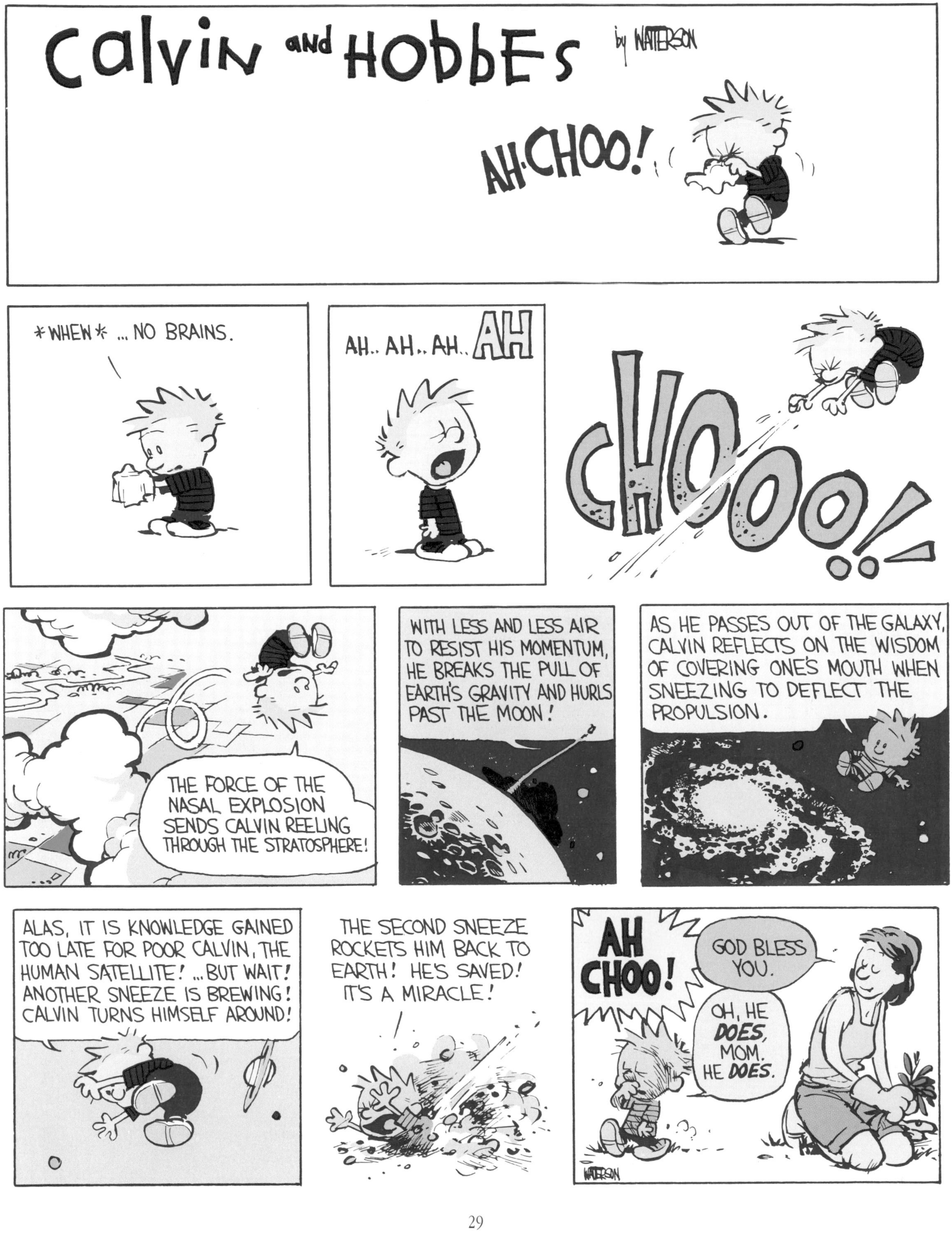
Calvin and HOBBES
by WATTERSON
AH-CHOO!
WHEW ... NO BRAINS.
AH.. AH.. AH.. AH
CHOOOO!!
THE FORCE OF THE NASAL EXPLOSION SENDS CALVIN REELING THROUGH THE STRATOSPHERE!
WITH LESS AND LESS AIR TO RESIST HIS MOMENTUM, HE BREAKS THE PULL OF EARTH'S GRAVITY AND HURLS PAST THE MOON!
AS HE PASSES OUT OF THE GALAXY, CALVIN REFLECTS ON THE WISDOM OF COVERING ONE'S MOUTH WHEN SNEEZING TO DEFLECT THE PROPULSION.
ALAS, IT IS KNOWLEDGE GAINED TOO LATE FOR POOR CALVIN, THE HUMAN SATELLITE! ...BUT WAIT! ANOTHER SNEEZE IS BREWING! CALVIN TURNS HIMSELF AROUND!
THE SECOND SNEEZE ROCKETS HIM BACK TO EARTH! HE'S SAVED! IT'S A MIRACLE!
AH CHOO!
GOD BLESS YOU.
OH, HE DOES, MOM. HE DOES.
WATTERSON

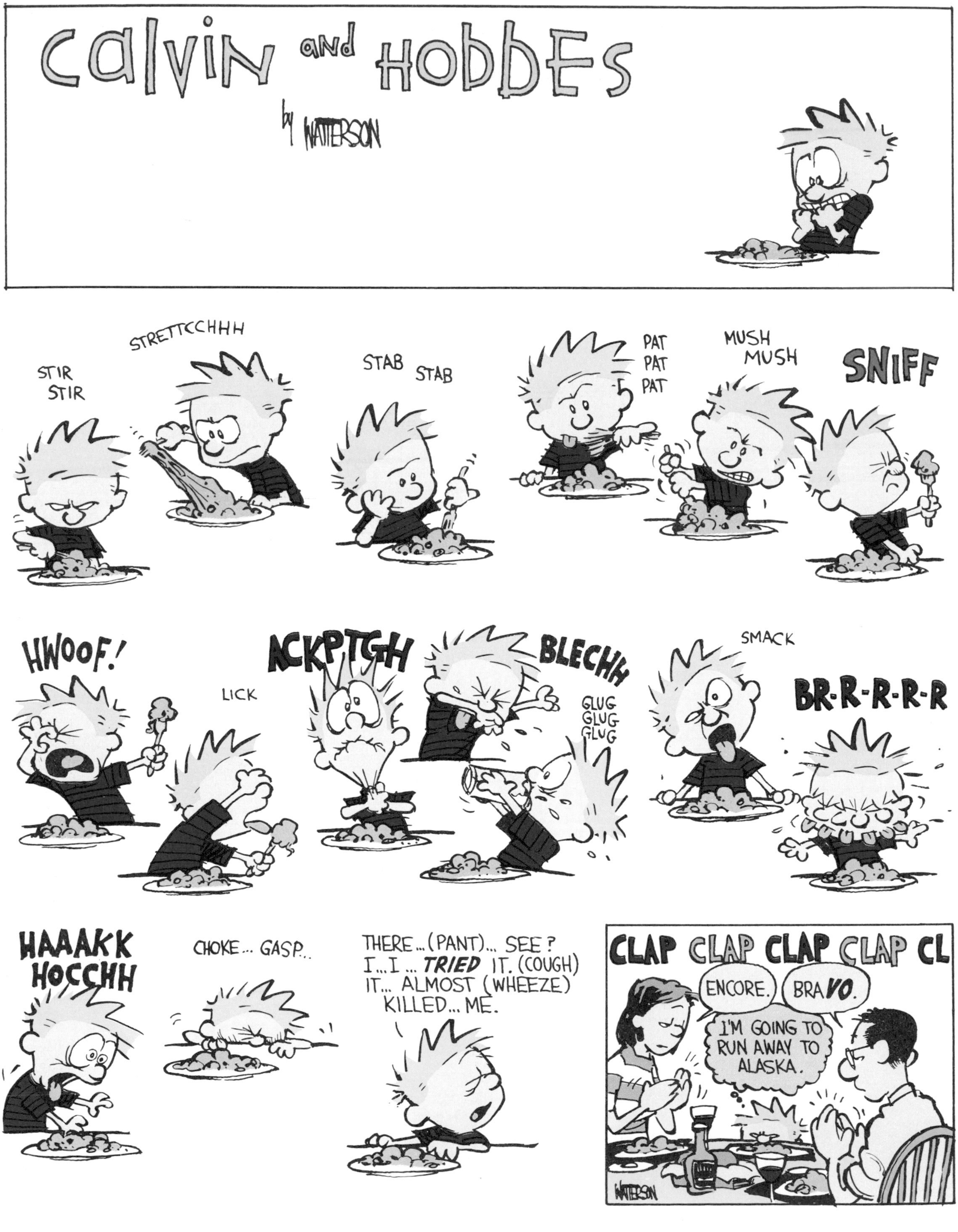
Calvin and Hobbes
by WATTERSON
STIR STIR
STRETTCCHHH
STAB STAB
PAT PAT PAT
MUSH MUSH
SNIFF
HWOOF!
LICK
ACKPTGH
BLECHH
GLUG GLUG GLUG
SMACK
BR-R-R-R-R
HAAAKK HOCCHH
CHOKE... GASP...
THERE... (PANT)... SEE? I... I... TRIED IT. (COUGH) IT... ALMOST (WHEEZE) KILLED... ME.
CLAP CLAP CLAP CLAP CL
ENCORE.
BRAVO.
I'M GOING TO RUN AWAY TO ALASKA.
WATTERSON

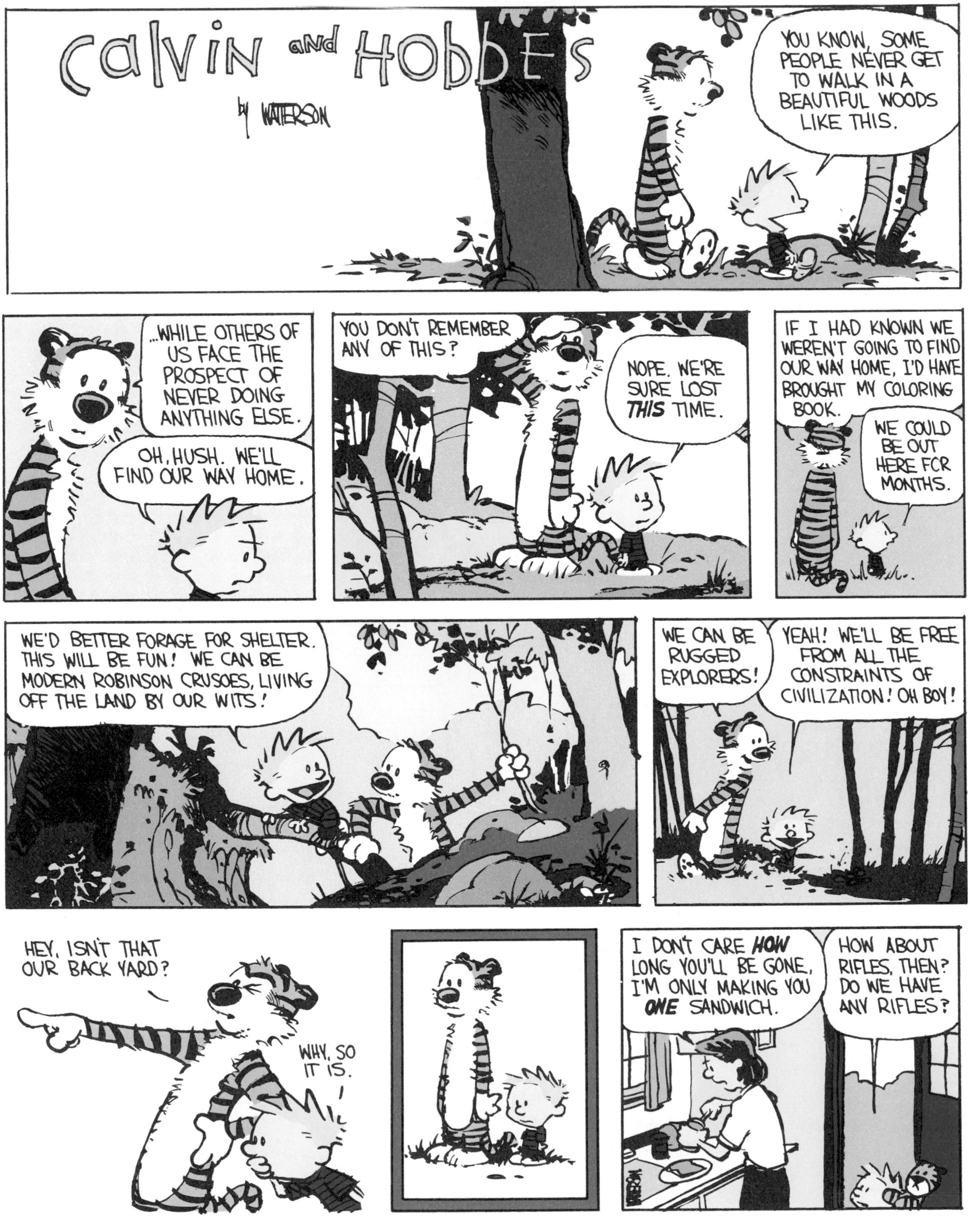
Calvin and HOBBES
by WATTERSON
YOU KNOW, SOME PEOPLE NEVER GET TO WALK IN A BEAUTIFUL WOODS LIKE THIS.
...WHILE OTHERS OF US FACE THE PROSPECT OF NEVER DOING ANYTHING ELSE.
OH, HUSH. WE'LL FIND OUR WAY HOME.
YOU DON'T REMEMBER ANY OF THIS?
NOPE. WE'RE SURE LOST **THIS** TIME.
IF I HAD KNOWN WE WEREN'T GOING TO FIND OUR WAY HOME, I'D HAVE BROUGHT MY COLORING BOOK.
WE COULD BE OUT HERE FOR MONTHS.
WE'D BETTER FORAGE FOR SHELTER. THIS WILL BE FUN! WE CAN BE MODERN ROBINSON CRUSOES, LIVING OFF THE LAND BY OUR WITS!
WE CAN BE RUGGED EXPLORERS!
YEAH! WE'LL BE FREE FROM ALL THE CONSTRAINTS OF CIVILIZATION! OH BOY!
HEY, ISN'T THAT OUR BACK YARD?
WHY, SO IT IS.
I DON'T CARE **HOW** LONG YOU'LL BE GONE, I'M ONLY MAKING YOU **ONE** SANDWICH.
HOW ABOUT RIFLES, THEN? DO WE HAVE ANY RIFLES?

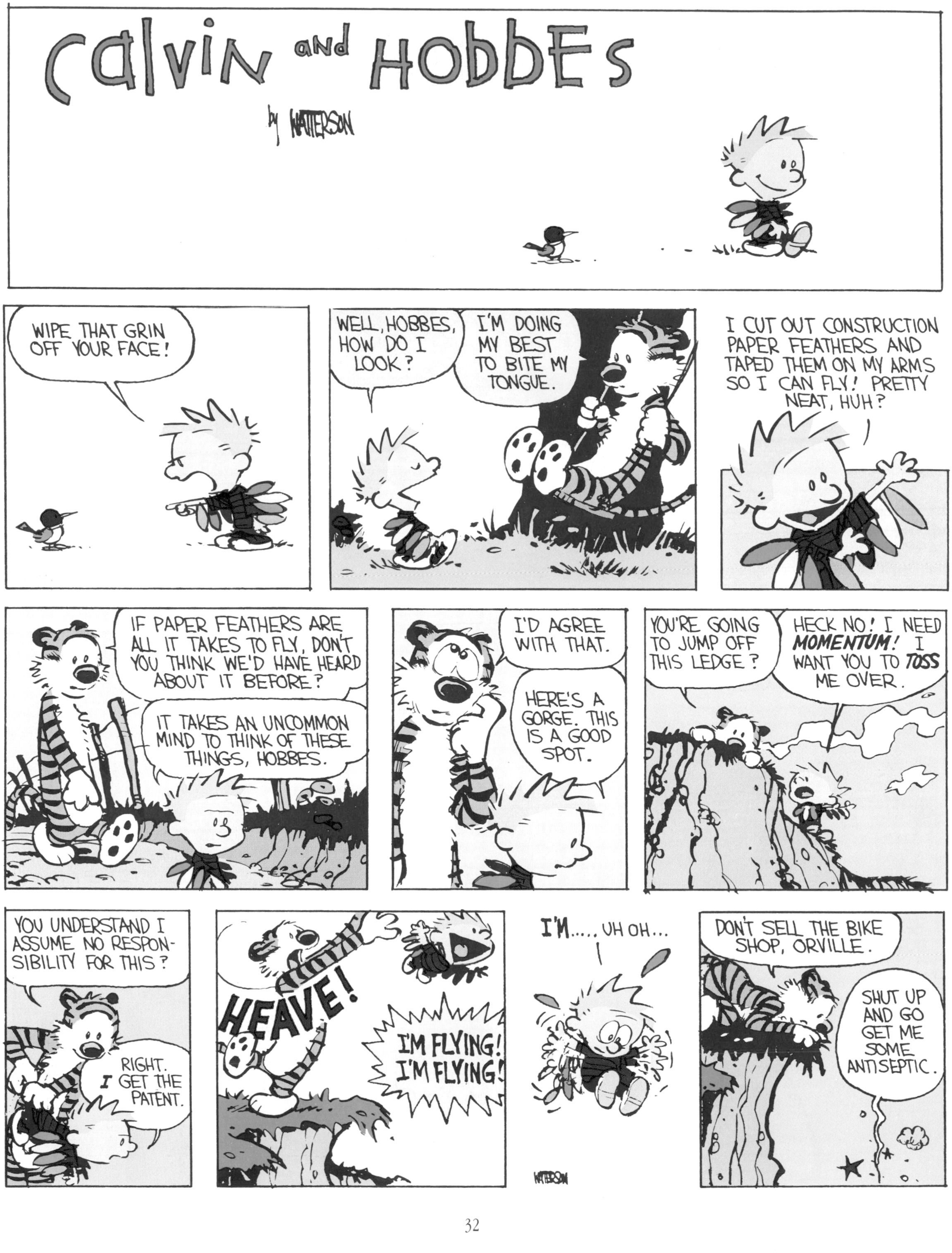
Calvin and HOBBES
by WATTERSON
WIPE THAT GRIN OFF YOUR FACE!
WELL, HOBBES, HOW DO I LOOK?
I'M DOING MY BEST TO BITE MY TONGUE.
I CUT OUT CONSTRUCTION PAPER FEATHERS AND TAPED THEM ON MY ARMS SO I CAN FLY! PRETTY NEAT, HUH?
IF PAPER FEATHERS ARE ALL IT TAKES TO FLY, DON'T YOU THINK WE'D HAVE HEARD ABOUT IT BEFORE?
IT TAKES AN UNCOMMON MIND TO THINK OF THESE THINGS, HOBBES.
I'D AGREE WITH THAT.
HERE'S A GORGE. THIS IS A GOOD SPOT.
YOU'RE GOING TO JUMP OFF THIS LEDGE?
HECK NO! I NEED MOMENTUM! I WANT YOU TO TOSS ME OVER.
YOU UNDERSTAND I ASSUME NO RESPONSIBILITY FOR THIS?
RIGHT. I GET THE PATENT.
HEAVE!
I'M FLYING! I'M FLYING!
I'M..... UH OH...
DON'T SELL THE BIKE SHOP, ORVILLE.
SHUT UP AND GO GET ME SOME ANTISEPTIC.
WATTERSON

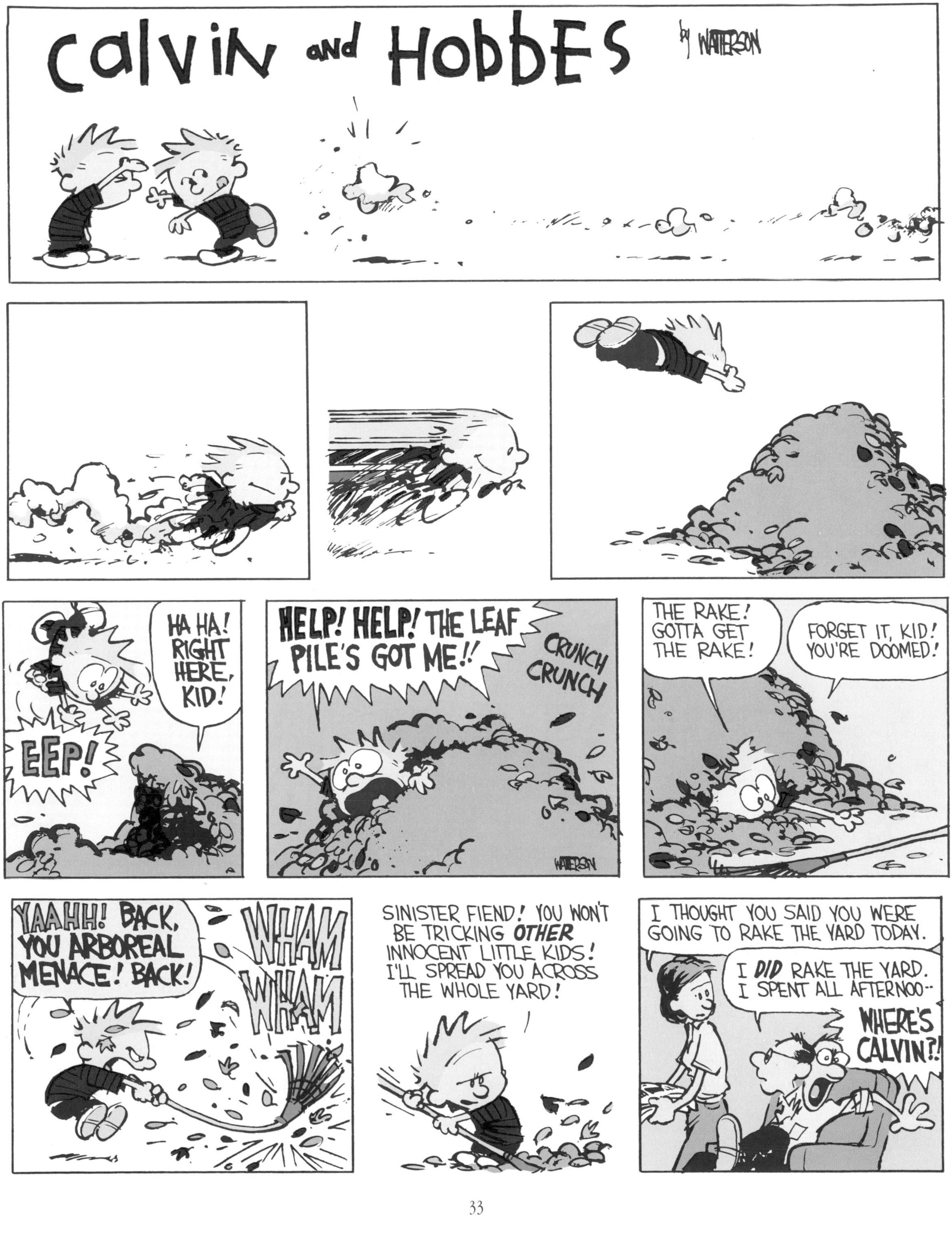
Calvin and HOBBES
by WATTERSON
HA HA! RIGHT HERE, KID!
EEP!
HELP! HELP! THE LEAF PILE'S GOT ME!!
CRUNCH CRUNCH
WATTERSON
THE RAKE! GOTTA GET THE RAKE!
FORGET IT, KID! YOU'RE DOOMED!
YAAHH! BACK, YOU ARBOREAL MENACE! BACK!
WHAM WHAM
SINISTER FIEND! YOU WON'T BE TRICKING OTHER INNOCENT LITTLE KIDS! I'LL SPREAD YOU ACROSS THE WHOLE YARD!
I THOUGHT YOU SAID YOU WERE GOING TO RAKE THE YARD TODAY.
I DID RAKE THE YARD. I SPENT ALL AFTERNOO--
WHERE'S CALVIN?!

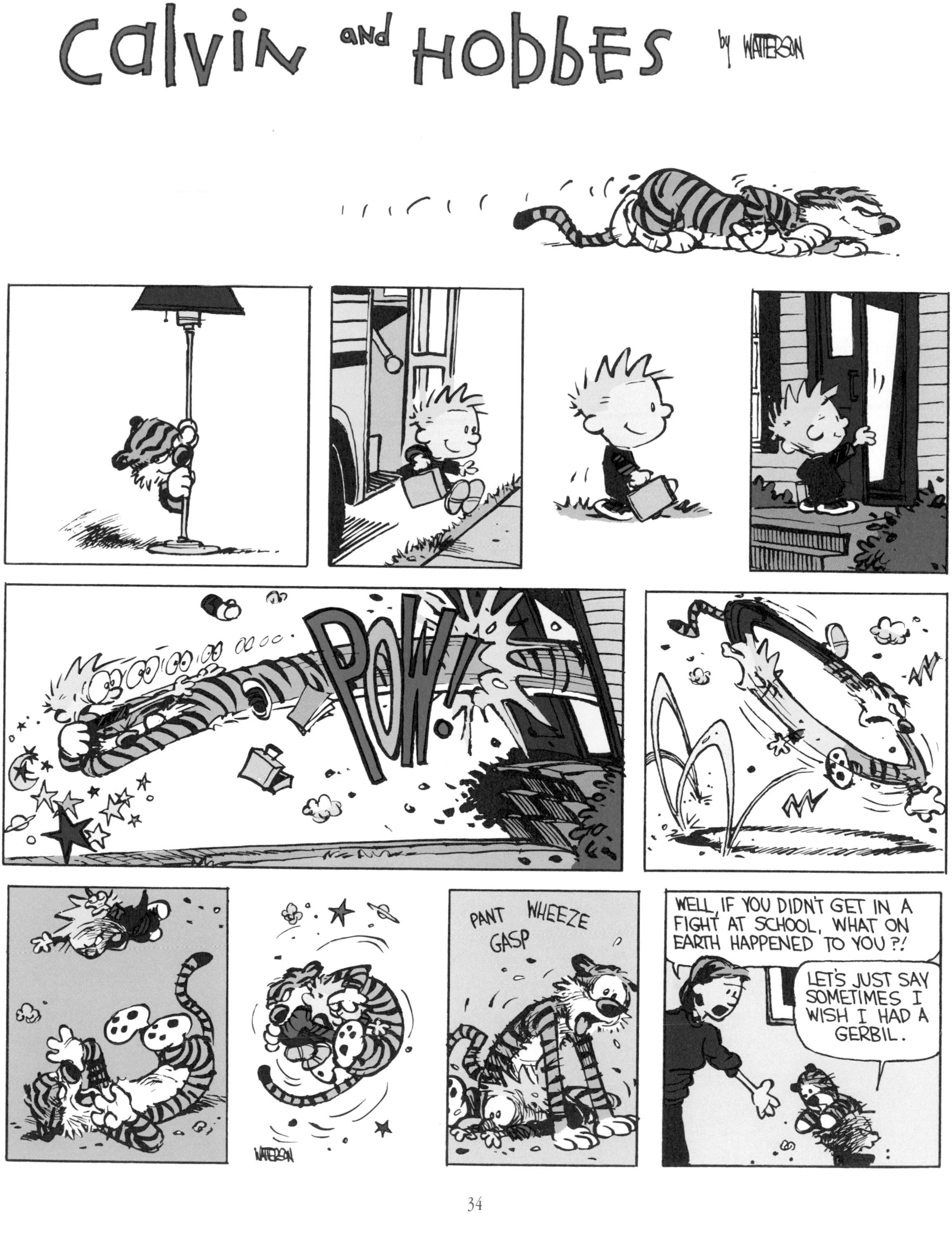

Calvin and HOBBES by WATTERSON
POW!
PANT WHEEZE
GASP
WELL, IF YOU DIDN'T GET IN A FIGHT AT SCHOOL, WHAT ON EARTH HAPPENED TO YOU ?!
LET'S JUST SAY SOMETIMES I WISH I HAD A GERBIL.
WATTERSON

CALVIN and HOBBES

A DAZED SPACEMAN SPIFF CRAWLS FROM THE SMOKING WRECKAGE OF HIS SHIP!

by WATERSON

OUR HERO NOW REGRETS NOT BUYING A TOWING RIDER ON HIS INSURANCE POLICY.

THE COURAGEOUS SPACEMAN SPIFF HAS BEEN CAPTURED BY THE HIDEOUS ZORGS OF PLANET X-13!

LED THROUGH THE DANK CORRIDORS OF THE DUNGEON, SPIFF LOOKS IN VAIN FOR AN OPPORTUNITY TO ESCAPE!

OUR HERO IS BROUGHT BEFORE THE ZORG DESPOT!

SO *THIS* IS THE FAMED SPACE EXPLORER SPIFF! I'VE WAITED A LONG TIME FOR THIS MOMENT, EARTHLING SCUM!

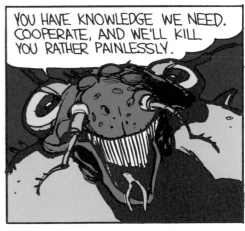

YOU HAVE KNOWLEDGE WE NEED. COOPERATE, AND WE'LL KILL YOU RATHER PAINLESSLY.

LET'S DISPENSE WITH THE PLEASANTRIES, YOU TWISTED SPACE CRUSTACEAN. WHAT IS IT YOU WANT FROM ME?

A SUMMARY OF LEWIS AND CLARK'S EXPEDITION TO THE PACIFIC!

HA! WILD ZONTARS COULDN'T DRAG THAT INFORMATION OUT OF ME! DO YOUR WORST!

YOU DIDN'T READ THE ASSIGNMENT, DID YOU, CALVIN?

WATERSON

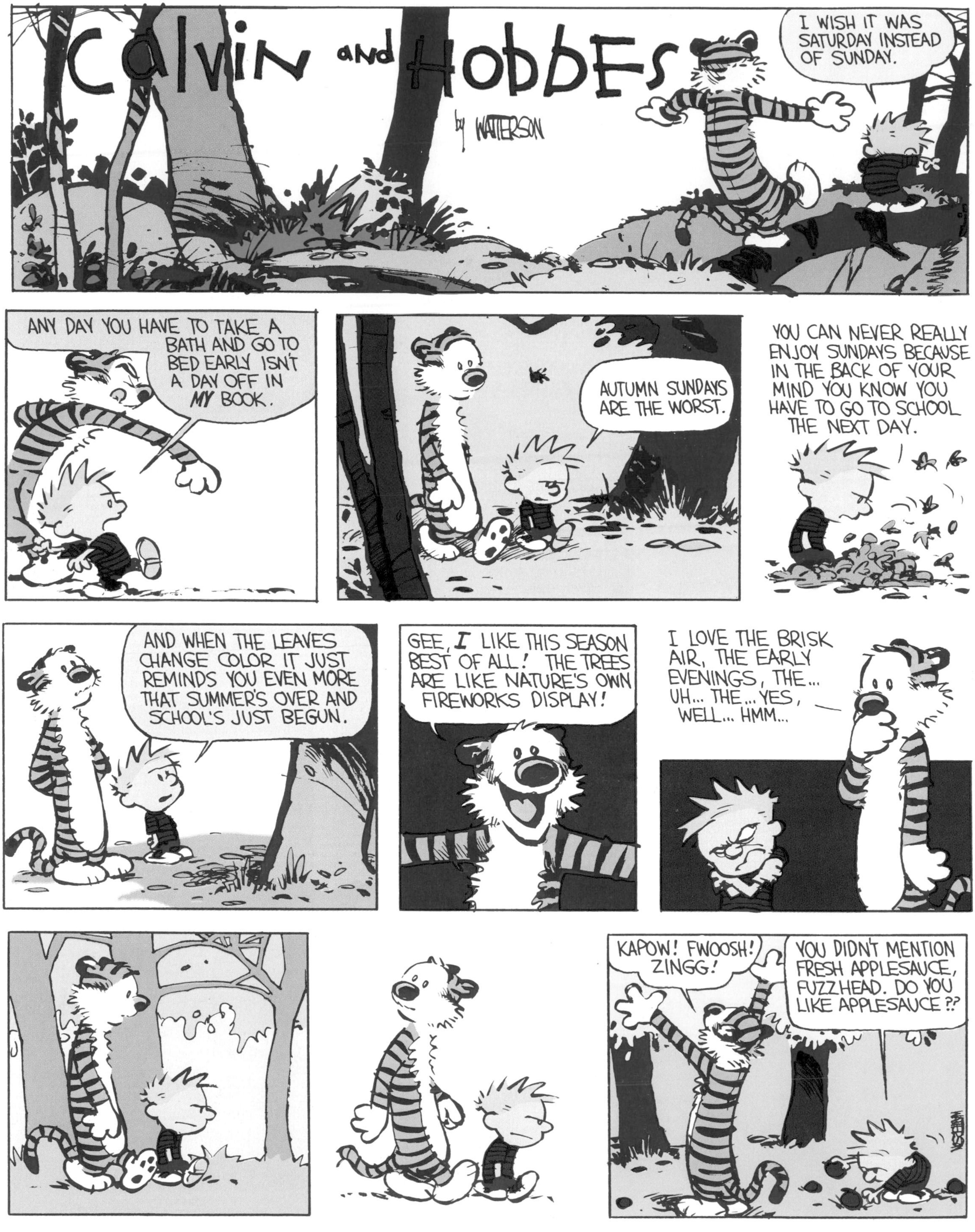
Calvin and Hobbes
by WATTERSON
I WISH IT WAS SATURDAY INSTEAD OF SUNDAY.
ANY DAY YOU HAVE TO TAKE A BATH AND GO TO BED EARLY ISN'T A DAY OFF IN MY BOOK.
AUTUMN SUNDAYS ARE THE WORST.
YOU CAN NEVER REALLY ENJOY SUNDAYS BECAUSE IN THE BACK OF YOUR MIND YOU KNOW YOU HAVE TO GO TO SCHOOL THE NEXT DAY.
AND WHEN THE LEAVES CHANGE COLOR IT JUST REMINDS YOU EVEN MORE THAT SUMMER'S OVER AND SCHOOL'S JUST BEGUN.
GEE, I LIKE THIS SEASON BEST OF ALL! THE TREES ARE LIKE NATURE'S OWN FIREWORKS DISPLAY!
I LOVE THE BRISK AIR, THE EARLY EVENINGS, THE... UH... THE... YES, WELL... HMM...
KAPOW! FWOOSH! ZINGG!
YOU DIDN'T MENTION FRESH APPLESAUCE, FUZZHEAD. DO YOU LIKE APPLESAUCE??

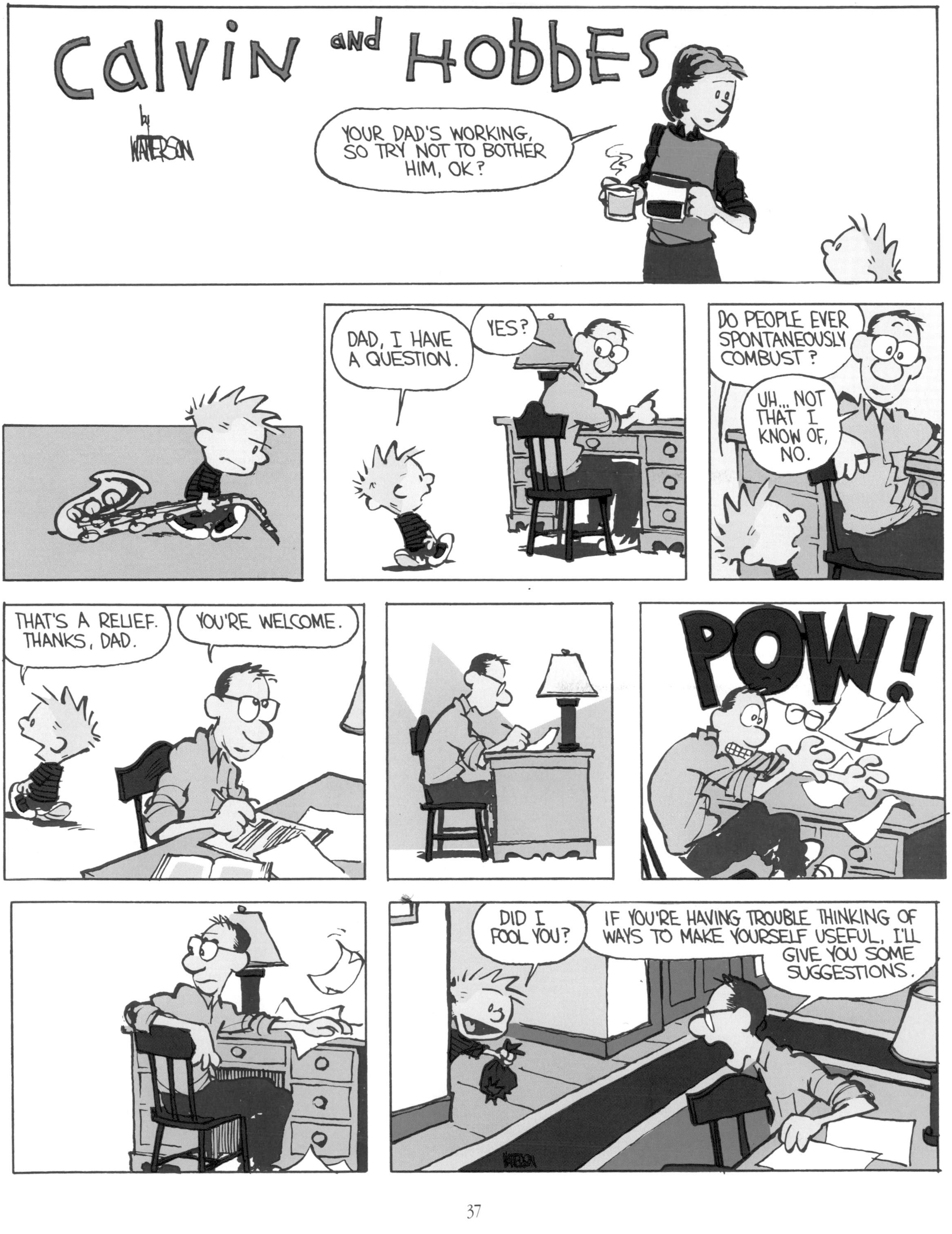
Calvin and HOBBES
by WATTERSON
YOUR DAD'S WORKING, SO TRY NOT TO BOTHER HIM, OK?
DAD, I HAVE A QUESTION.
YES?
DO PEOPLE EVER SPONTANEOUSLY COMBUST?
UH... NOT THAT I KNOW OF, NO.
THAT'S A RELIEF. THANKS, DAD.
YOU'RE WELCOME.
POW!
DID I FOOL YOU?
IF YOU'RE HAVING TROUBLE THINKING OF WAYS TO MAKE YOURSELF USEFUL, I'LL GIVE YOU SOME SUGGESTIONS.

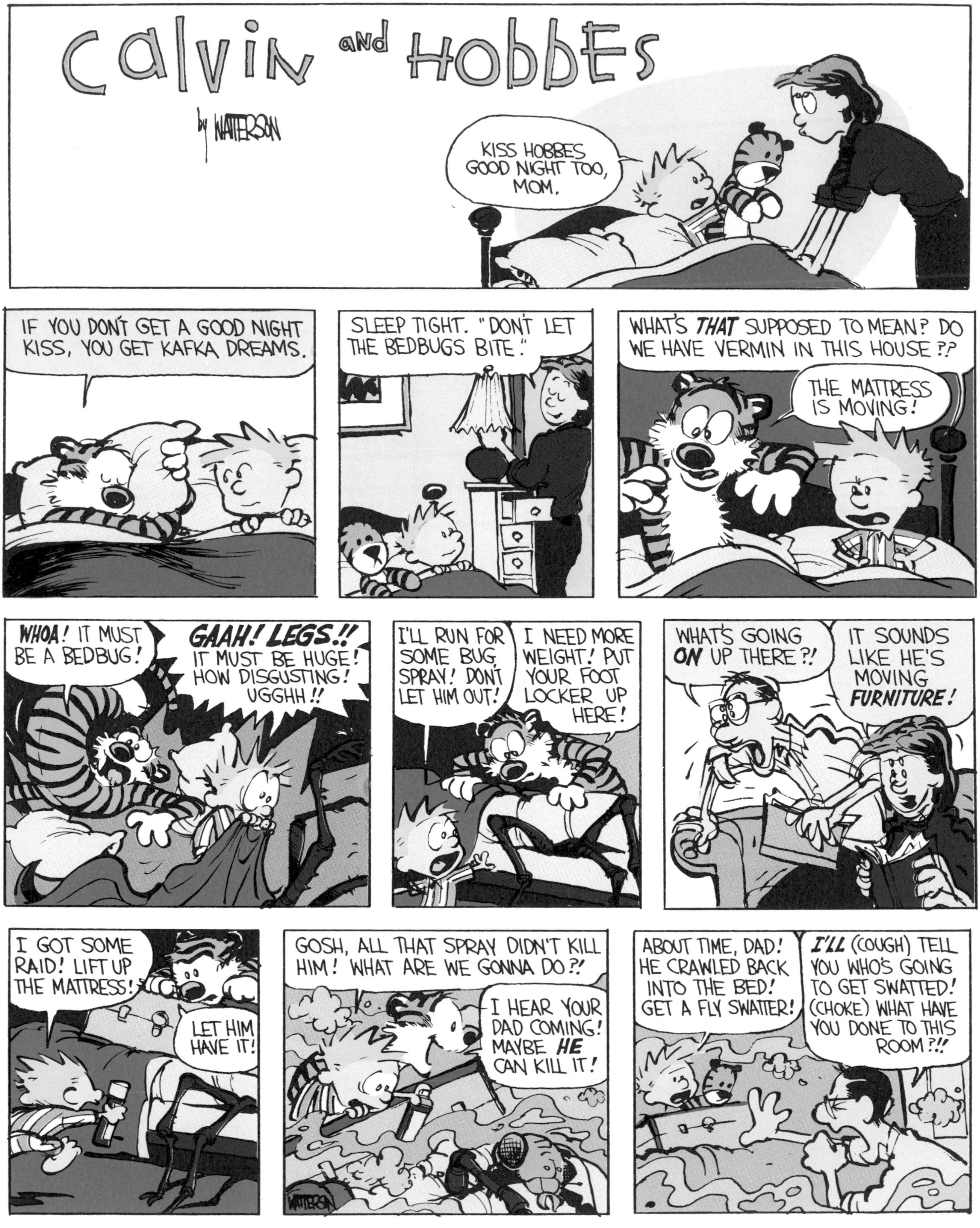
Calvin and HOBBES
by WATTERSON
KISS HOBBES GOOD NIGHT TOO, MOM.
IF YOU DON'T GET A GOOD NIGHT KISS, YOU GET KAFKA DREAMS.
SLEEP TIGHT. "DON'T LET THE BEDBUGS BITE."
WHAT'S *THAT* SUPPOSED TO MEAN? DO WE HAVE VERMIN IN THIS HOUSE ?!?
THE MATTRESS IS MOVING!
WHOA! IT MUST BE A BEDBUG!
GAAH! LEGS!! IT MUST BE HUGE! HOW DISGUSTING! UGGHH!!
I'LL RUN FOR SOME BUG SPRAY! DON'T LET HIM OUT!
I NEED MORE WEIGHT! PUT YOUR FOOT LOCKER UP HERE!
WHAT'S GOING **ON** UP THERE?!
IT SOUNDS LIKE HE'S MOVING **FURNITURE**!
I GOT SOME RAID! LIFT UP THE MATTRESS!
LET HIM HAVE IT!
GOSH, ALL THAT SPRAY DIDN'T KILL HIM! WHAT ARE WE GONNA DO?!
I HEAR YOUR DAD COMING! MAYBE ***HE*** CAN KILL IT!
WATTERSON
ABOUT TIME, DAD! HE CRAWLED BACK INTO THE BED! GET A FLY SWATTER!
I'LL (COUGH) TELL YOU WHO'S GOING TO GET SWATTED! (CHOKE) WHAT HAVE YOU DONE TO THIS ROOM?!!

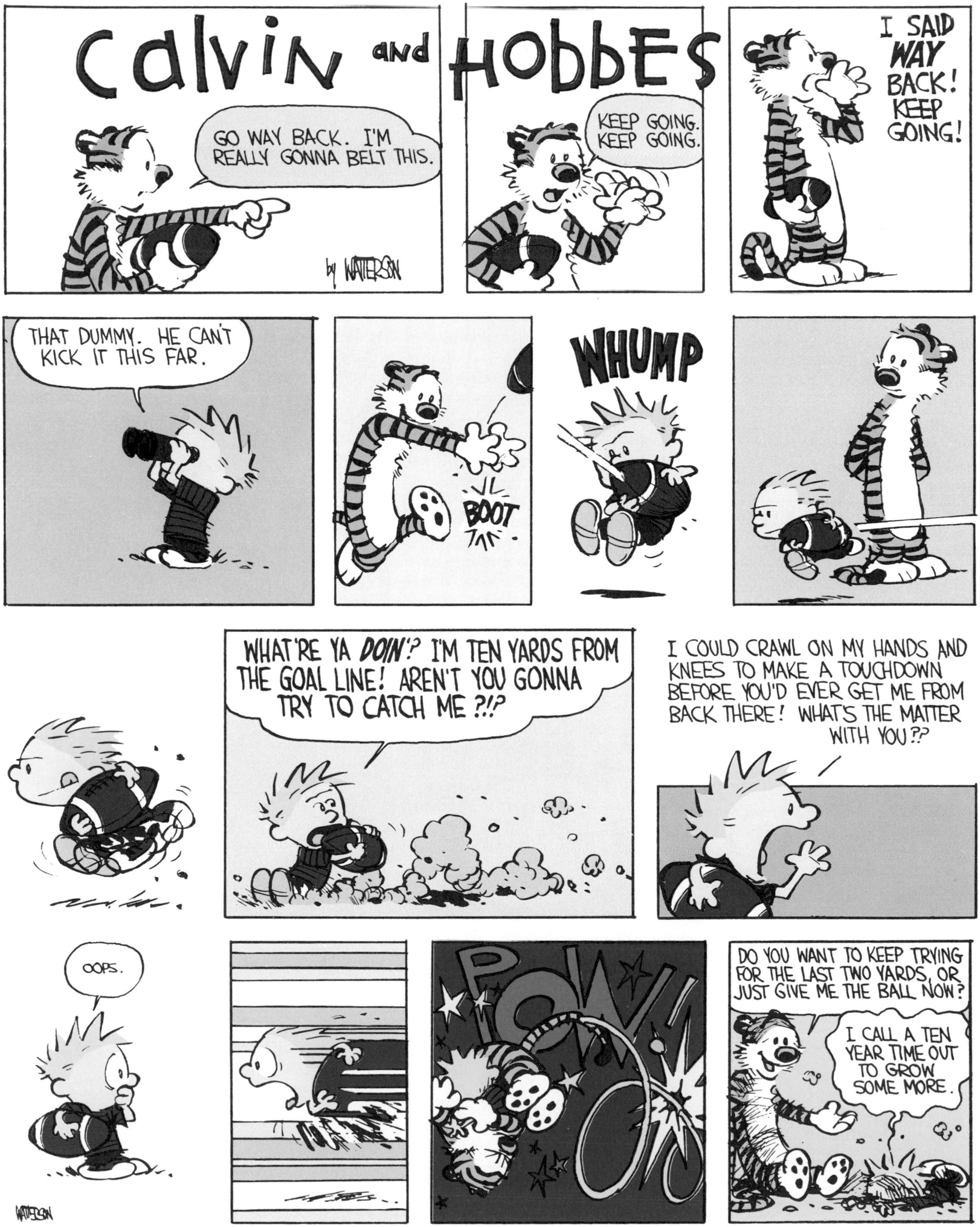
Calvin and HOBBES
by WATTERSON
GO WAY BACK. I'M REALLY GONNA BELT THIS.
KEEP GOING. KEEP GOING.
I SAID WAY BACK! KEEP GOING!
THAT DUMMY. HE CAN'T KICK IT THIS FAR.
BOOT
WHUMP
WHAT'RE YA DOIN'? I'M TEN YARDS FROM THE GOAL LINE! AREN'T YOU GONNA TRY TO CATCH ME ?!?
I COULD CRAWL ON MY HANDS AND KNEES TO MAKE A TOUCHDOWN BEFORE YOU'D EVER GET ME FROM BACK THERE! WHAT'S THE MATTER WITH YOU ??
OOPS.
WATTERSON
POW!
DO YOU WANT TO KEEP TRYING FOR THE LAST TWO YARDS, OR JUST GIVE ME THE BALL NOW?
I CALL A TEN YEAR TIME OUT TO GROW SOME MORE.

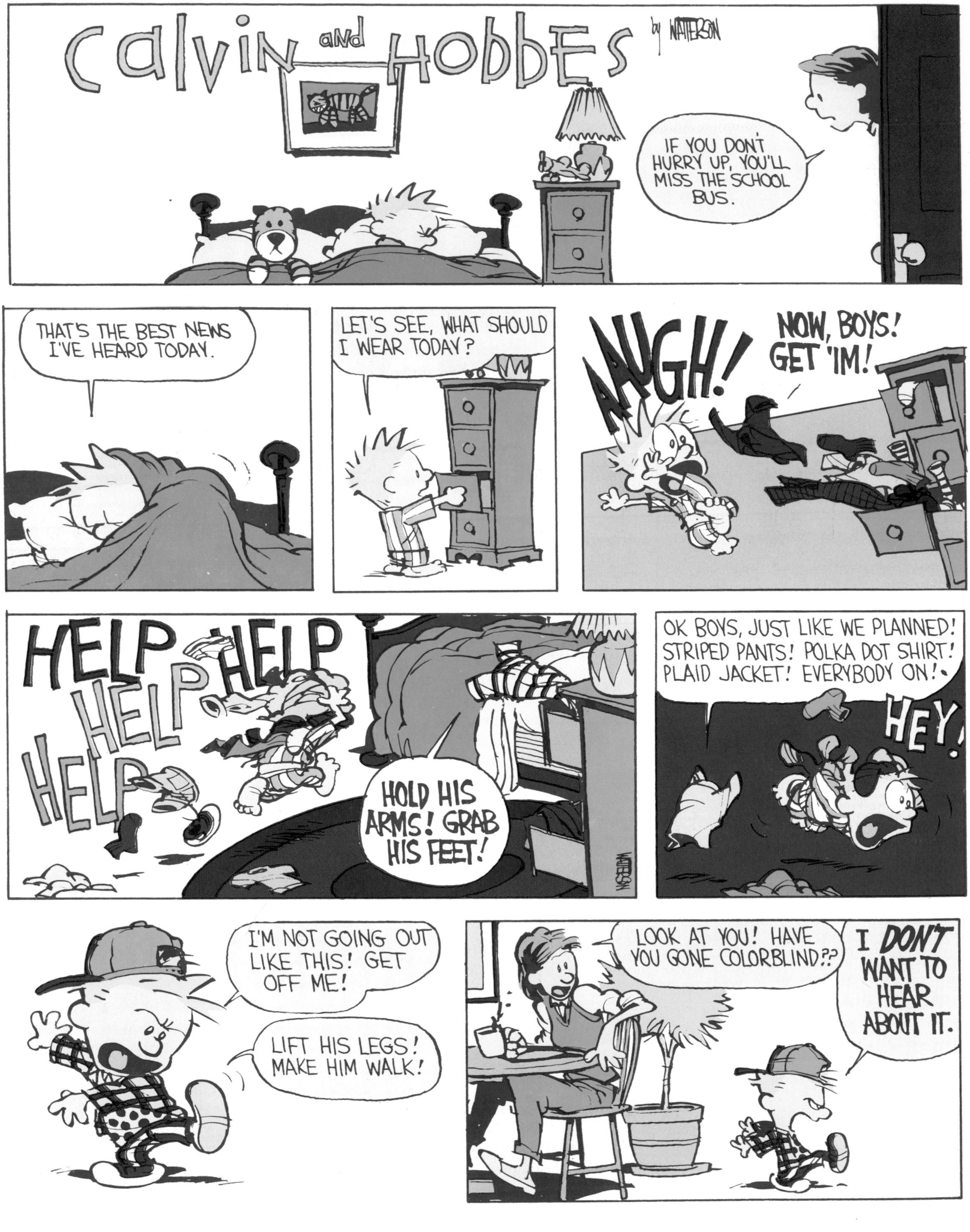
Calvin and HOBBES
by WATTERSON
IF YOU DON'T HURRY UP, YOU'LL MISS THE SCHOOL BUS.
THAT'S THE BEST NEWS I'VE HEARD TODAY.
LET'S SEE, WHAT SHOULD I WEAR TODAY?
AAUGH!
NOW, BOYS! GET 'IM!
HELP HELP HELP HELP
HOLD HIS ARMS! GRAB HIS FEET!
WATTERSON
OK BOYS, JUST LIKE WE PLANNED! STRIPED PANTS! POLKA DOT SHIRT! PLAID JACKET! EVERYBODY ON!
HEY!
I'M NOT GOING OUT LIKE THIS! GET OFF ME!
LIFT HIS LEGS! MAKE HIM WALK!
LOOK AT YOU! HAVE YOU GONE COLORBLIND?!?
I DON'T WANT TO HEAR ABOUT IT.

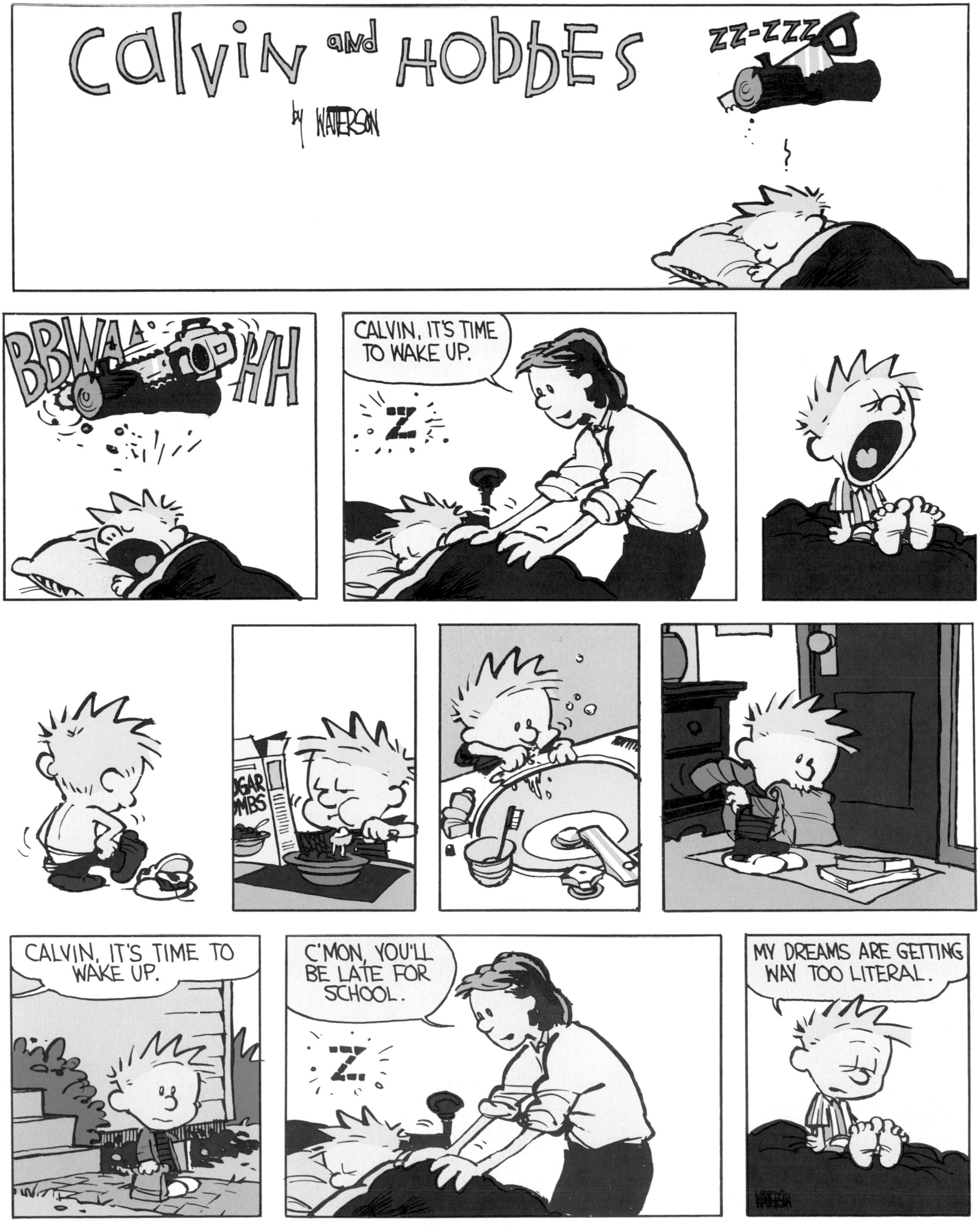

Calvin and HOBBES
by WATTERSON
ZZ-ZZZ
BBWAAAHH
CALVIN, IT'S TIME TO WAKE UP.
Z
SUGAR BOMBS
CALVIN, IT'S TIME TO WAKE UP.
C'MON, YOU'LL BE LATE FOR SCHOOL.
Z
MY DREAMS ARE GETTING WAY TOO LITERAL.

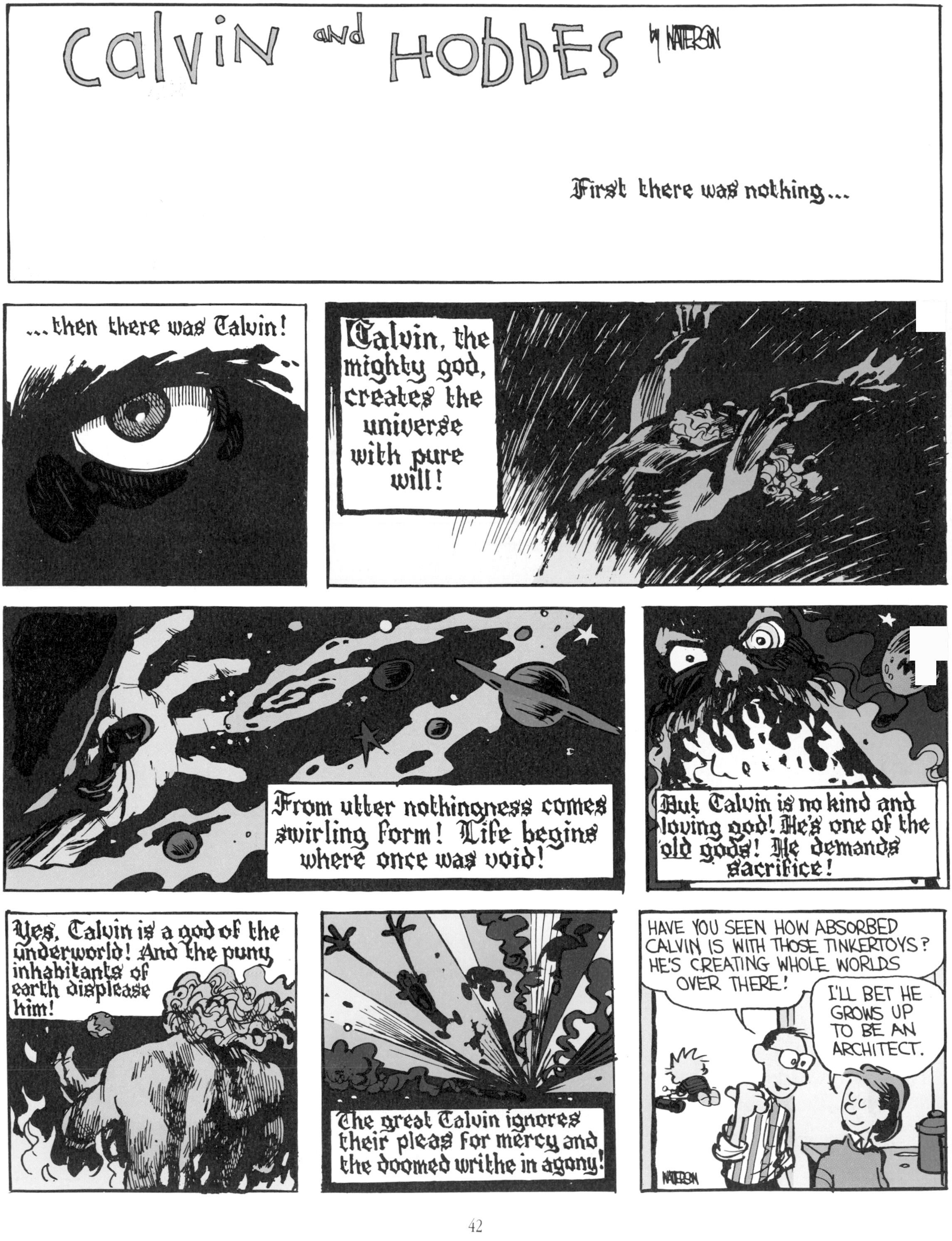
Calvin and Hobbes by WATTERSON
First there was nothing...
...then there was Calvin!
Calvin, the mighty god, creates the universe with pure will!
From utter nothingness comes swirling form! Life begins where once was void!
But Calvin is no kind and loving god! He's one of the old gods! He demands sacrifice!
Yes, Calvin is a god of the underworld! And the puny inhabitants of earth displease him!
The great Calvin ignores their pleas for mercy and the doomed writhe in agony!
HAVE YOU SEEN HOW ABSORBED CALVIN IS WITH THOSE TINKERTOYS? HE'S CREATING WHOLE WORLDS OVER THERE!
I'LL BET HE GROWS UP TO BE AN ARCHITECT.
WATTERSON

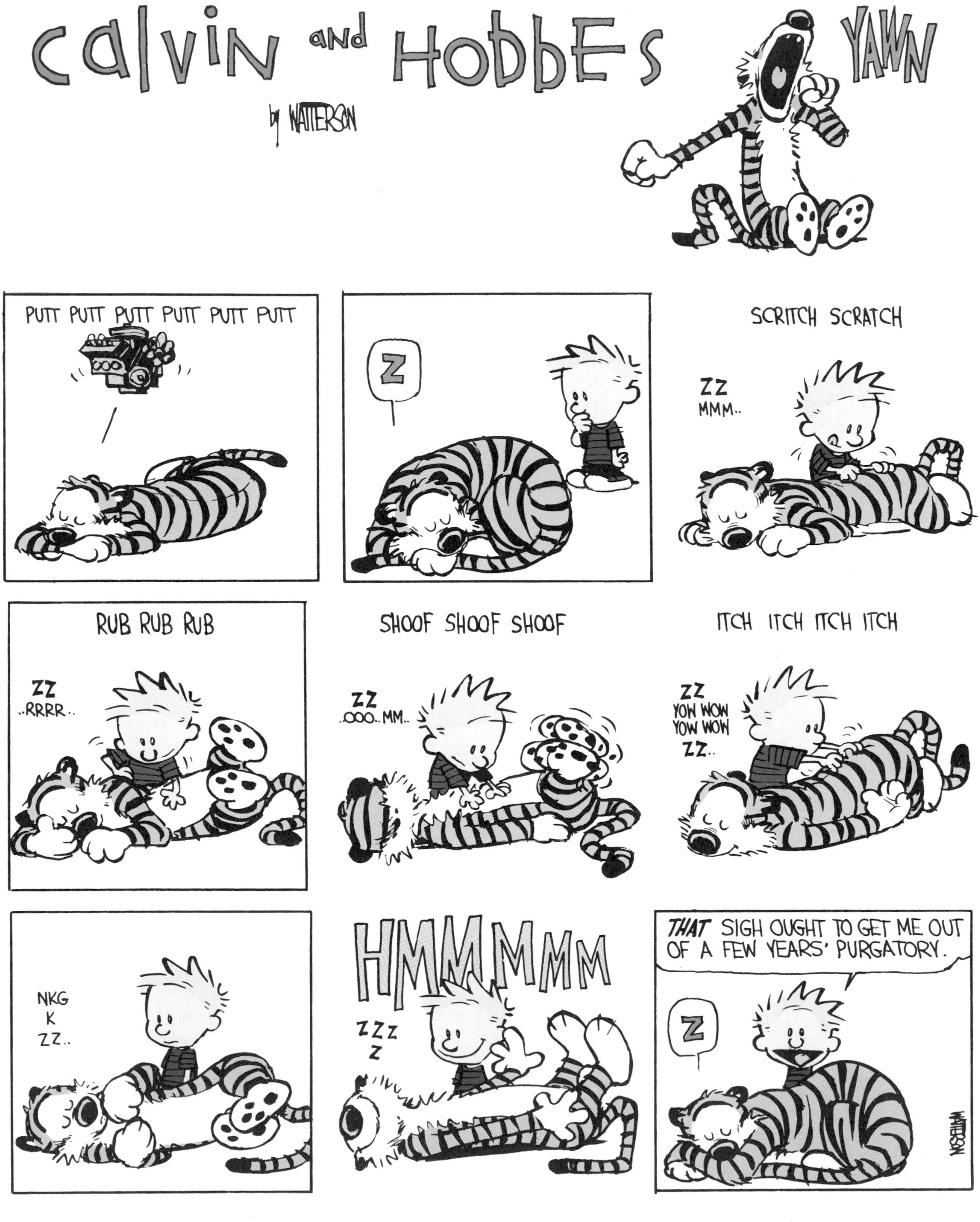
Calvin and HOBBES
by WATTERSON
YAWN
PUTT PUTT PUTT PUTT PUTT PUTT
Z
SCRITCH SCRATCH
ZZ MMM..
RUB RUB RUB
ZZ ..RRRR..
SHOOF SHOOF SHOOF
ZZ .OOO..MM..
ITCH ITCH ITCH ITCH
ZZ YOW WOW YOW WOW ZZ..
NKG K ZZ..
HMMMMM
ZZZ Z
THAT SIGH OUGHT TO GET ME OUT OF A FEW YEARS' PURGATORY.
Z
WATTERSON

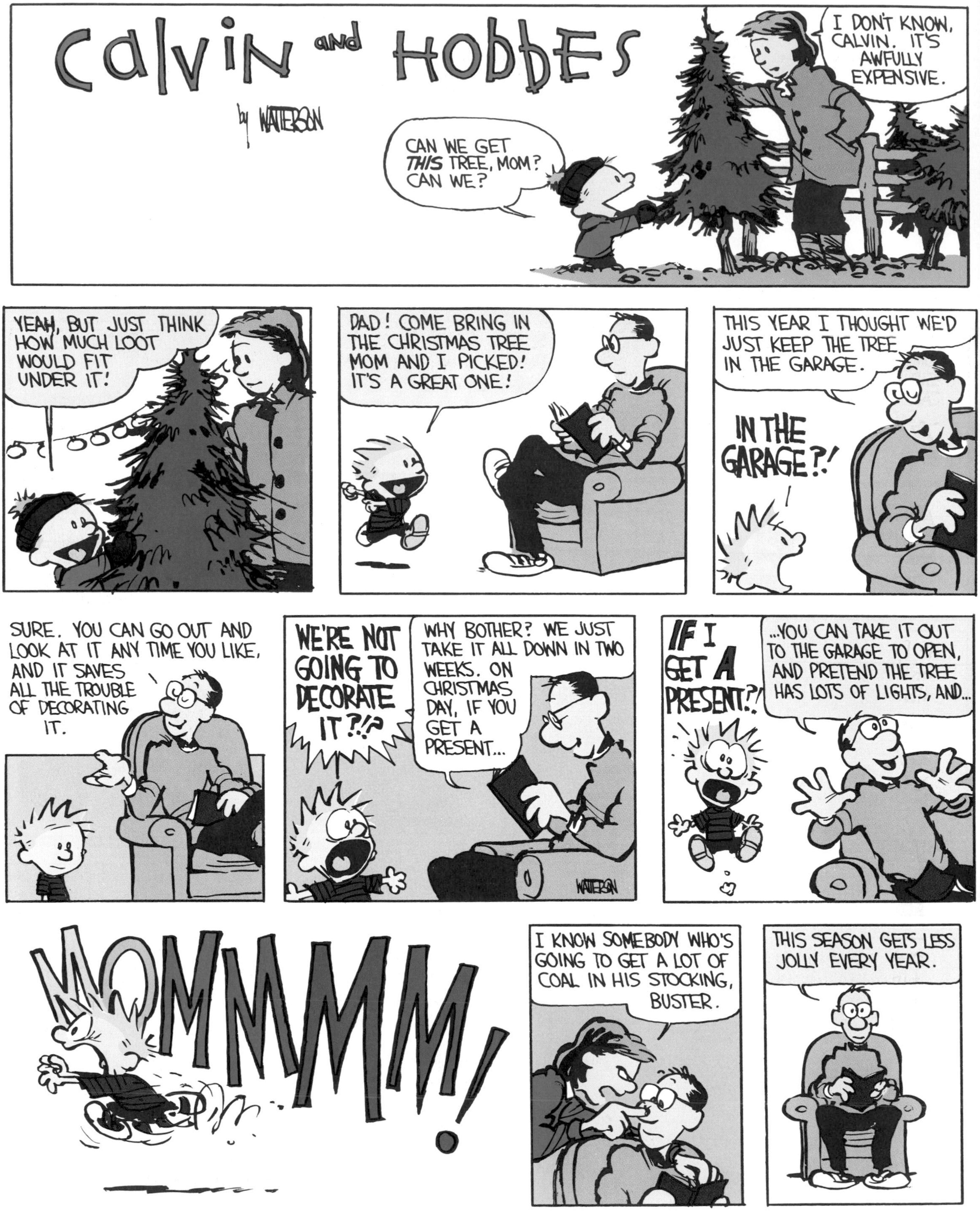
Calvin and HOBBES
by WATTERSON
CAN WE GET THIS TREE, MOM? CAN WE?
I DON'T KNOW, CALVIN. IT'S AWFULLY EXPENSIVE.
YEAH, BUT JUST THINK HOW MUCH LOOT WOULD FIT UNDER IT!
DAD! COME BRING IN THE CHRISTMAS TREE MOM AND I PICKED! IT'S A GREAT ONE!
THIS YEAR I THOUGHT WE'D JUST KEEP THE TREE IN THE GARAGE.
IN THE GARAGE?!
SURE. YOU CAN GO OUT AND LOOK AT IT ANY TIME YOU LIKE, AND IT SAVES ALL THE TROUBLE OF DECORATING IT.
WE'RE NOT GOING TO DECORATE IT?!?
WHY BOTHER? WE JUST TAKE IT ALL DOWN IN TWO WEEKS. ON CHRISTMAS DAY, IF YOU GET A PRESENT...
WATTERSON
IF I GET A PRESENT?!
...YOU CAN TAKE IT OUT TO THE GARAGE TO OPEN, AND PRETEND THE TREE HAS LOTS OF LIGHTS, AND...
MOMMMM!
I KNOW SOMEBODY WHO'S GOING TO GET A LOT OF COAL IN HIS STOCKING, BUSTER.
THIS SEASON GETS LESS JOLLY EVERY YEAR.

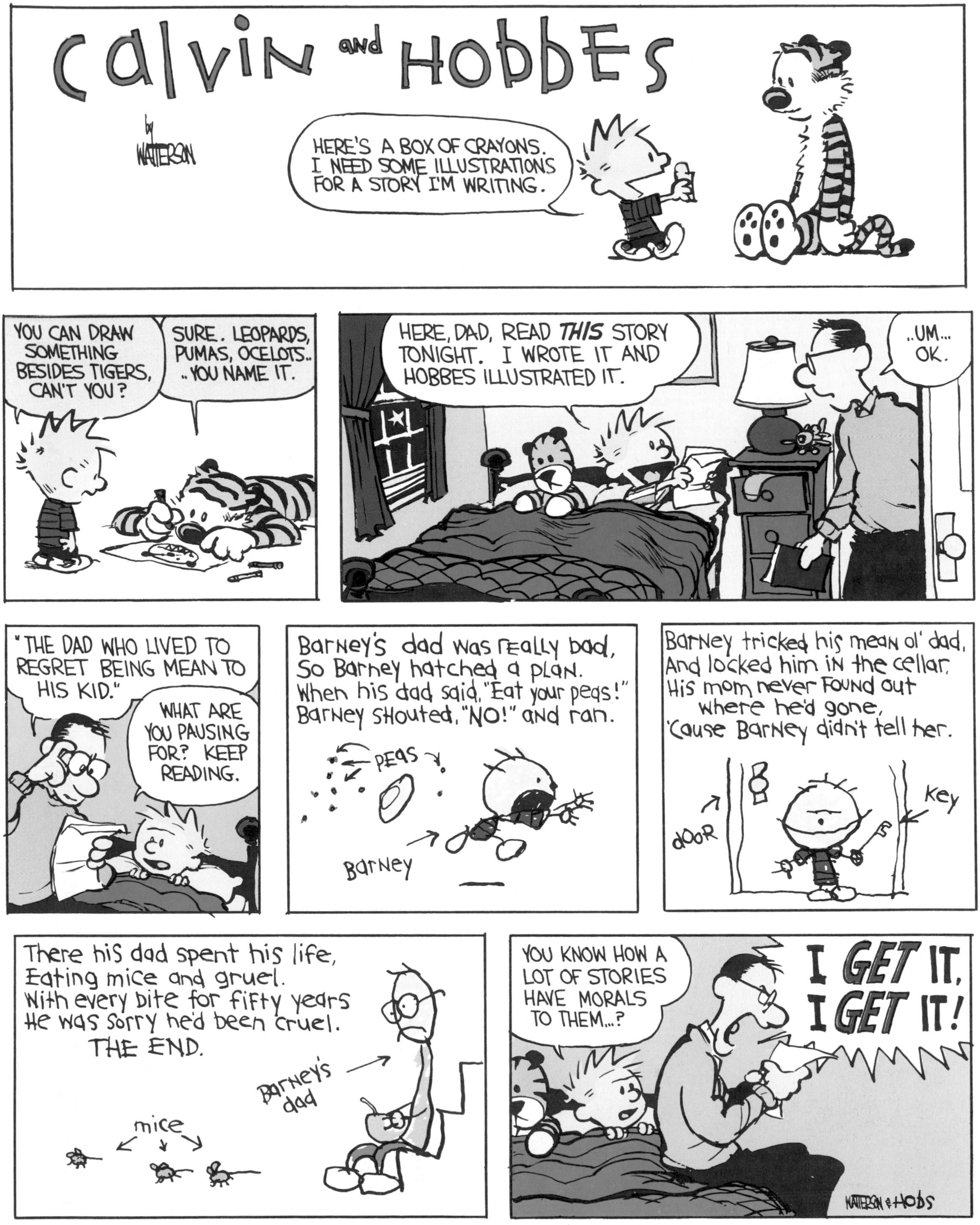
Calvin and Hobbes
by WATTERSON
HERE'S A BOX OF CRAYONS. I NEED SOME ILLUSTRATIONS FOR A STORY I'M WRITING.
YOU CAN DRAW SOMETHING BESIDES TIGERS, CAN'T YOU?
SURE. LEOPARDS, PUMAS, OCELOTS.. ..YOU NAME IT.
HERE, DAD, READ THIS STORY TONIGHT. I WROTE IT AND HOBBES ILLUSTRATED IT.
..UM... OK.
"THE DAD WHO LIVED TO REGRET BEING MEAN TO HIS KID."
WHAT ARE YOU PAUSING FOR? KEEP READING.
Barney's dad was really bad, So Barney hatched a plan. When his dad said, "Eat your peas!" Barney shouted, "NO!" and ran.
peas
Barney
Barney tricked his mean ol' dad, And locked him in the cellar. His mom never found out where he'd gone, 'Cause Barney didn't tell her.
door
key
There his dad spent his life, Eating mice and gruel. With every bite for fifty years He was sorry he'd been cruel. THE END.
Barney's dad
mice
YOU KNOW HOW A LOT OF STORIES HAVE MORALS TO THEM...?
I GET IT, I GET IT!
WATTERSON & HOBS

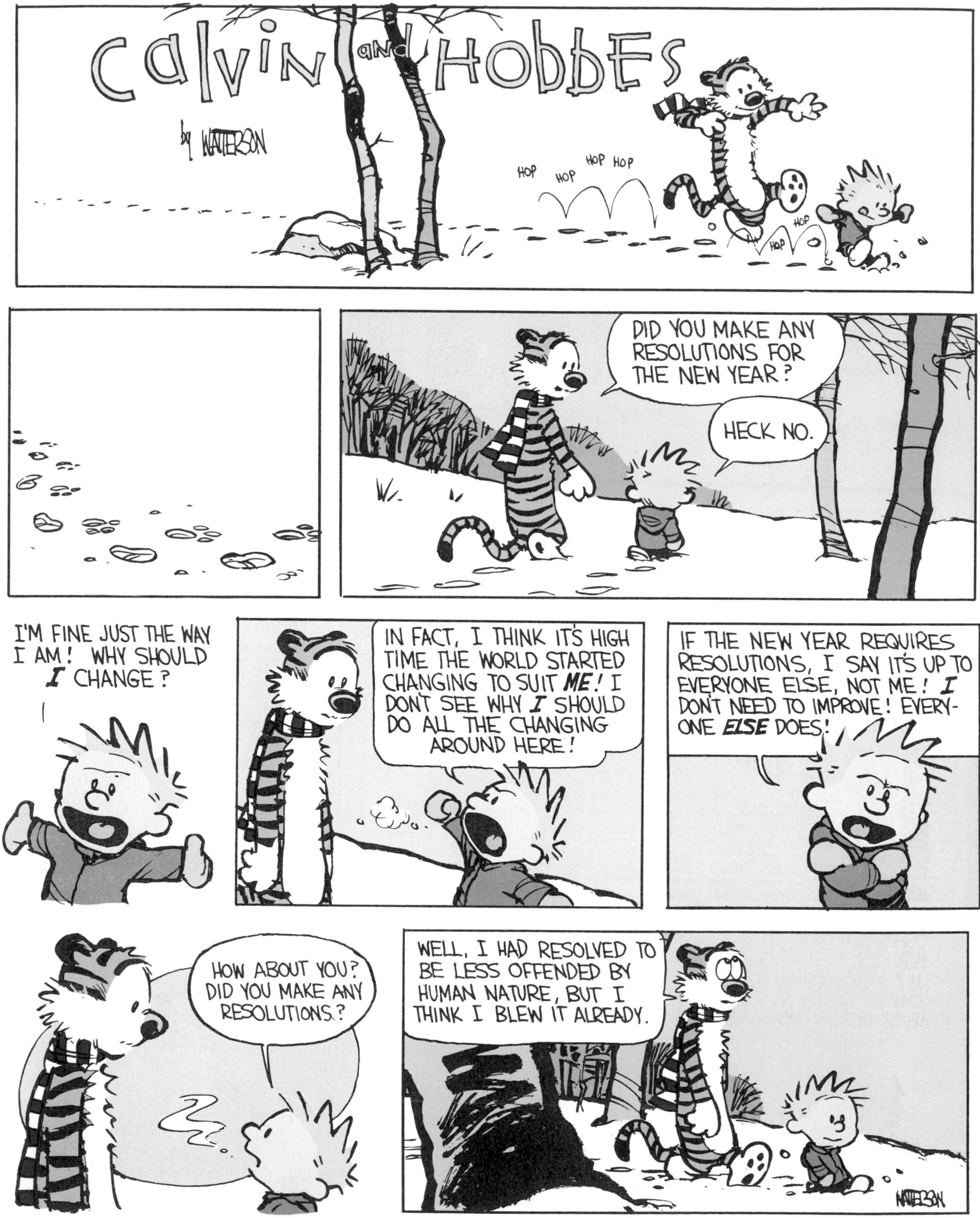
Calvin and HOBBES
by WATTERSON
HOP HOP HOP HOP
HOP HOP
DID YOU MAKE ANY RESOLUTIONS FOR THE NEW YEAR?
HECK NO.
I'M FINE JUST THE WAY I AM! WHY SHOULD *I* CHANGE?
IN FACT, I THINK IT'S HIGH TIME THE WORLD STARTED CHANGING TO SUIT *ME*! I DON'T SEE WHY *I* SHOULD DO ALL THE CHANGING AROUND HERE!
IF THE NEW YEAR REQUIRES RESOLUTIONS, I SAY IT'S UP TO EVERYONE ELSE, NOT ME! *I* DON'T NEED TO IMPROVE! EVERYONE *ELSE* DOES!
HOW ABOUT YOU? DID YOU MAKE ANY RESOLUTIONS?
WELL, I HAD RESOLVED TO BE LESS OFFENDED BY HUMAN NATURE, BUT I THINK I BLEW IT ALREADY.
WATTERSON

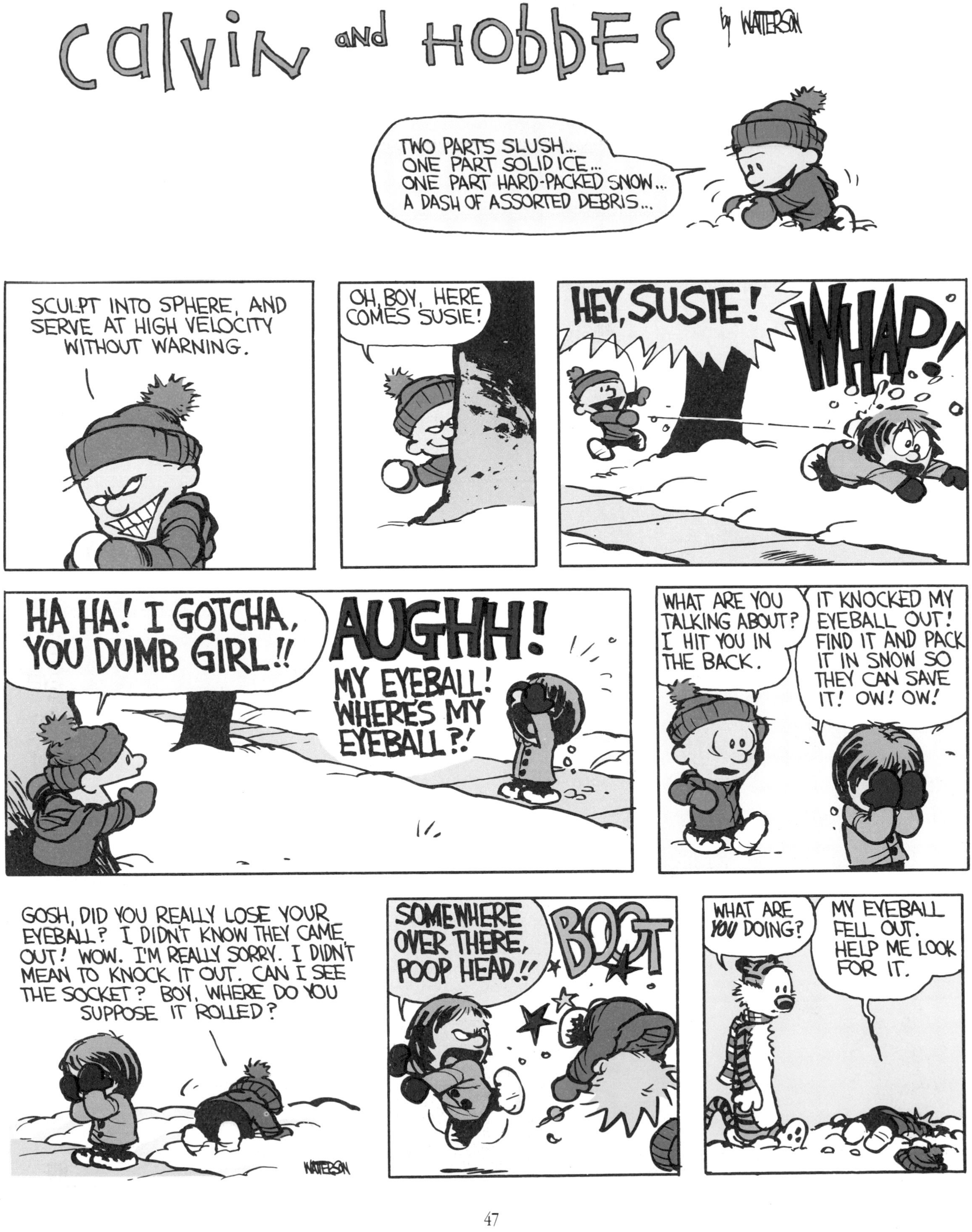
Calvin and HOBBES by WATTERSON
TWO PARTS SLUSH... ONE PART SOLID ICE... ONE PART HARD-PACKED SNOW... A DASH OF ASSORTED DEBRIS...
SCULPT INTO SPHERE, AND SERVE AT HIGH VELOCITY WITHOUT WARNING.
OH, BOY, HERE COMES SUSIE!
HEY, SUSIE!
WHAP!
HA HA! I GOTCHA, YOU DUMB GIRL!!
AUGHH!
MY EYEBALL! WHERE'S MY EYEBALL?!
WHAT ARE YOU TALKING ABOUT? I HIT YOU IN THE BACK.
IT KNOCKED MY EYEBALL OUT! FIND IT AND PACK IT IN SNOW SO THEY CAN SAVE IT! OW! OW!
GOSH, DID YOU REALLY LOSE YOUR EYEBALL? I DIDN'T KNOW THEY CAME OUT! WOW. I'M REALLY SORRY. I DIDN'T MEAN TO KNOCK IT OUT. CAN I SEE THE SOCKET? BOY, WHERE DO YOU SUPPOSE IT ROLLED?
WATTERSON
SOMEWHERE OVER THERE, POOP HEAD!!
BOOT
WHAT ARE YOU DOING?
MY EYEBALL FELL OUT. HELP ME LOOK FOR IT.

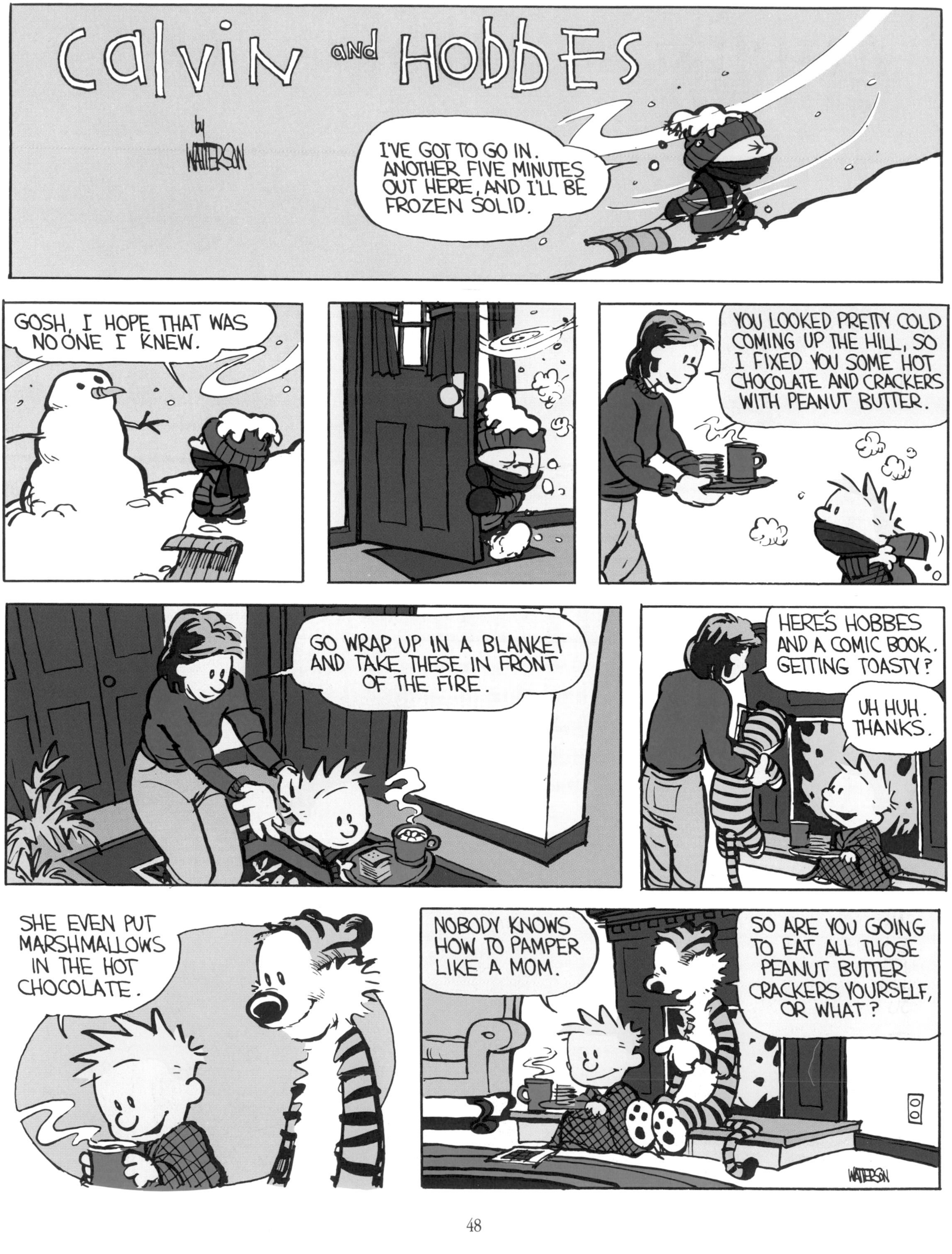
Calvin and HOBBES
by WATTERSON
I'VE GOT TO GO IN. ANOTHER FIVE MINUTES OUT HERE, AND I'LL BE FROZEN SOLID.
GOSH, I HOPE THAT WAS NO ONE I KNEW.
YOU LOOKED PRETTY COLD COMING UP THE HILL, SO I FIXED YOU SOME HOT CHOCOLATE AND CRACKERS WITH PEANUT BUTTER.
GO WRAP UP IN A BLANKET AND TAKE THESE IN FRONT OF THE FIRE.
HERE'S HOBBES AND A COMIC BOOK. GETTING TOASTY?
UH HUH. THANKS.
SHE EVEN PUT MARSHMALLOWS IN THE HOT CHOCOLATE.
NOBODY KNOWS HOW TO PAMPER LIKE A MOM.
SO ARE YOU GOING TO EAT ALL THOSE PEANUT BUTTER CRACKERS YOURSELF, OR WHAT?
WATTERSON

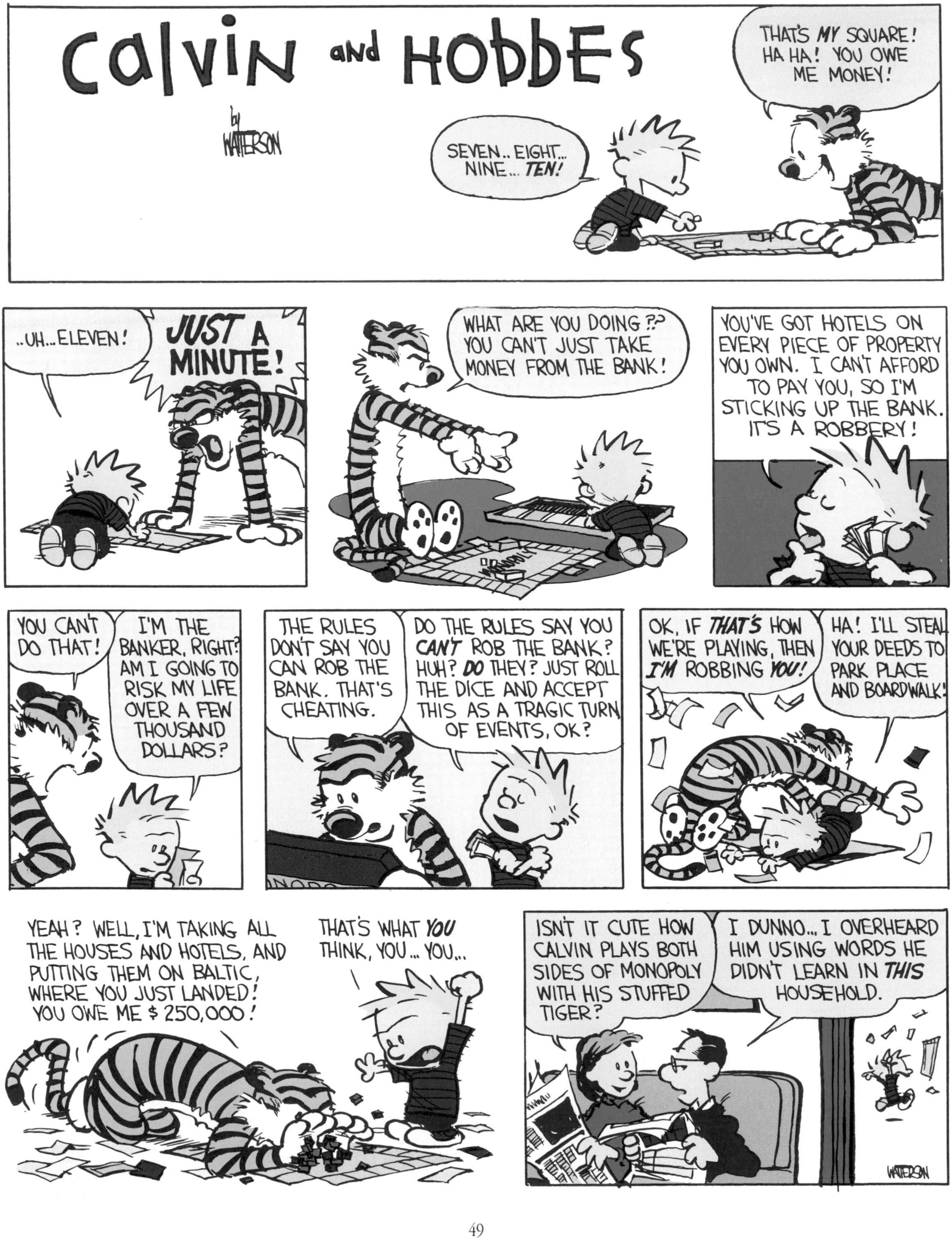

Calvin and Hobbes
by WATTERSON
SEVEN.. EIGHT... NINE... TEN!
THAT'S MY SQUARE! HA HA! YOU OWE ME MONEY!
..UH...ELEVEN!
JUST A MINUTE!
WHAT ARE YOU DOING ?!? YOU CAN'T JUST TAKE MONEY FROM THE BANK!
YOU'VE GOT HOTELS ON EVERY PIECE OF PROPERTY YOU OWN. I CAN'T AFFORD TO PAY YOU, SO I'M STICKING UP THE BANK. IT'S A ROBBERY!
YOU CAN'T DO THAT!
I'M THE BANKER, RIGHT? AM I GOING TO RISK MY LIFE OVER A FEW THOUSAND DOLLARS?
THE RULES DON'T SAY YOU CAN ROB THE BANK. THAT'S CHEATING.
DO THE RULES SAY YOU CAN'T ROB THE BANK? HUH? DO THEY? JUST ROLL THE DICE AND ACCEPT THIS AS A TRAGIC TURN OF EVENTS, OK?
OK, IF THAT'S HOW WE'RE PLAYING, THEN I'M ROBBING YOU!
HA! I'LL STEAL YOUR DEEDS TO PARK PLACE AND BOARDWALK!
YEAH? WELL, I'M TAKING ALL THE HOUSES AND HOTELS, AND PUTTING THEM ON BALTIC, WHERE YOU JUST LANDED! YOU OWE ME $ 250,000!
THAT'S WHAT YOU THINK, YOU... YOU...
ISN'T IT CUTE HOW CALVIN PLAYS BOTH SIDES OF MONOPOLY WITH HIS STUFFED TIGER?
I DUNNO... I OVERHEARD HIM USING WORDS HE DIDN'T LEARN IN THIS HOUSEHOLD.
WATTERSON

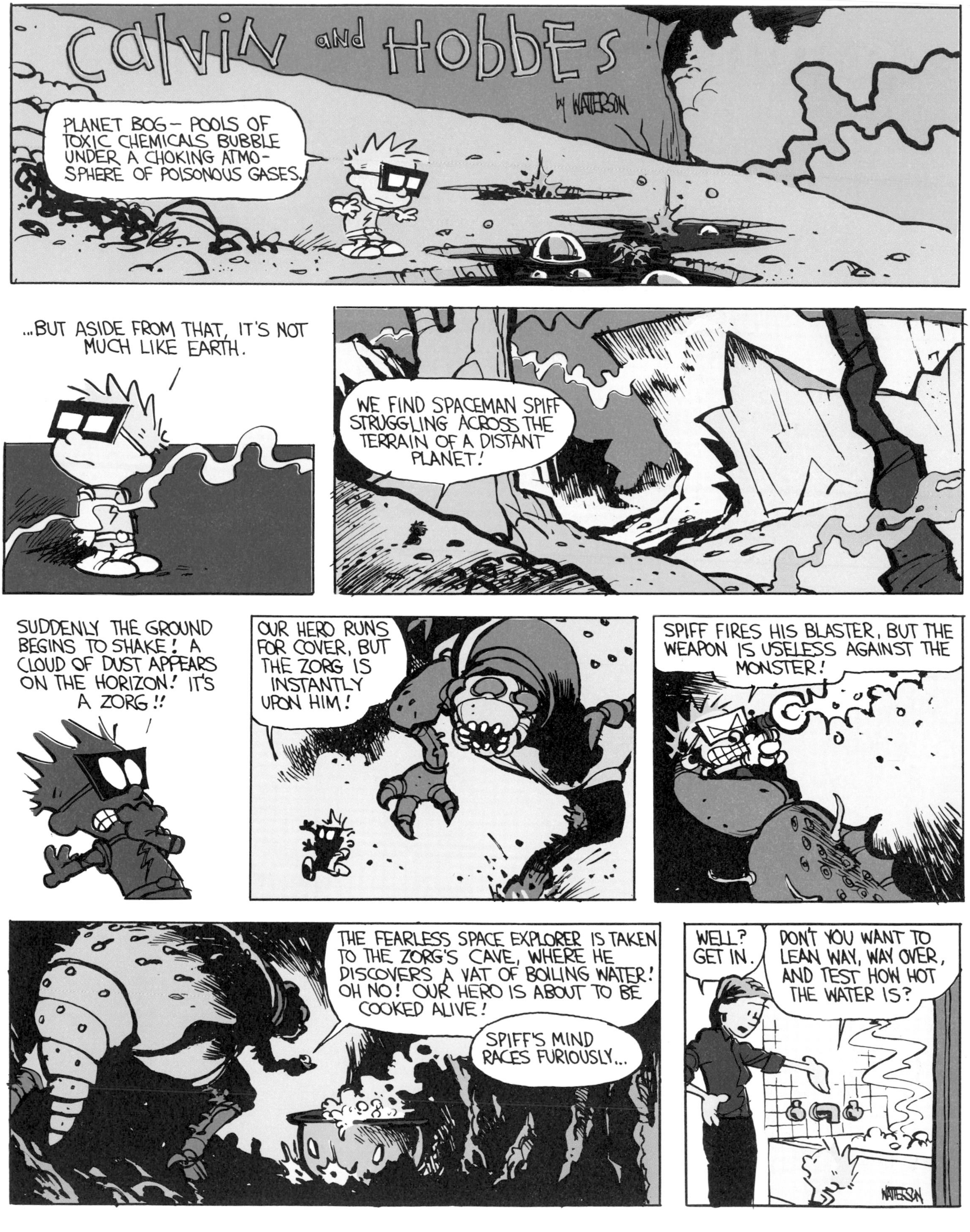
Calvin and Hobbes
by WATTERSON
PLANET BOG – POOLS OF TOXIC CHEMICALS BUBBLE UNDER A CHOKING ATMOSPHERE OF POISONOUS GASES...
...BUT ASIDE FROM THAT, IT'S NOT MUCH LIKE EARTH.
WE FIND SPACEMAN SPIFF STRUGGLING ACROSS THE TERRAIN OF A DISTANT PLANET!
SUDDENLY THE GROUND BEGINS TO SHAKE! A CLOUD OF DUST APPEARS ON THE HORIZON! IT'S A ZORG!!
OUR HERO RUNS FOR COVER, BUT THE ZORG IS INSTANTLY UPON HIM!
SPIFF FIRES HIS BLASTER, BUT THE WEAPON IS USELESS AGAINST THE MONSTER!
THE FEARLESS SPACE EXPLORER IS TAKEN TO THE ZORG'S CAVE, WHERE HE DISCOVERS A VAT OF BOILING WATER! OH NO! OUR HERO IS ABOUT TO BE COOKED ALIVE!
SPIFF'S MIND RACES FURIOUSLY...
WELL? GET IN.
DON'T YOU WANT TO LEAN WAY, WAY OVER, AND TEST HOW HOT THE WATER IS?
WATTERSON

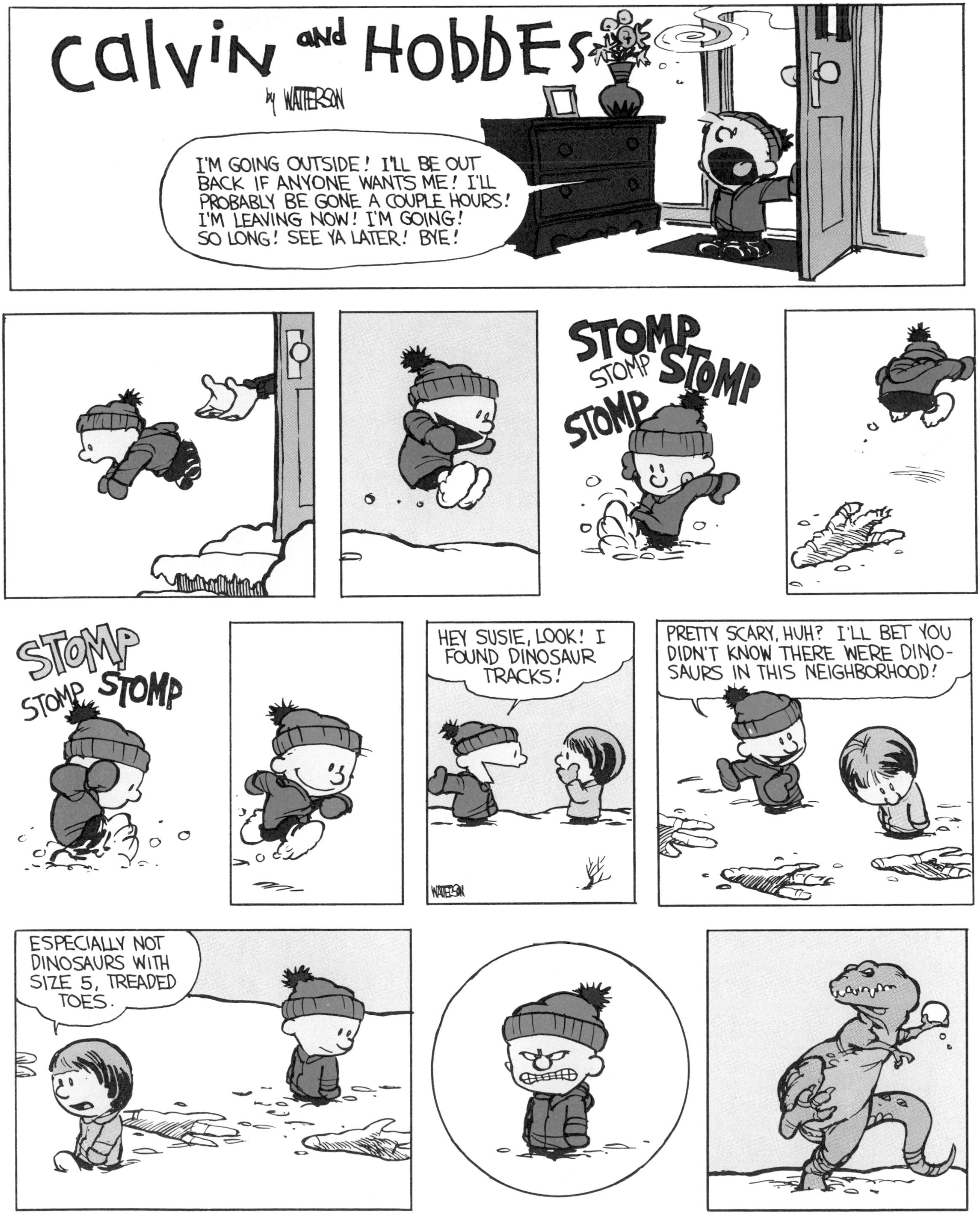
Calvin and Hobbes
by WATTERSON
I'M GOING OUTSIDE! I'LL BE OUT BACK IF ANYONE WANTS ME! I'LL PROBABLY BE GONE A COUPLE HOURS! I'M LEAVING NOW! I'M GOING! SO LONG! SEE YA LATER! BYE!
STOMP STOMP STOMP STOMP
STOMP STOMP STOMP
HEY SUSIE, LOOK! I FOUND DINOSAUR TRACKS!
WATTERSON
PRETTY SCARY, HUH? I'LL BET YOU DIDN'T KNOW THERE WERE DINOSAURS IN THIS NEIGHBORHOOD!
ESPECIALLY NOT DINOSAURS WITH SIZE 5, TREADED TOES.

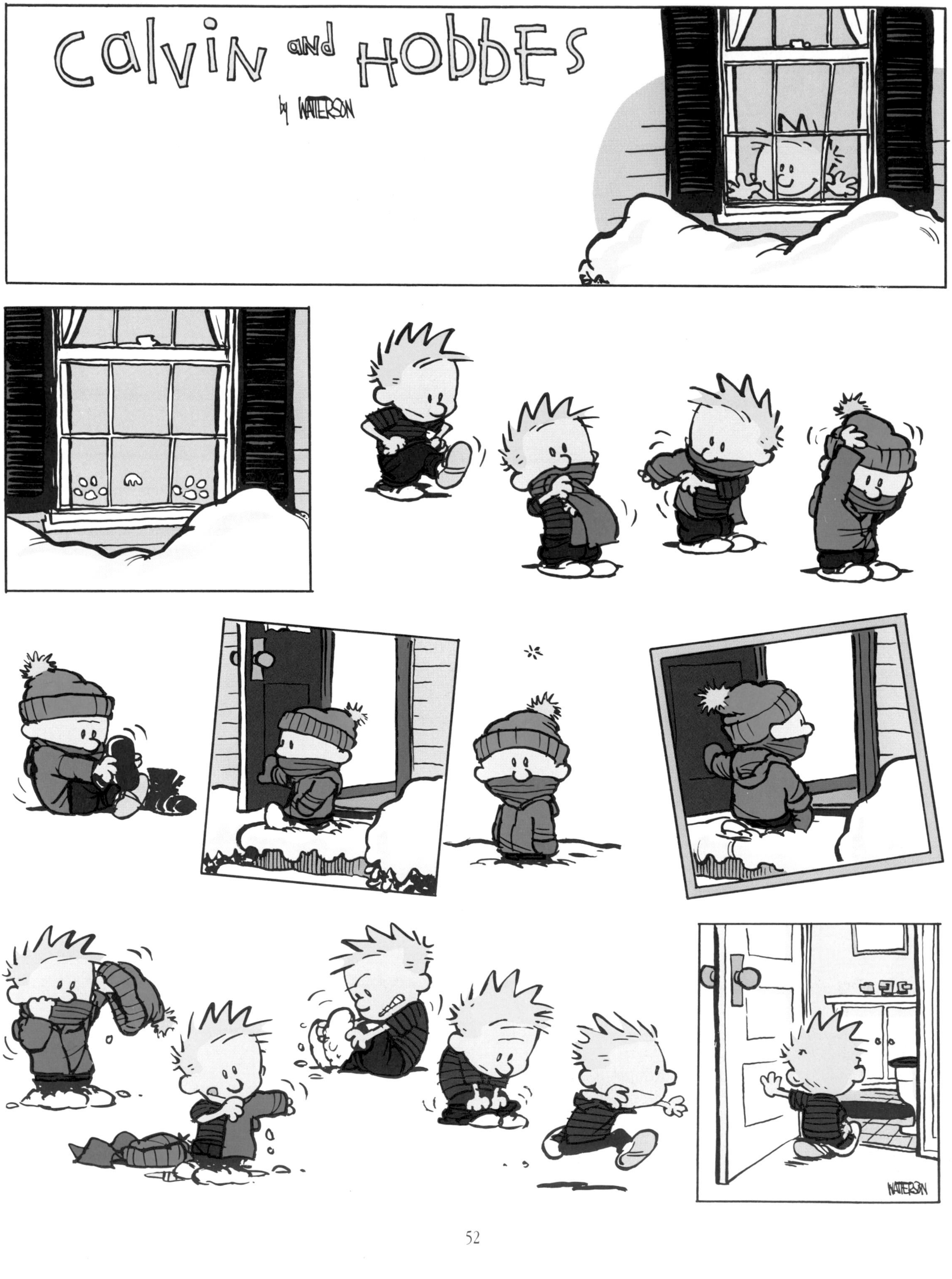
Calvin and HOBBES
by WATTERSON
WATTERSON

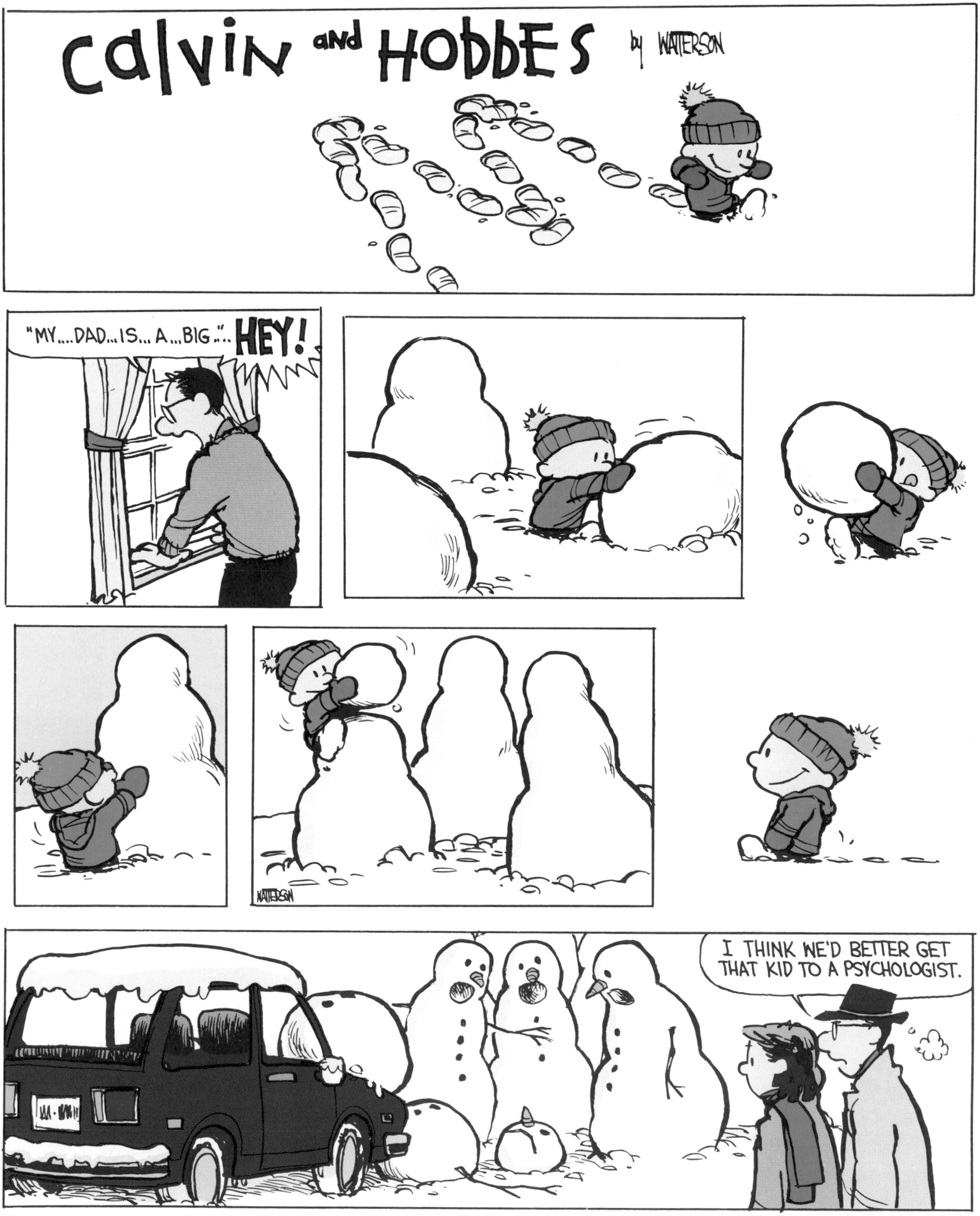
Calvin and HOBBES
by WATTERSON
"MY....DAD...IS... A...BIG...".. HEY!
WATTERSON
I THINK WE'D BETTER GET THAT KID TO A PSYCHOLOGIST.

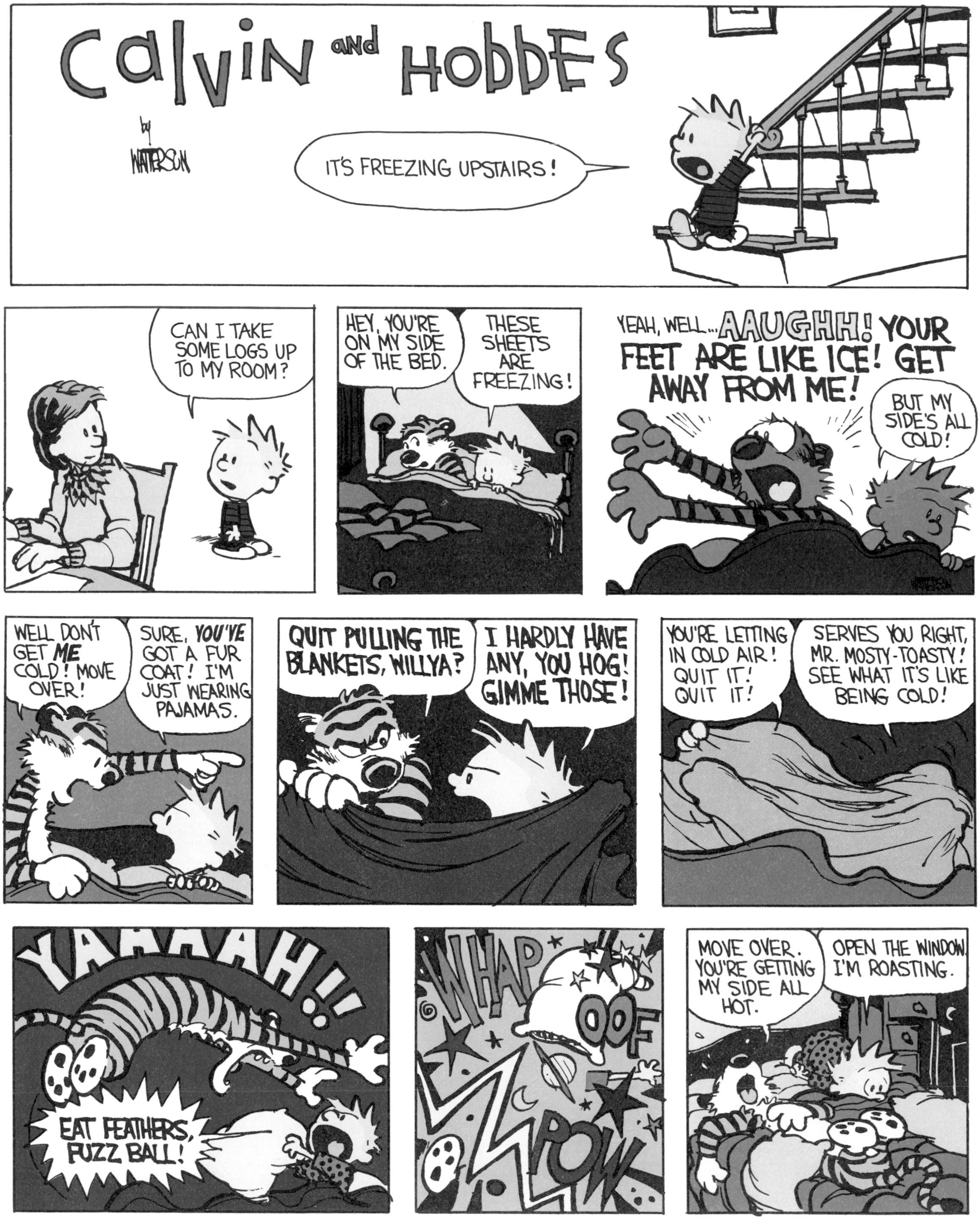
Calvin and Hobbes
by WATTERSON
IT'S FREEZING UPSTAIRS!
CAN I TAKE SOME LOGS UP TO MY ROOM?
HEY, YOU'RE ON MY SIDE OF THE BED.
THESE SHEETS ARE FREEZING!
YEAH, WELL... AAUGHH! YOUR FEET ARE LIKE ICE! GET AWAY FROM ME!
BUT MY SIDE'S ALL COLD!
WELL DON'T GET ME COLD! MOVE OVER!
SURE, YOU'VE GOT A FUR COAT! I'M JUST WEARING PAJAMAS.
QUIT PULLING THE BLANKETS, WILLYA?
I HARDLY HAVE ANY, YOU HOG! GIMME THOSE!
YOU'RE LETTING IN COLD AIR! QUIT IT! QUIT IT!
SERVES YOU RIGHT, MR. MOSTY-TOASTY! SEE WHAT IT'S LIKE BEING COLD!
YAAAAH!!!
EAT FEATHERS, FUZZ BALL!
WHAP
OOF
POW
MOVE OVER. YOU'RE GETTING MY SIDE ALL HOT.
OPEN THE WINDOW. I'M ROASTING.

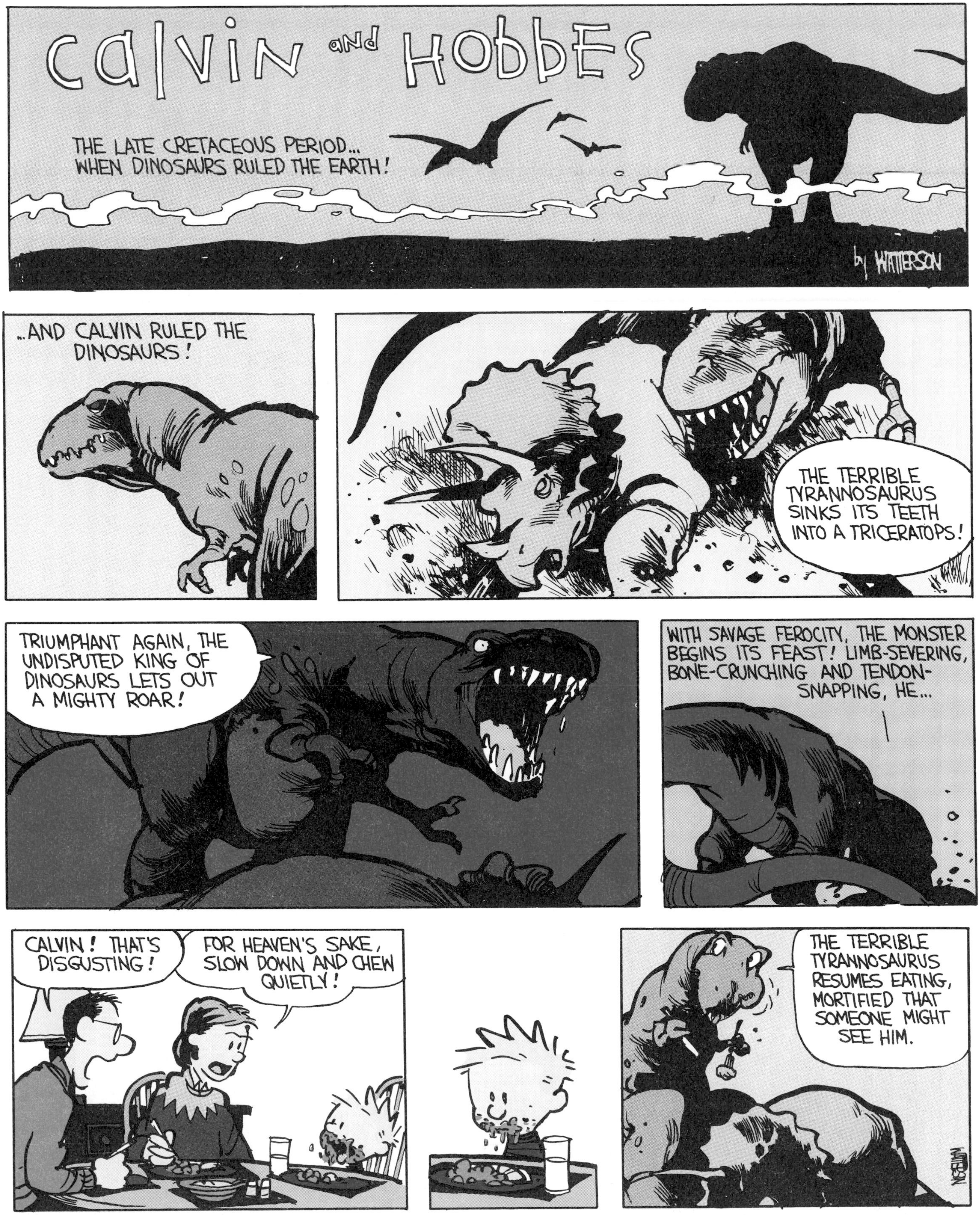

Calvin and Hobbes
THE LATE CRETACEOUS PERIOD... WHEN DINOSAURS RULED THE EARTH!
by WATTERSON
..AND CALVIN RULED THE DINOSAURS!
THE TERRIBLE TYRANNOSAURUS SINKS ITS TEETH INTO A TRICERATOPS!
TRIUMPHANT AGAIN, THE UNDISPUTED KING OF DINOSAURS LETS OUT A MIGHTY ROAR!
WITH SAVAGE FEROCITY, THE MONSTER BEGINS ITS FEAST! LIMB-SEVERING, BONE-CRUNCHING AND TENDON-SNAPPING, HE...
CALVIN! THAT'S DISGUSTING!
FOR HEAVEN'S SAKE, SLOW DOWN AND CHEW QUIETLY!
THE TERRIBLE TYRANNOSAURUS RESUMES EATING, MORTIFIED THAT SOMEONE MIGHT SEE HIM.

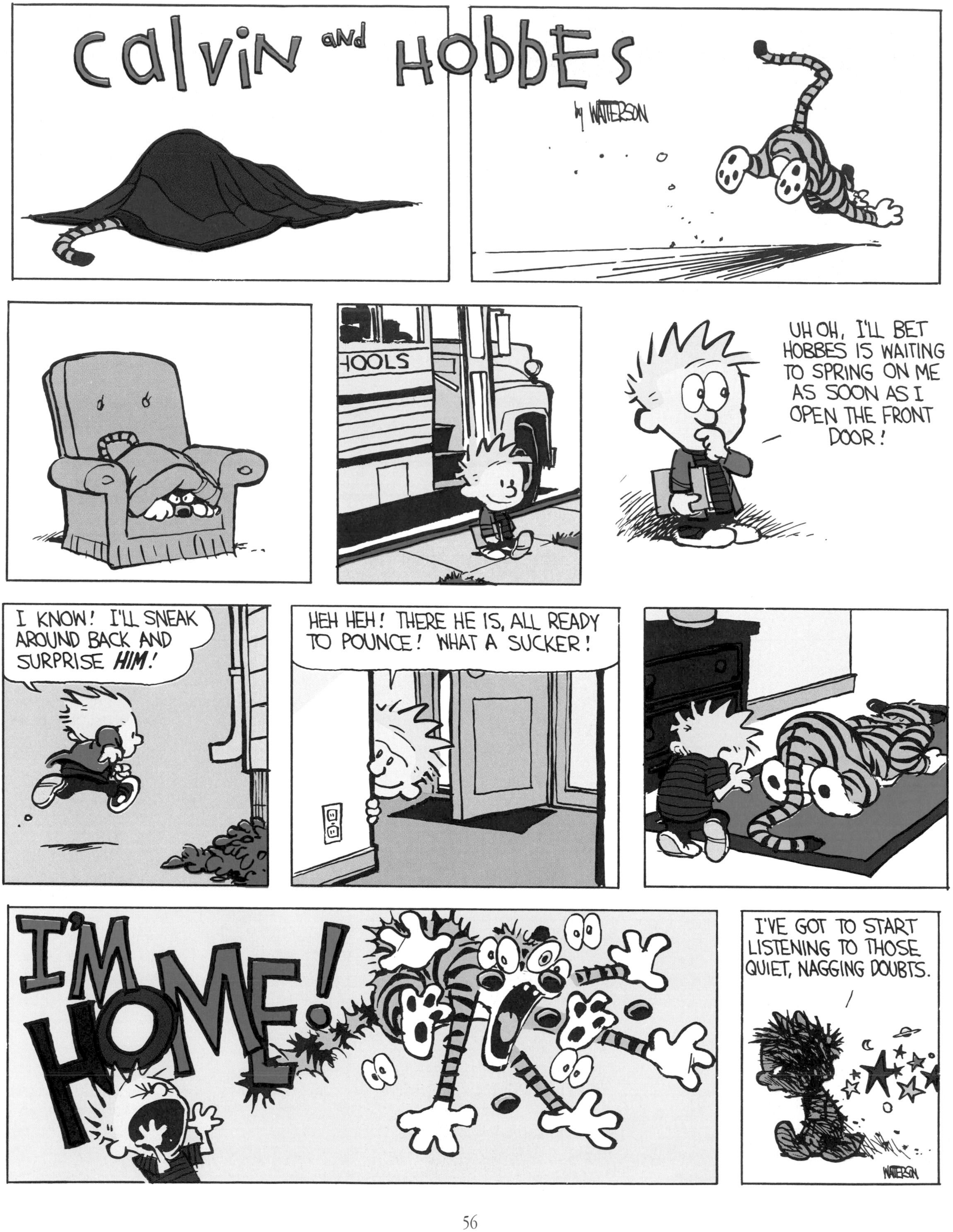
Calvin and HOBBES
by WATTERSON
HOOLS
UH OH, I'LL BET HOBBES IS WAITING TO SPRING ON ME AS SOON AS I OPEN THE FRONT DOOR!
I KNOW! I'LL SNEAK AROUND BACK AND SURPRISE HIM!
HEH HEH! THERE HE IS, ALL READY TO POUNCE! WHAT A SUCKER!
I'M HOME!
I'VE GOT TO START LISTENING TO THOSE QUIET, NAGGING DOUBTS.
WATTERSON

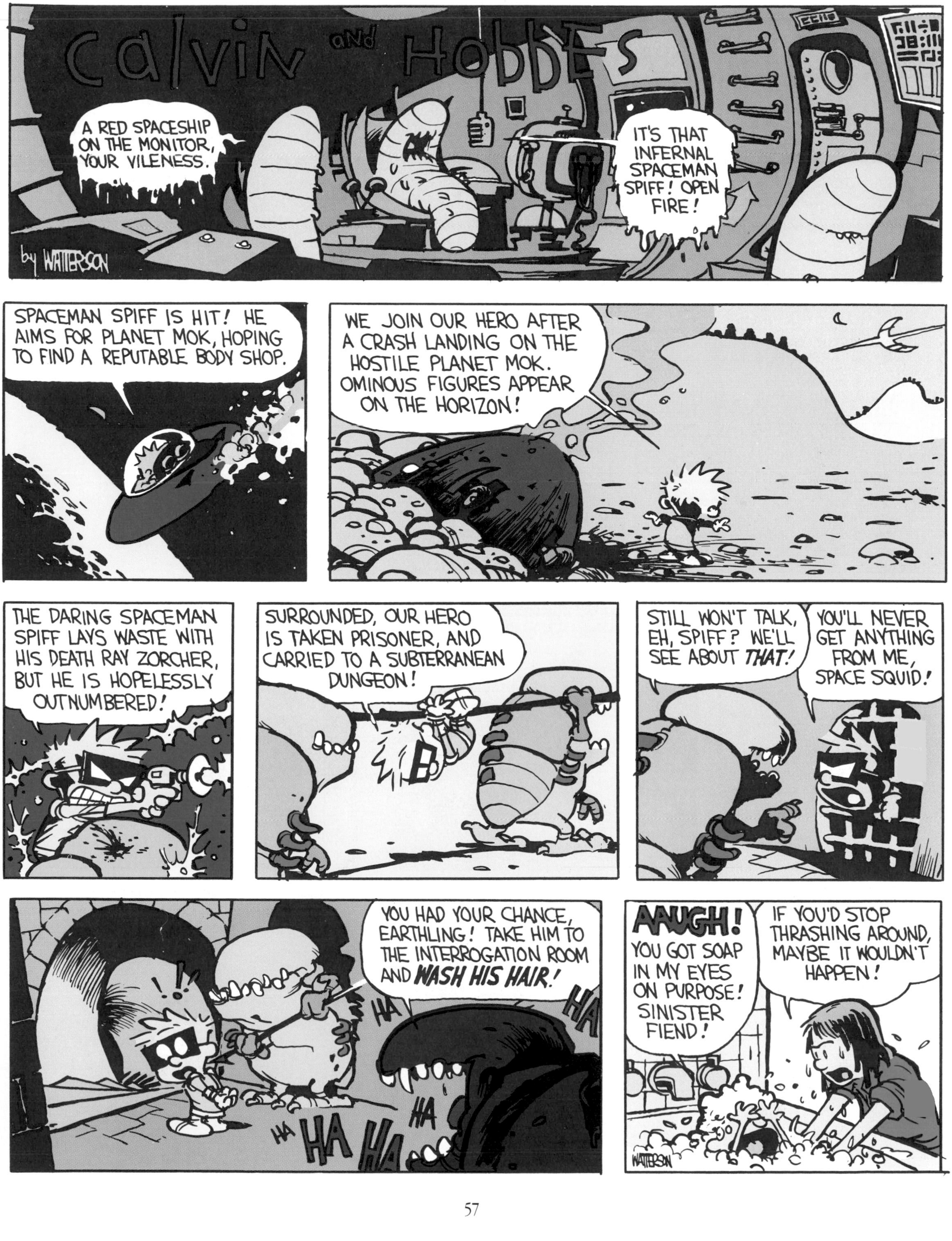

Calvin and Hobbes
by WATTERSON
A RED SPACESHIP ON THE MONITOR, YOUR VILENESS.
IT'S THAT INFERNAL SPACEMAN SPIFF! OPEN FIRE!
SPACEMAN SPIFF IS HIT! HE AIMS FOR PLANET MOK, HOPING TO FIND A REPUTABLE BODY SHOP.
WE JOIN OUR HERO AFTER A CRASH LANDING ON THE HOSTILE PLANET MOK. OMINOUS FIGURES APPEAR ON THE HORIZON!
THE DARING SPACEMAN SPIFF LAYS WASTE WITH HIS DEATH RAY ZORCHER, BUT HE IS HOPELESSLY OUTNUMBERED!
SURROUNDED, OUR HERO IS TAKEN PRISONER, AND CARRIED TO A SUBTERRANEAN DUNGEON!
STILL WON'T TALK, EH, SPIFF? WE'LL SEE ABOUT THAT!
YOU'LL NEVER GET ANYTHING FROM ME, SPACE SQUID!
YOU HAD YOUR CHANCE, EARTHLING! TAKE HIM TO THE INTERROGATION ROOM AND WASH HIS HAIR!
HA HA HA HA HA HA
AAUGH! YOU GOT SOAP IN MY EYES ON PURPOSE! SINISTER FIEND!
IF YOU'D STOP THRASHING AROUND, MAYBE IT WOULDN'T HAPPEN!
WATTERSON

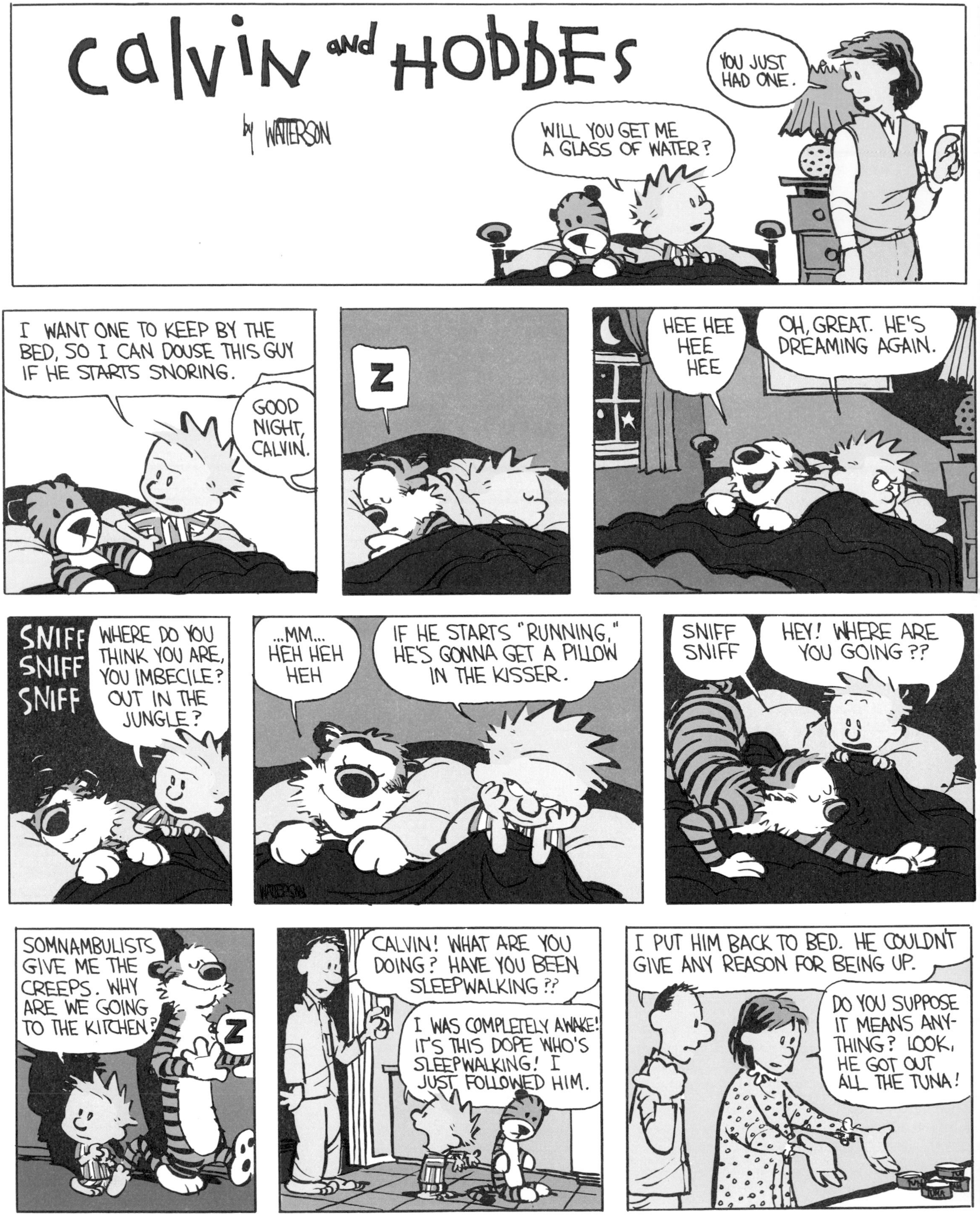
Calvin and HOBBES
by WATTERSON
WILL YOU GET ME A GLASS OF WATER?
YOU JUST HAD ONE.
I WANT ONE TO KEEP BY THE BED, SO I CAN DOUSE THIS GUY IF HE STARTS SNORING.
GOOD NIGHT, CALVIN.
Z
HEE HEE HEE HEE
OH, GREAT. HE'S DREAMING AGAIN.
SNIFF SNIFF SNIFF
WHERE DO YOU THINK YOU ARE, YOU IMBECILE? OUT IN THE JUNGLE?
...MM... HEH HEH HEH
IF HE STARTS "RUNNING," HE'S GONNA GET A PILLOW IN THE KISSER.
SNIFF SNIFF
HEY! WHERE ARE YOU GOING??
SOMNAMBULISTS GIVE ME THE CREEPS. WHY ARE WE GOING TO THE KITCHEN?
Z
CALVIN! WHAT ARE YOU DOING? HAVE YOU BEEN SLEEPWALKING??
I WAS COMPLETELY AWAKE! IT'S THIS DOPE WHO'S SLEEPWALKING! I JUST FOLLOWED HIM.
I PUT HIM BACK TO BED. HE COULDN'T GIVE ANY REASON FOR BEING UP.
DO YOU SUPPOSE IT MEANS ANYTHING? LOOK, HE GOT OUT ALL THE TUNA!

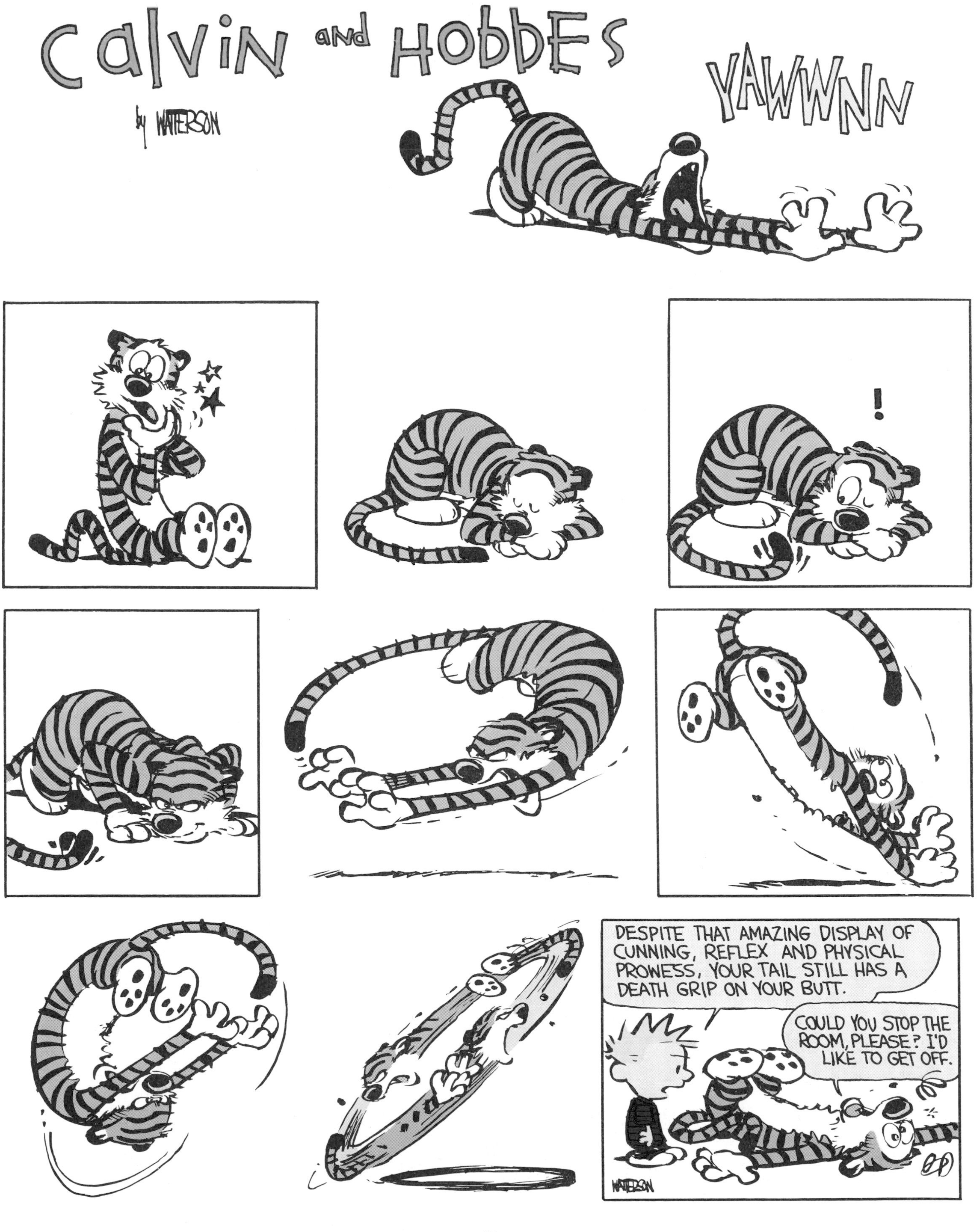
Calvin and HOBBES
by WATTERSON
YAWWNN
!
DESPITE THAT AMAZING DISPLAY OF CUNNING, REFLEX AND PHYSICAL PROWESS, YOUR TAIL STILL HAS A DEATH GRIP ON YOUR BUTT.
COULD YOU STOP THE ROOM, PLEASE? I'D LIKE TO GET OFF.
WATTERSON

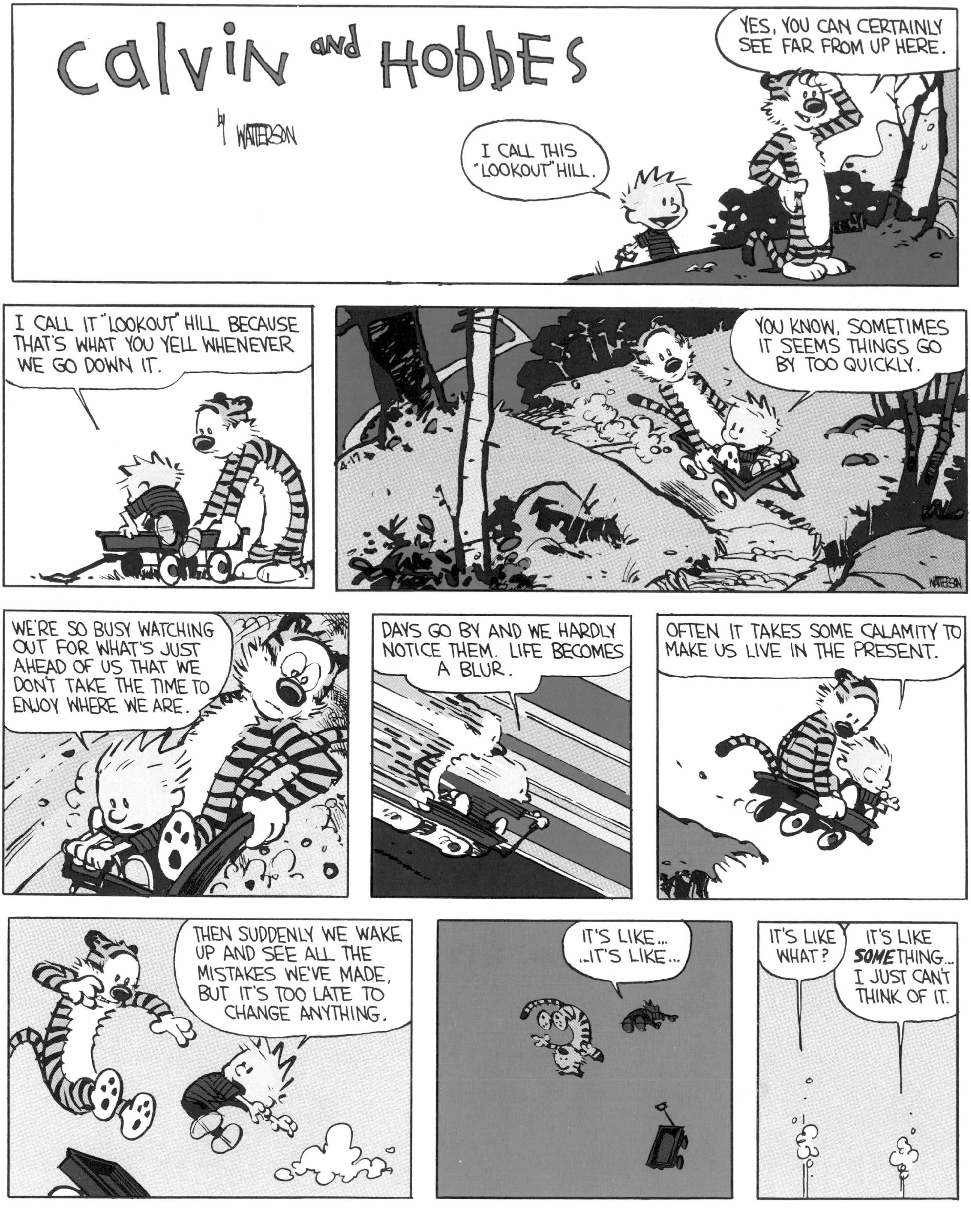
Calvin and HOBBES
by WATTERSON
I CALL THIS "LOOKOUT" HILL.
YES, YOU CAN CERTAINLY SEE FAR FROM UP HERE.
I CALL IT "LOOKOUT" HILL BECAUSE THAT'S WHAT YOU YELL WHENEVER WE GO DOWN IT.
4-17
YOU KNOW, SOMETIMES IT SEEMS THINGS GO BY TOO QUICKLY.
WATTERSON
WE'RE SO BUSY WATCHING OUT FOR WHAT'S JUST AHEAD OF US THAT WE DON'T TAKE THE TIME TO ENJOY WHERE WE ARE.
DAYS GO BY AND WE HARDLY NOTICE THEM. LIFE BECOMES A BLUR.
OFTEN IT TAKES SOME CALAMITY TO MAKE US LIVE IN THE PRESENT.
THEN SUDDENLY WE WAKE UP AND SEE ALL THE MISTAKES WE'VE MADE, BUT IT'S TOO LATE TO CHANGE ANYTHING.
IT'S LIKE... ..IT'S LIKE...
IT'S LIKE WHAT?
IT'S LIKE **SOME**THING... I JUST CAN'T THINK OF IT.

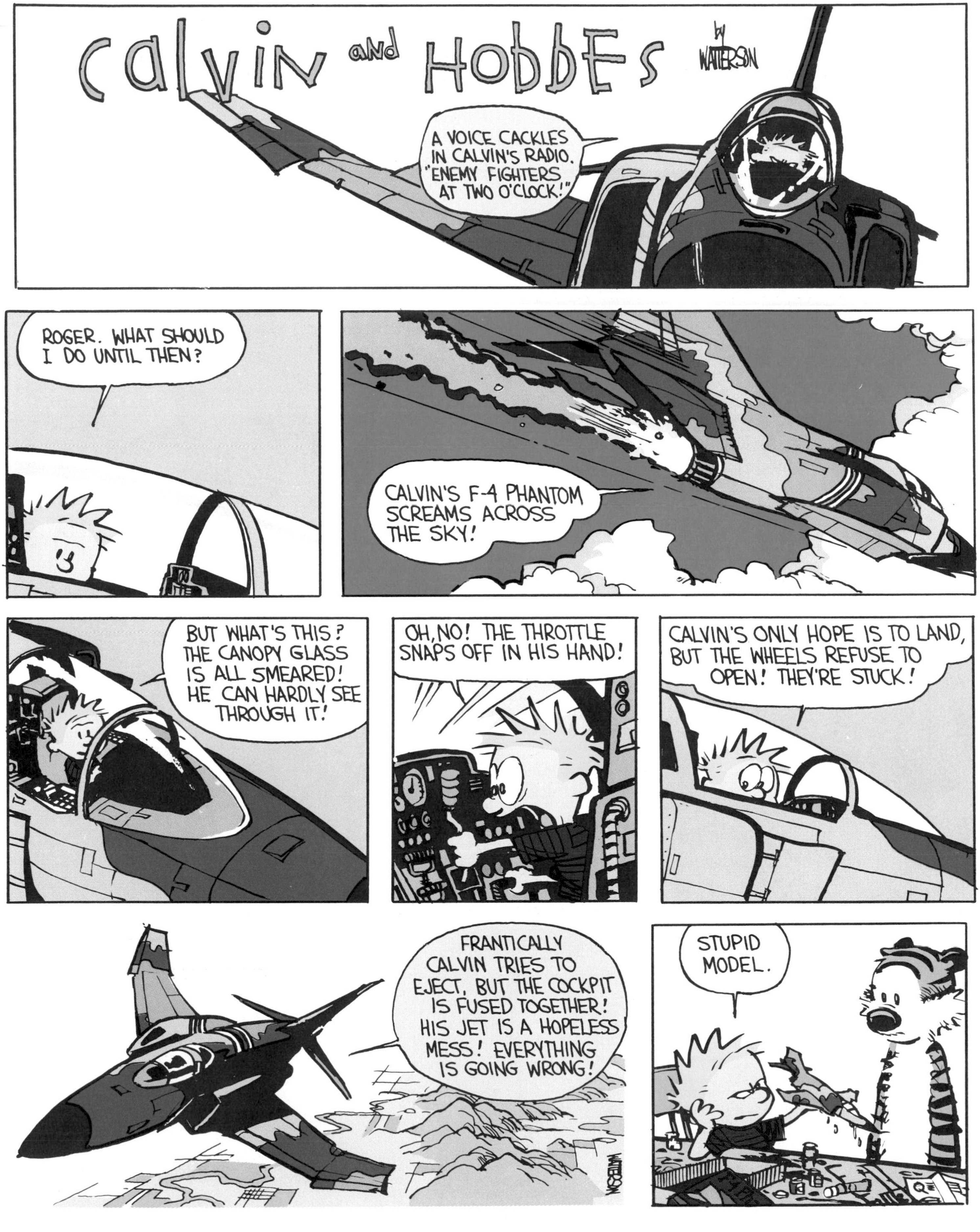
Calvin and HOBBES
by WATTERSON
A VOICE CACKLES IN CALVIN'S RADIO. "ENEMY FIGHTERS AT TWO O'CLOCK!"
ROGER. WHAT SHOULD I DO UNTIL THEN?
CALVIN'S F-4 PHANTOM SCREAMS ACROSS THE SKY!
BUT WHAT'S THIS? THE CANOPY GLASS IS ALL SMEARED! HE CAN HARDLY SEE THROUGH IT!
OH, NO! THE THROTTLE SNAPS OFF IN HIS HAND!
CALVIN'S ONLY HOPE IS TO LAND, BUT THE WHEELS REFUSE TO OPEN! THEY'RE STUCK!
FRANTICALLY CALVIN TRIES TO EJECT, BUT THE COCKPIT IS FUSED TOGETHER! HIS JET IS A HOPELESS MESS! EVERYTHING IS GOING WRONG!
WATTERSON
STUPID MODEL.

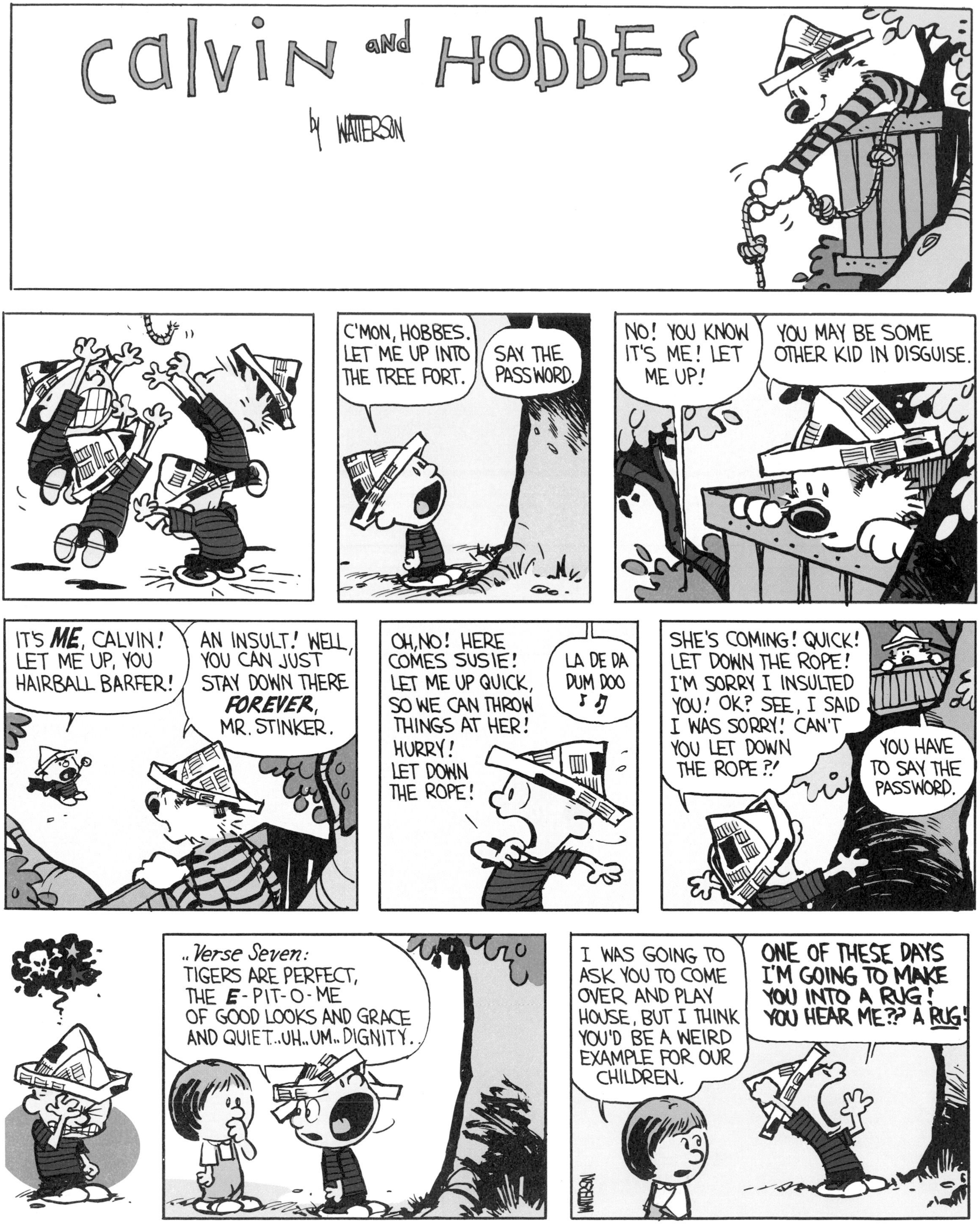

Calvin and HOBBES
by WATTERSON
C'MON, HOBBES. LET ME UP INTO THE TREE FORT.
SAY THE PASSWORD.
NO! YOU KNOW IT'S ME! LET ME UP!
YOU MAY BE SOME OTHER KID IN DISGUISE.
IT'S **ME**, CALVIN! LET ME UP, YOU HAIRBALL BARFER!
AN INSULT! WELL, YOU CAN JUST STAY DOWN THERE ***FOREVER***, MR. STINKER.
OH, NO! HERE COMES SUSIE! LET ME UP QUICK, SO WE CAN THROW THINGS AT HER! HURRY! LET DOWN THE ROPE!
LA DE DA DUM DOO
SHE'S COMING! QUICK! LET DOWN THE ROPE! I'M SORRY I INSULTED YOU! OK? SEE, I SAID I WAS SORRY! CAN'T YOU LET DOWN THE ROPE?!
YOU HAVE TO SAY THE PASSWORD.
..*Verse Seven:* TIGERS ARE PERFECT, THE **E**-PIT-O-ME OF GOOD LOOKS AND GRACE AND QUIET..UH..UM..DIGNITY..
I WAS GOING TO ASK YOU TO COME OVER AND PLAY HOUSE, BUT I THINK YOU'D BE A WEIRD EXAMPLE FOR OUR CHILDREN.
ONE OF THESE DAYS I'M GOING TO MAKE YOU INTO A RUG! YOU HEAR ME?? A RUG!
WATTERSON

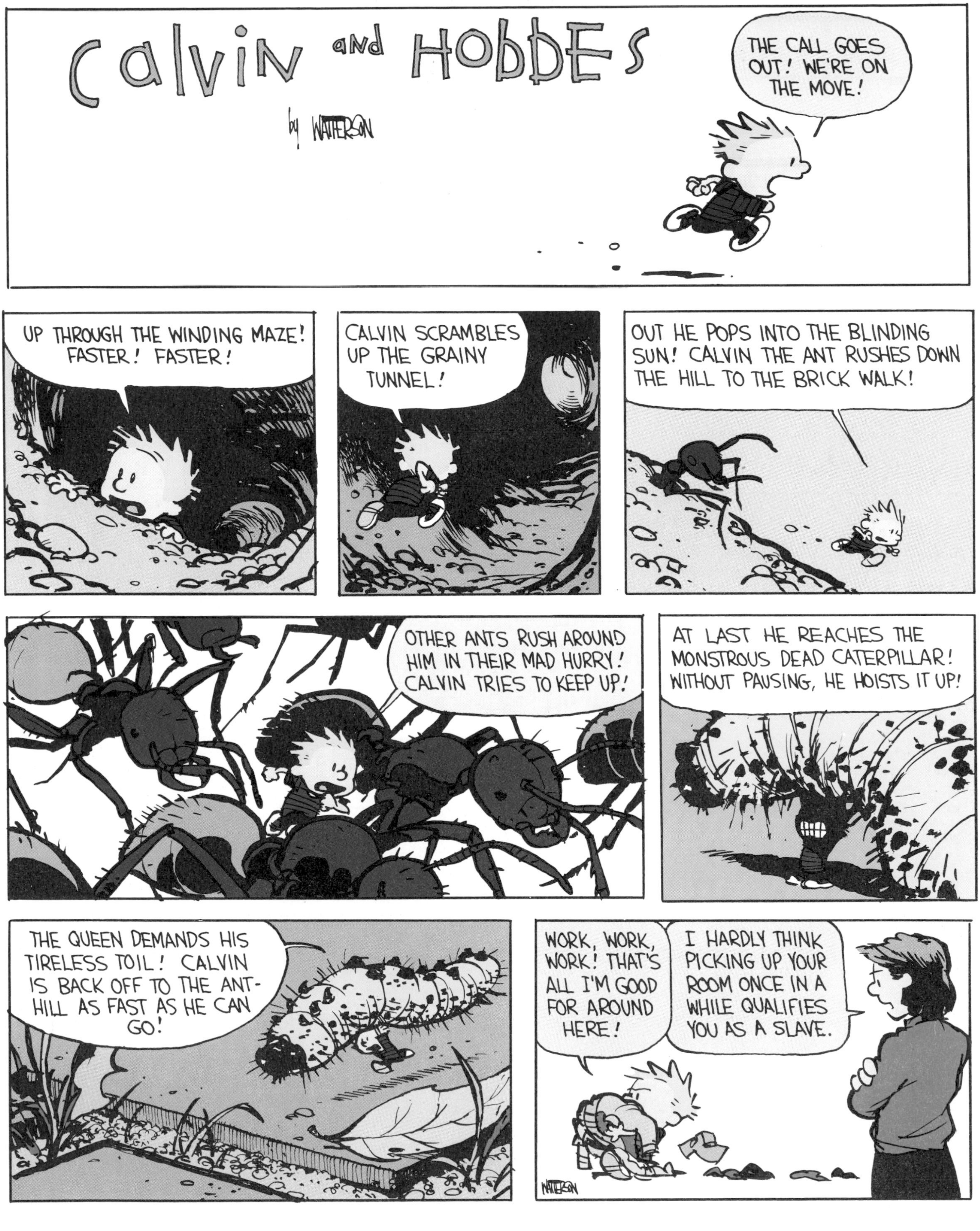
Calvin and HOBBES
by WATTERSON
THE CALL GOES OUT! WE'RE ON THE MOVE!
UP THROUGH THE WINDING MAZE! FASTER! FASTER!
CALVIN SCRAMBLES UP THE GRAINY TUNNEL!
OUT HE POPS INTO THE BLINDING SUN! CALVIN THE ANT RUSHES DOWN THE HILL TO THE BRICK WALK!
OTHER ANTS RUSH AROUND HIM IN THEIR MAD HURRY! CALVIN TRIES TO KEEP UP!
AT LAST HE REACHES THE MONSTROUS DEAD CATERPILLAR! WITHOUT PAUSING, HE HOISTS IT UP!
THE QUEEN DEMANDS HIS TIRELESS TOIL! CALVIN IS BACK OFF TO THE ANT-HILL AS FAST AS HE CAN GO!
WORK, WORK, WORK! THAT'S ALL I'M GOOD FOR AROUND HERE!
I HARDLY THINK PICKING UP YOUR ROOM ONCE IN A WHILE QUALIFIES YOU AS A SLAVE.
WATTERSON

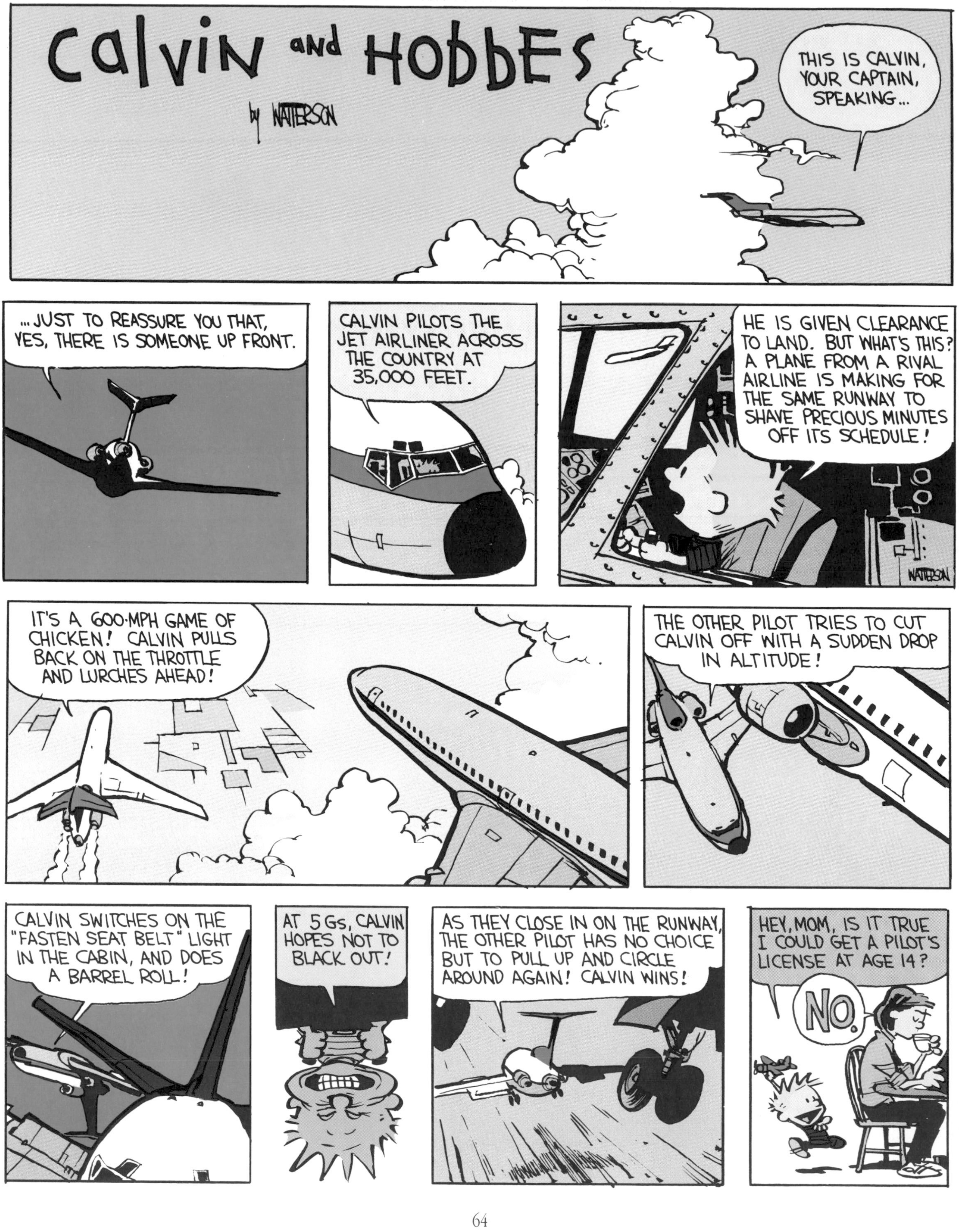
Calvin and HOBBES
by WATTERSON
THIS IS CALVIN, YOUR CAPTAIN, SPEAKING...
...JUST TO REASSURE YOU THAT, YES, THERE IS SOMEONE UP FRONT.
CALVIN PILOTS THE JET AIRLINER ACROSS THE COUNTRY AT 35,000 FEET.
HE IS GIVEN CLEARANCE TO LAND. BUT WHAT'S THIS? A PLANE FROM A RIVAL AIRLINE IS MAKING FOR THE SAME RUNWAY TO SHAVE PRECIOUS MINUTES OFF ITS SCHEDULE!
WATTERSON
IT'S A 600-MPH GAME OF CHICKEN! CALVIN PULLS BACK ON THE THROTTLE AND LURCHES AHEAD!
THE OTHER PILOT TRIES TO CUT CALVIN OFF WITH A SUDDEN DROP IN ALTITUDE!
CALVIN SWITCHES ON THE "FASTEN SEAT BELT" LIGHT IN THE CABIN, AND DOES A BARREL ROLL!
AT 5 Gs, CALVIN HOPES NOT TO BLACK OUT!
AS THEY CLOSE IN ON THE RUNWAY, THE OTHER PILOT HAS NO CHOICE BUT TO PULL UP AND CIRCLE AROUND AGAIN! CALVIN WINS!
HEY, MOM, IS IT TRUE I COULD GET A PILOT'S LICENSE AT AGE 14?
NO.

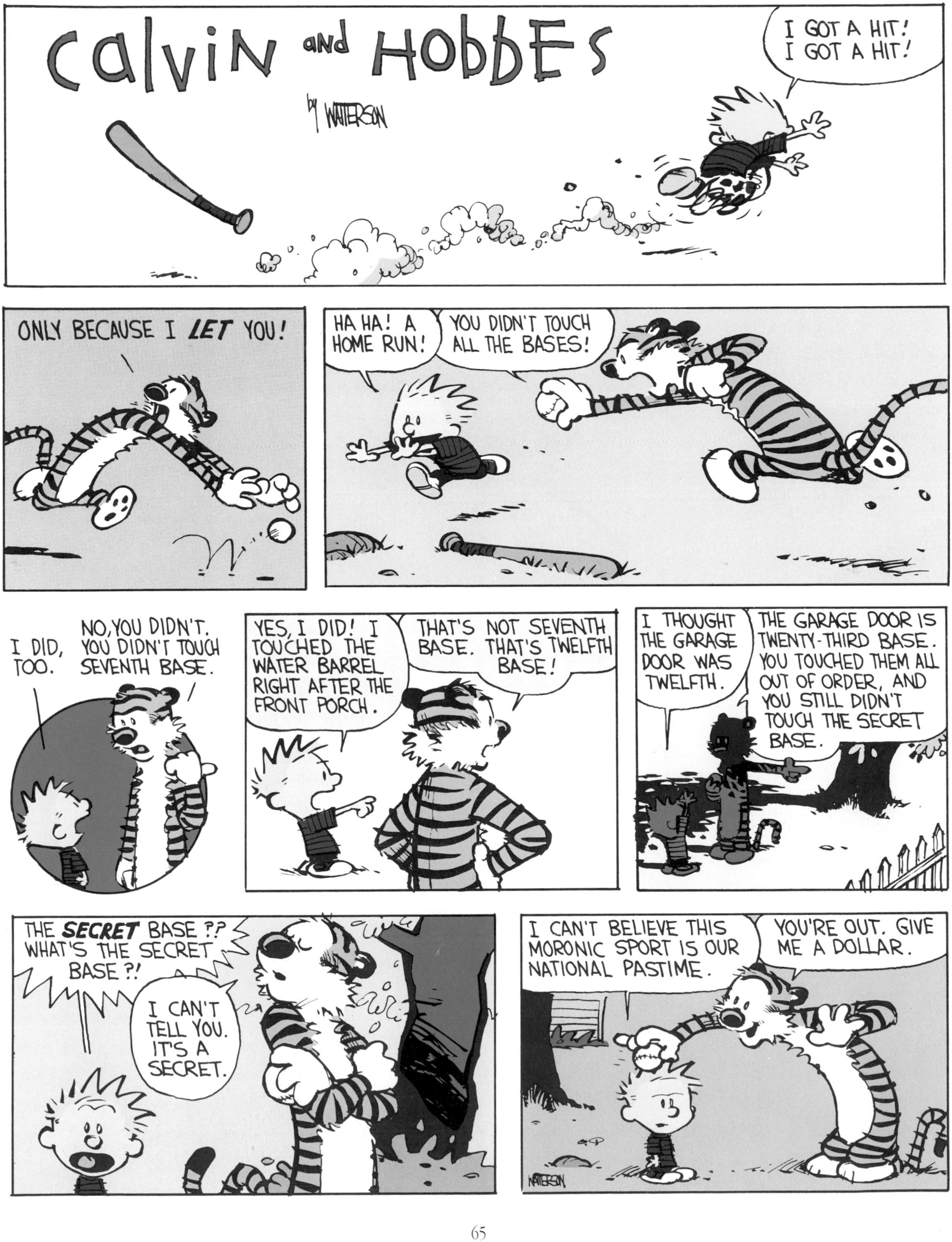
Calvin and Hobbes
by WATTERSON
I GOT A HIT! I GOT A HIT!
ONLY BECAUSE I LET YOU!
HA HA! A HOME RUN!
YOU DIDN'T TOUCH ALL THE BASES!
I DID, TOO.
NO, YOU DIDN'T. YOU DIDN'T TOUCH SEVENTH BASE.
YES, I DID! I TOUCHED THE WATER BARREL RIGHT AFTER THE FRONT PORCH.
THAT'S NOT SEVENTH BASE. THAT'S TWELFTH BASE!
I THOUGHT THE GARAGE DOOR WAS TWELFTH.
THE GARAGE DOOR IS TWENTY-THIRD BASE. YOU TOUCHED THEM ALL OUT OF ORDER, AND YOU STILL DIDN'T TOUCH THE SECRET BASE.
THE SECRET BASE ?? WHAT'S THE SECRET BASE ?!
I CAN'T TELL YOU. IT'S A SECRET.
I CAN'T BELIEVE THIS MORONIC SPORT IS OUR NATIONAL PASTIME.
YOU'RE OUT. GIVE ME A DOLLAR.
WATTERSON

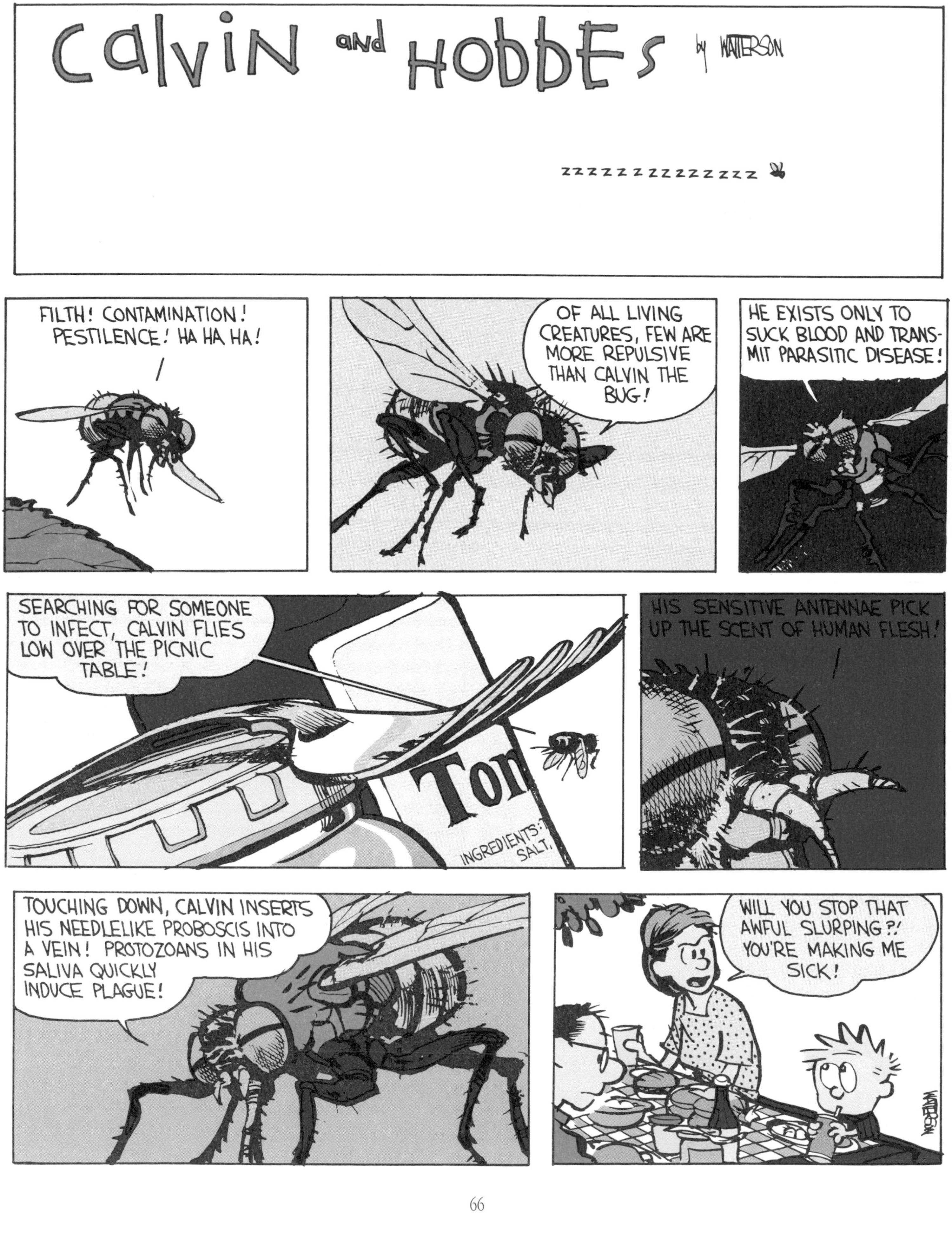
Calvin and HobbEs by WATTERSON
zzzzzzzzzzzzzz
FILTH! CONTAMINATION! PESTILENCE! HA HA HA!
OF ALL LIVING CREATURES, FEW ARE MORE REPULSIVE THAN CALVIN THE BUG!
HE EXISTS ONLY TO SUCK BLOOD AND TRANSMIT PARASITIC DISEASE!
SEARCHING FOR SOMEONE TO INFECT, CALVIN FLIES LOW OVER THE PICNIC TABLE!
Ton
INGREDIENTS:
SALT,
HIS SENSITIVE ANTENNAE PICK UP THE SCENT OF HUMAN FLESH!
TOUCHING DOWN, CALVIN INSERTS HIS NEEDLELIKE PROBOSCIS INTO A VEIN! PROTOZOANS IN HIS SALIVA QUICKLY INDUCE PLAGUE!
WILL YOU STOP THAT AWFUL SLURPING?! YOU'RE MAKING ME SICK!
WATTERSON

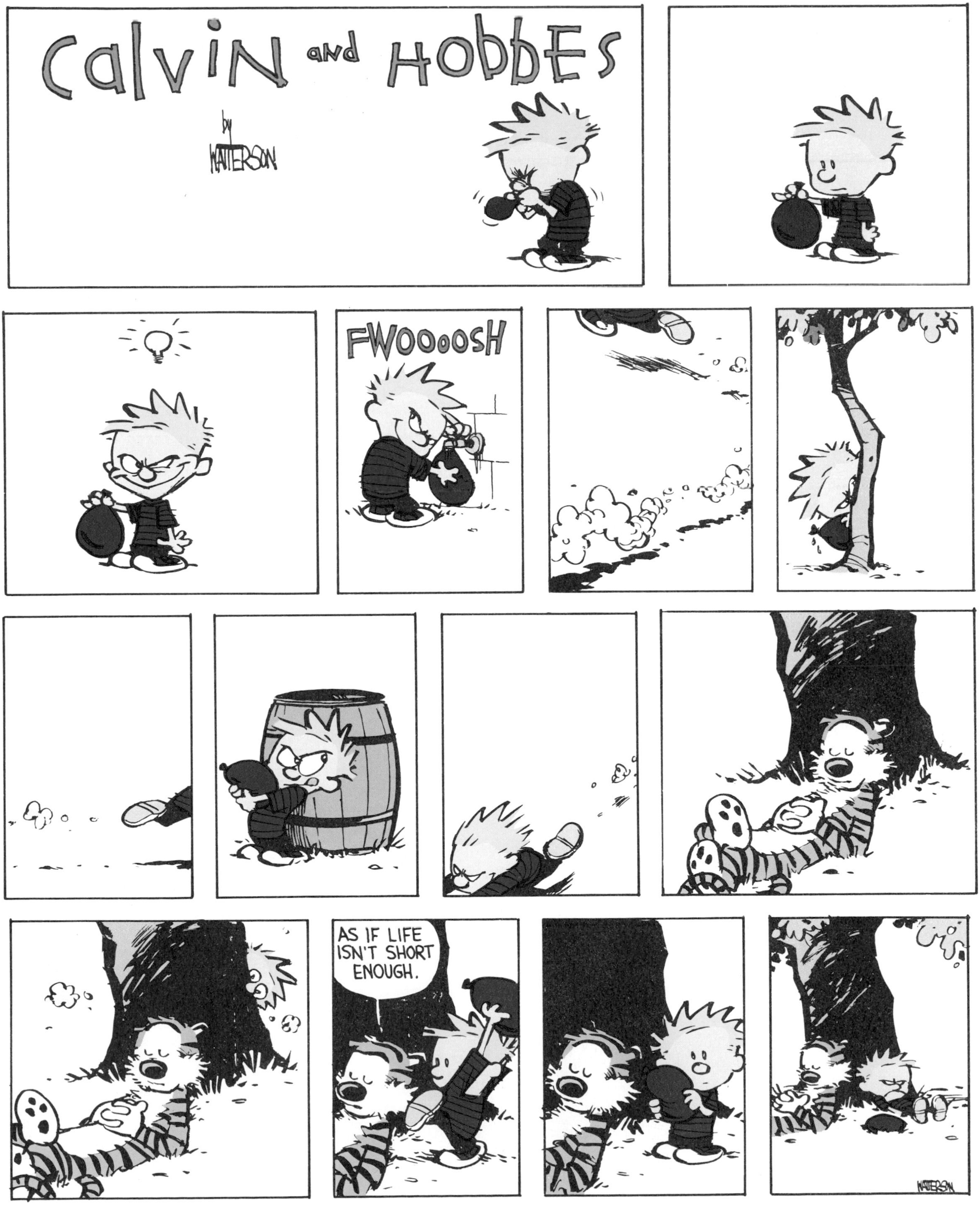
Calvin and HOBBES
by WATTERSON
FWOOOOSH
AS IF LIFE ISN'T SHORT ENOUGH.
WATTERSON

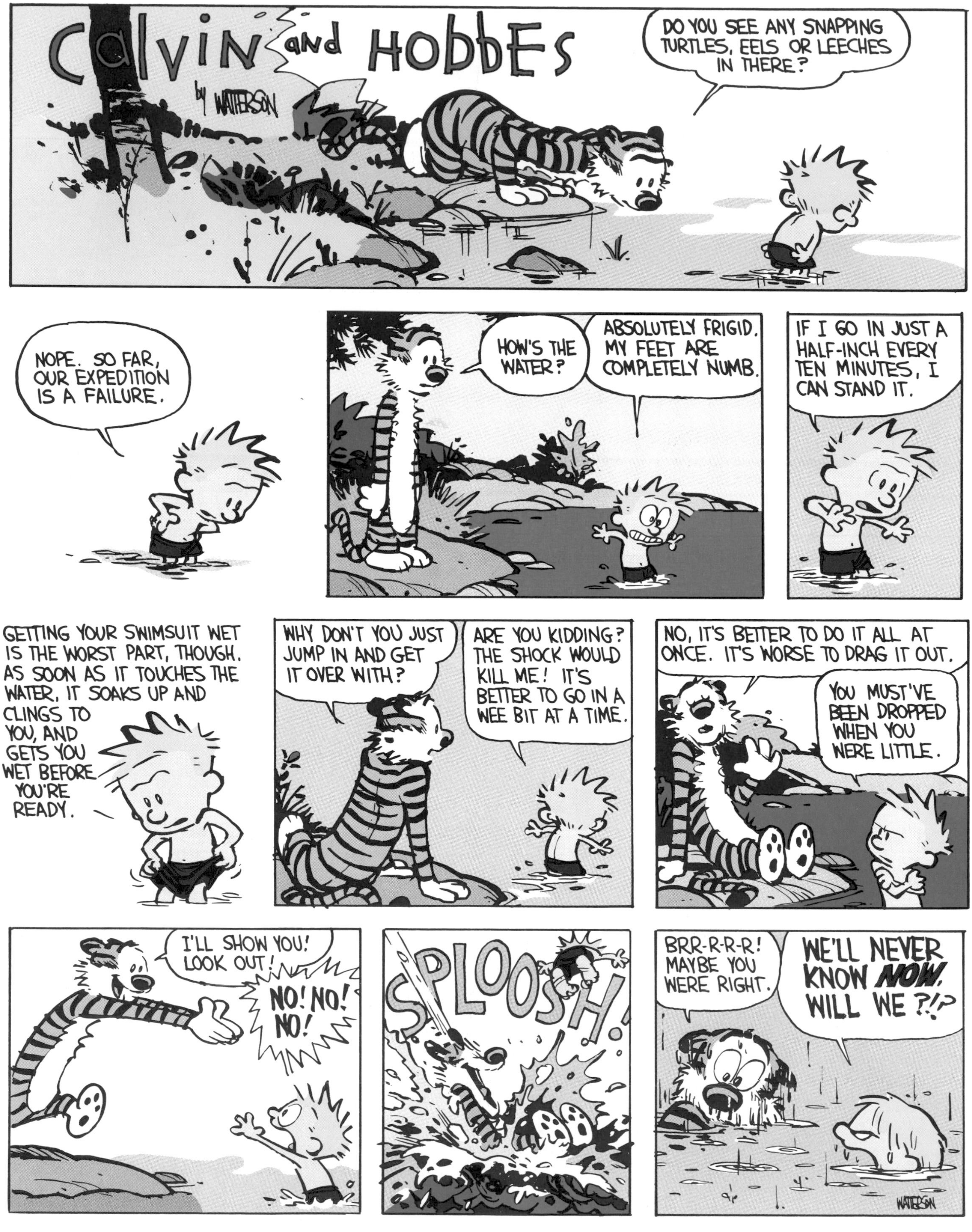

Calvin and HOBBES
by WATTERSON
DO YOU SEE ANY SNAPPING TURTLES, EELS OR LEECHES IN THERE?
NOPE. SO FAR, OUR EXPEDITION IS A FAILURE.
HOW'S THE WATER?
ABSOLUTELY FRIGID. MY FEET ARE COMPLETELY NUMB.
IF I GO IN JUST A HALF-INCH EVERY TEN MINUTES, I CAN STAND IT.
GETTING YOUR SWIMSUIT WET IS THE WORST PART, THOUGH. AS SOON AS IT TOUCHES THE WATER, IT SOAKS UP AND CLINGS TO YOU, AND GETS YOU WET BEFORE YOU'RE READY.
WHY DON'T YOU JUST JUMP IN AND GET IT OVER WITH?
ARE YOU KIDDING? THE SHOCK WOULD KILL ME! IT'S BETTER TO GO IN A WEE BIT AT A TIME.
NO, IT'S BETTER TO DO IT ALL AT ONCE. IT'S WORSE TO DRAG IT OUT.
YOU MUST'VE BEEN DROPPED WHEN YOU WERE LITTLE.
I'LL SHOW YOU! LOOK OUT!
NO! NO! NO!
SPLOOSH!
BRR-R-R-R! MAYBE YOU WERE RIGHT.
WE'LL NEVER KNOW NOW, WILL WE ?!?
WATTERSON

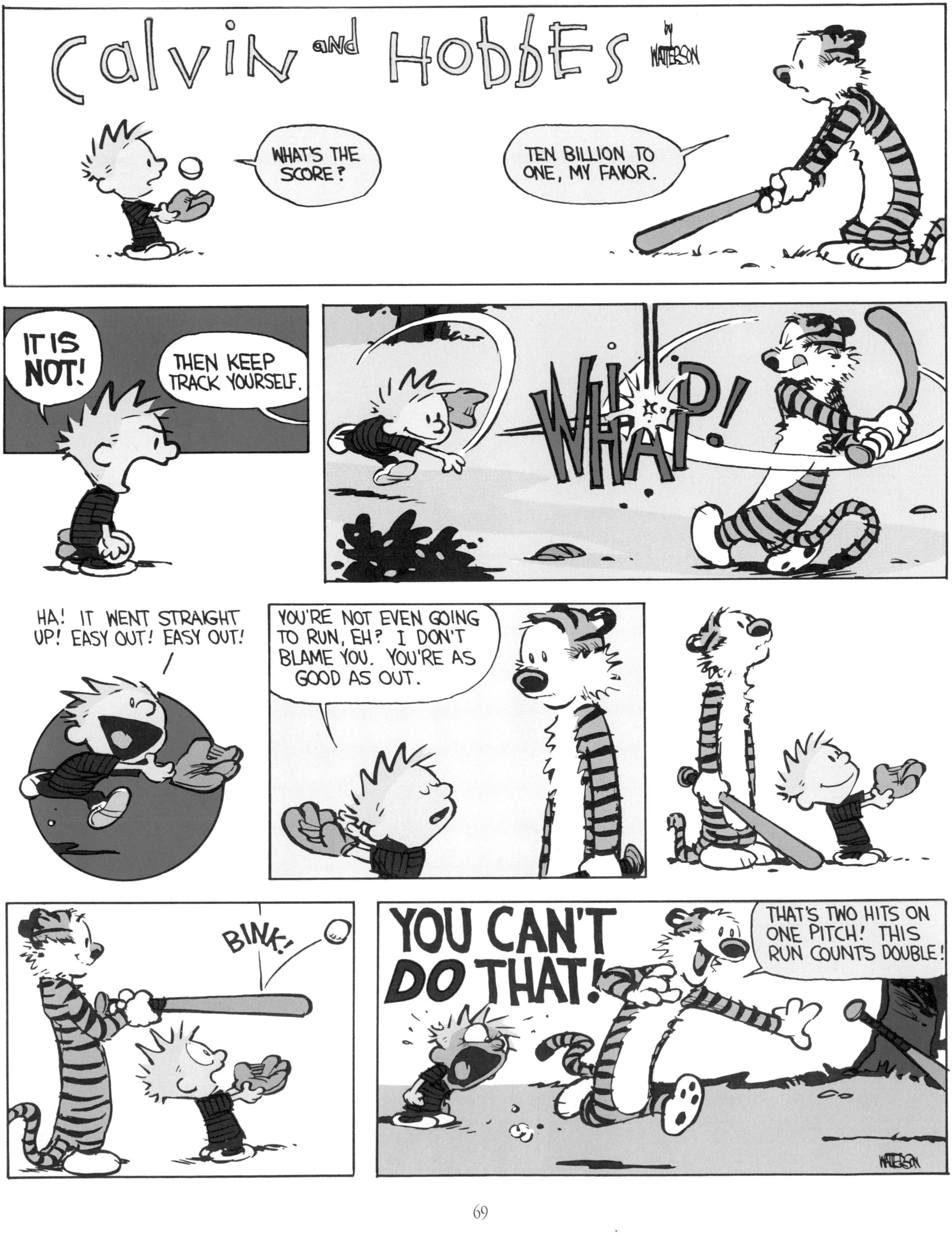
Calvin and Hobbes
by WATTERSON
WHAT'S THE SCORE?
TEN BILLION TO ONE, MY FAVOR.
IT IS NOT!
THEN KEEP TRACK YOURSELF.
WHAP!
HA! IT WENT STRAIGHT UP! EASY OUT! EASY OUT!
YOU'RE NOT EVEN GOING TO RUN, EH? I DON'T BLAME YOU. YOU'RE AS GOOD AS OUT.
BINK!
YOU CAN'T DO THAT!
THAT'S TWO HITS ON ONE PITCH! THIS RUN COUNTS DOUBLE!
WATTERSON

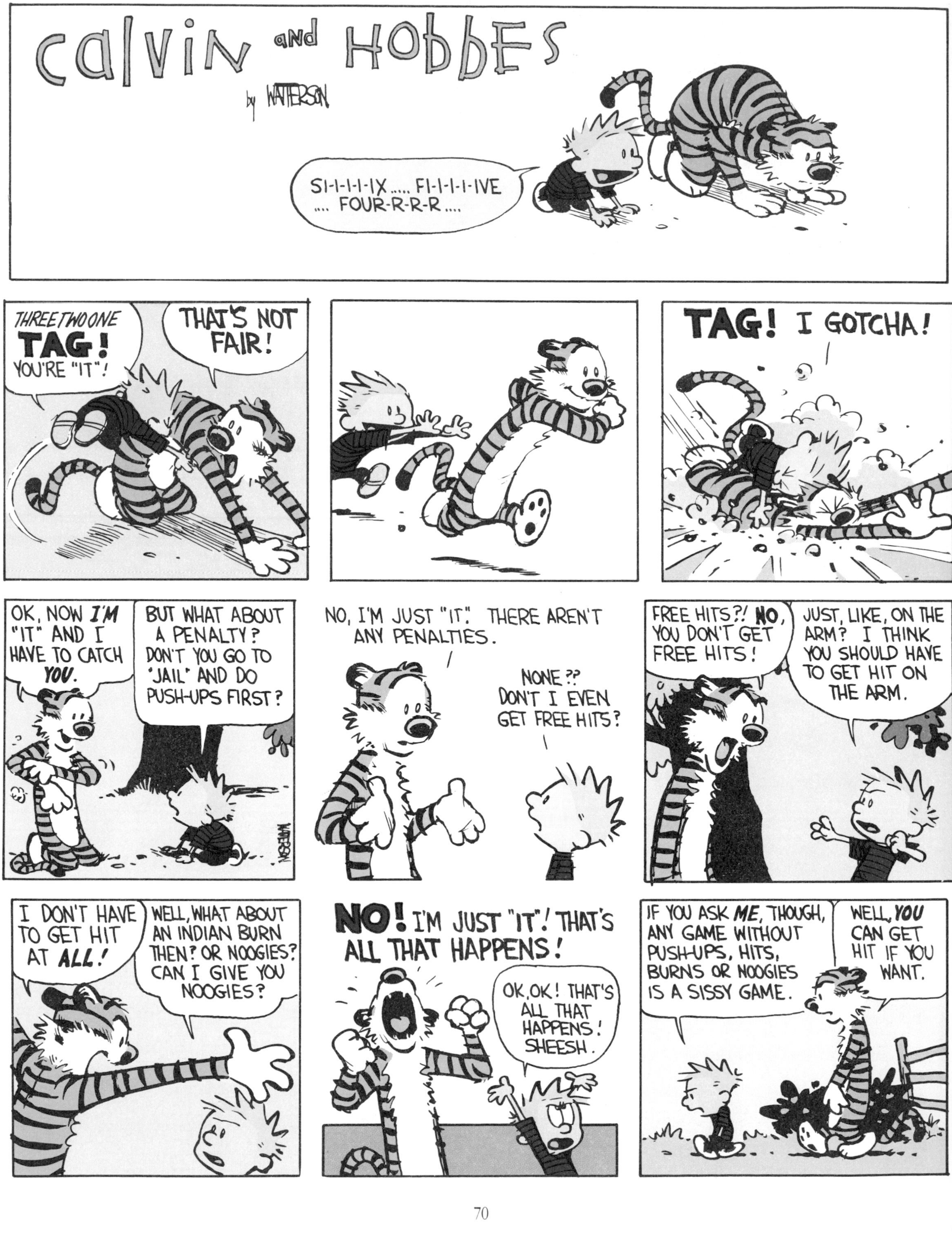

Calvin and Hobbes
by WATTERSON
SI-I-I-I-IX..... FI-I-I-I-IVE .... FOUR-R-R-R....
THREETWOONE TAG! YOU'RE "IT"!
THAT'S NOT FAIR!
TAG! I GOTCHA!
OK, NOW I'M "IT" AND I HAVE TO CATCH YOU.
BUT WHAT ABOUT A PENALTY? DON'T YOU GO TO 'JAIL' AND DO PUSH-UPS FIRST?
WATTERSON
NO, I'M JUST "IT". THERE AREN'T ANY PENALTIES.
NONE?? DON'T I EVEN GET FREE HITS?
FREE HITS?! NO, YOU DON'T GET FREE HITS!
JUST, LIKE, ON THE ARM? I THINK YOU SHOULD HAVE TO GET HIT ON THE ARM.
I DON'T HAVE TO GET HIT AT ALL!
WELL, WHAT ABOUT AN INDIAN BURN THEN? OR NOOGIES? CAN I GIVE YOU NOOGIES?
NO! I'M JUST "IT"! THAT'S ALL THAT HAPPENS!
OK, OK! THAT'S ALL THAT HAPPENS! SHEESH.
IF YOU ASK ME, THOUGH, ANY GAME WITHOUT PUSH-UPS, HITS, BURNS OR NOOGIES IS A SISSY GAME.
WELL, YOU CAN GET HIT IF YOU WANT.

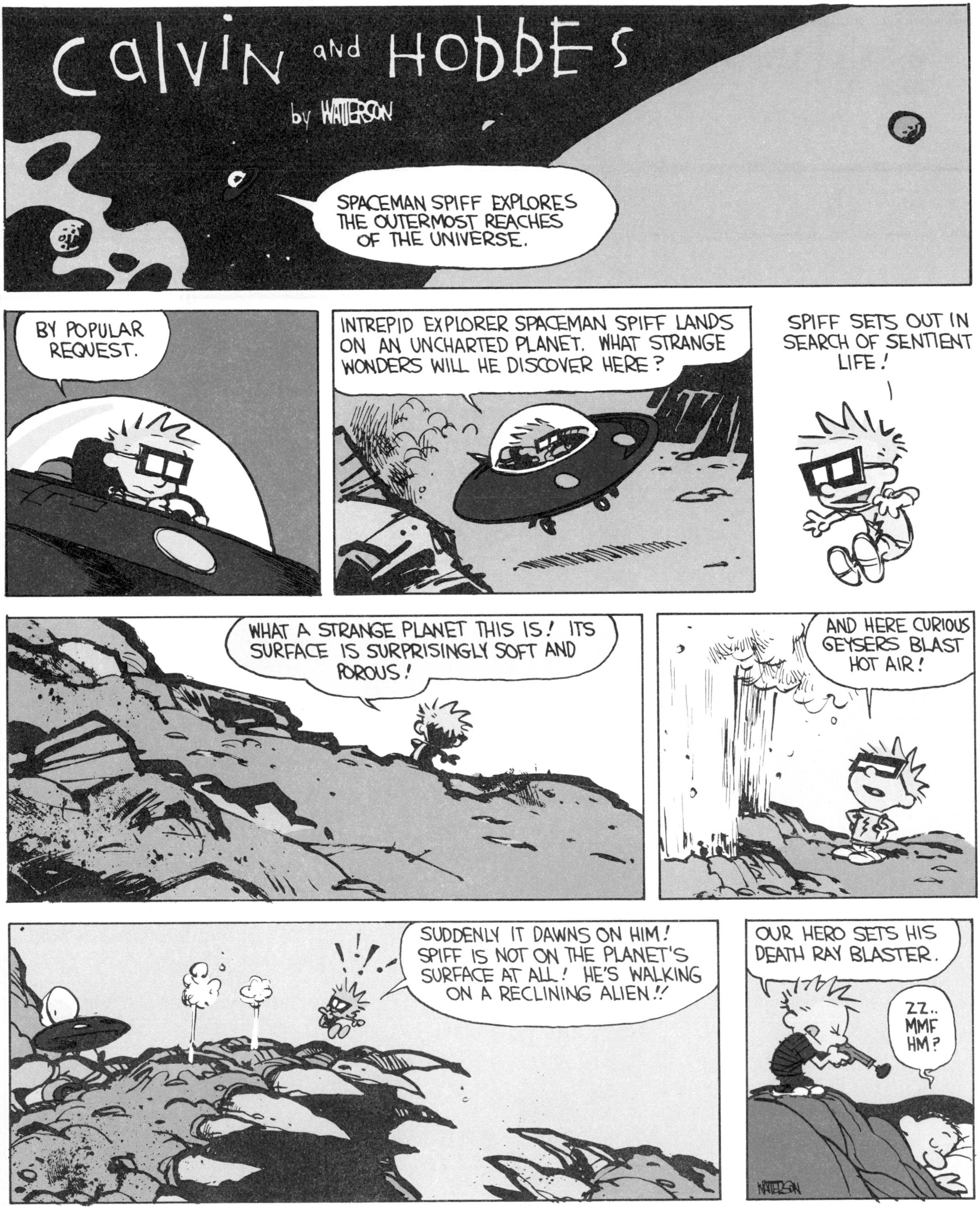
Calvin and HOBBES
by WATTERSON
SPACEMAN SPIFF EXPLORES THE OUTERMOST REACHES OF THE UNIVERSE.
BY POPULAR REQUEST.
INTREPID EXPLORER SPACEMAN SPIFF LANDS ON AN UNCHARTED PLANET. WHAT STRANGE WONDERS WILL HE DISCOVER HERE?
SPIFF SETS OUT IN SEARCH OF SENTIENT LIFE!
WHAT A STRANGE PLANET THIS IS! ITS SURFACE IS SURPRISINGLY SOFT AND POROUS!
AND HERE CURIOUS GEYSERS BLAST HOT AIR!
!?!
SUDDENLY IT DAWNS ON HIM! SPIFF IS NOT ON THE PLANET'S SURFACE AT ALL! HE'S WALKING ON A RECLINING ALIEN!!
OUR HERO SETS HIS DEATH RAY BLASTER.
ZZ.. MMF HM?
WATTERSON

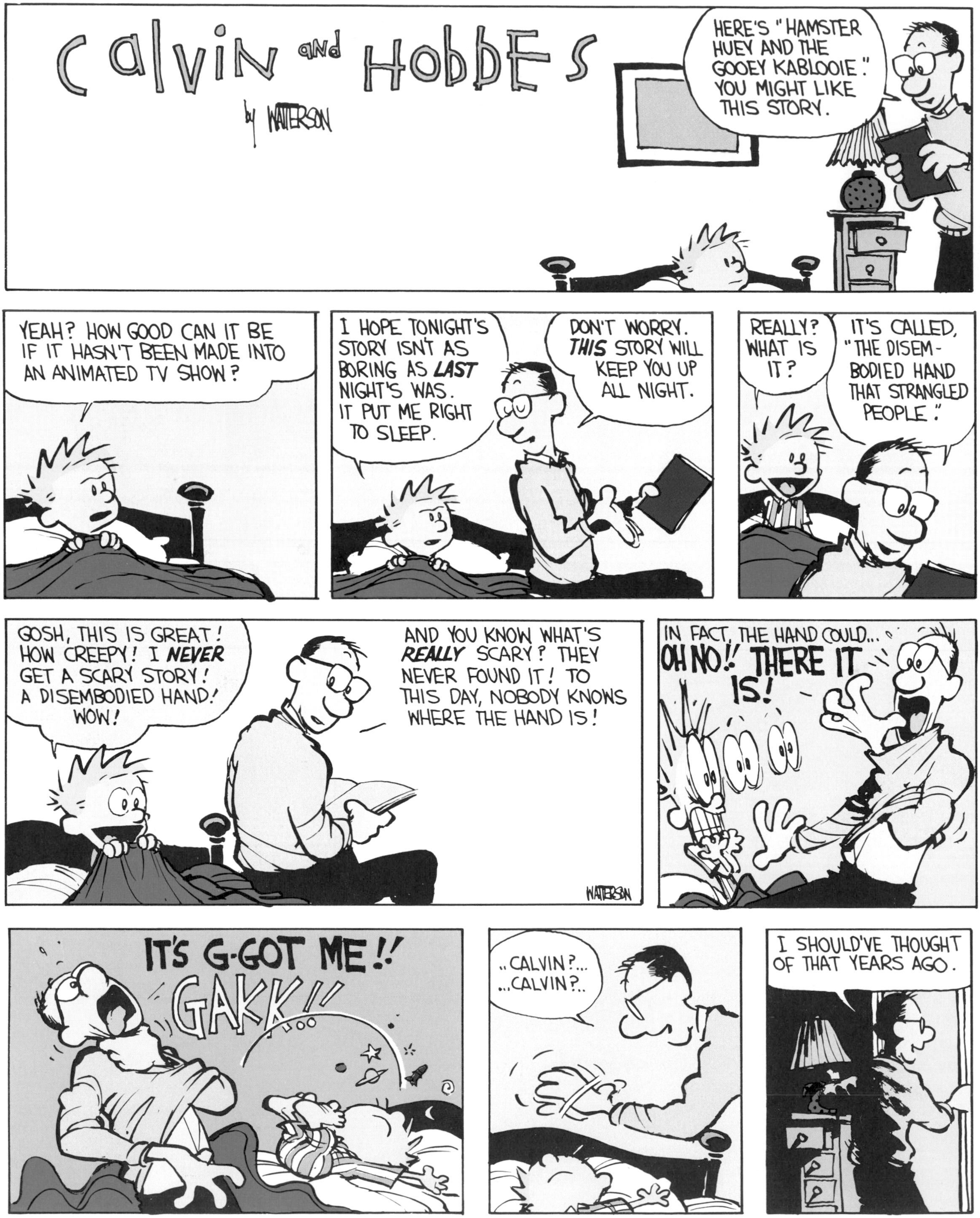
Calvin and Hobbes
by WATTERSON
HERE'S "HAMSTER HUEY AND THE GOOEY KABLOOIE." YOU MIGHT LIKE THIS STORY.
YEAH? HOW GOOD CAN IT BE IF IT HASN'T BEEN MADE INTO AN ANIMATED TV SHOW?
I HOPE TONIGHT'S STORY ISN'T AS BORING AS LAST NIGHT'S WAS. IT PUT ME RIGHT TO SLEEP.
DON'T WORRY. THIS STORY WILL KEEP YOU UP ALL NIGHT.
REALLY? WHAT IS IT?
IT'S CALLED, "THE DISEMBODIED HAND THAT STRANGLED PEOPLE."
GOSH, THIS IS GREAT! HOW CREEPY! I NEVER GET A SCARY STORY! A DISEMBODIED HAND! WOW!
AND YOU KNOW WHAT'S REALLY SCARY? THEY NEVER FOUND IT! TO THIS DAY, NOBODY KNOWS WHERE THE HAND IS!
WATTERSON
IN FACT, THE HAND COULD... OH NO!! THERE IT IS!
IT'S G-GOT ME!!
GAKK!!
..CALVIN?... ...CALVIN?..
I SHOULD'VE THOUGHT OF THAT YEARS AGO.

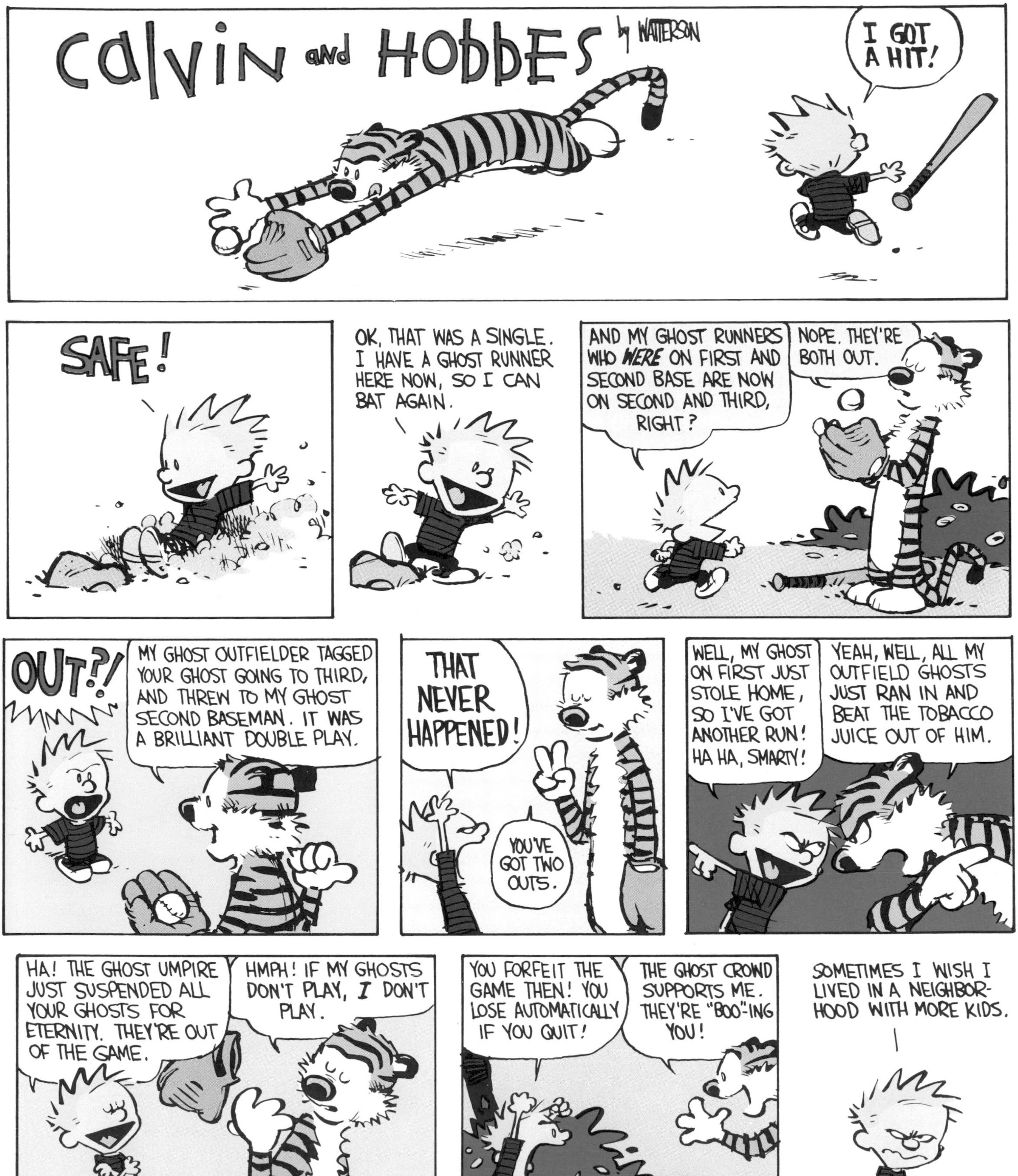
Calvin and HOBBES
by WATTERSON
I GOT A HIT!
SAFE!
OK, THAT WAS A SINGLE. I HAVE A GHOST RUNNER HERE NOW, SO I CAN BAT AGAIN.
AND MY GHOST RUNNERS WHO WERE ON FIRST AND SECOND BASE ARE NOW ON SECOND AND THIRD, RIGHT?
NOPE. THEY'RE BOTH OUT.
OUT?!
MY GHOST OUTFIELDER TAGGED YOUR GHOST GOING TO THIRD, AND THREW TO MY GHOST SECOND BASEMAN. IT WAS A BRILLIANT DOUBLE PLAY.
THAT NEVER HAPPENED!
YOU'VE GOT TWO OUTS.
WELL, MY GHOST ON FIRST JUST STOLE HOME, SO I'VE GOT ANOTHER RUN! HA HA, SMARTY!
YEAH, WELL, ALL MY OUTFIELD GHOSTS JUST RAN IN AND BEAT THE TOBACCO JUICE OUT OF HIM.
HA! THE GHOST UMPIRE JUST SUSPENDED ALL YOUR GHOSTS FOR ETERNITY. THEY'RE OUT OF THE GAME.
HMPH! IF MY GHOSTS DON'T PLAY, I DON'T PLAY.
YOU FORFEIT THE GAME THEN! YOU LOSE AUTOMATICALLY IF YOU QUIT!
THE GHOST CROWD SUPPORTS ME. THEY'RE "BOO"-ING YOU!
SOMETIMES I WISH I LIVED IN A NEIGHBORHOOD WITH MORE KIDS.
WATTERSON

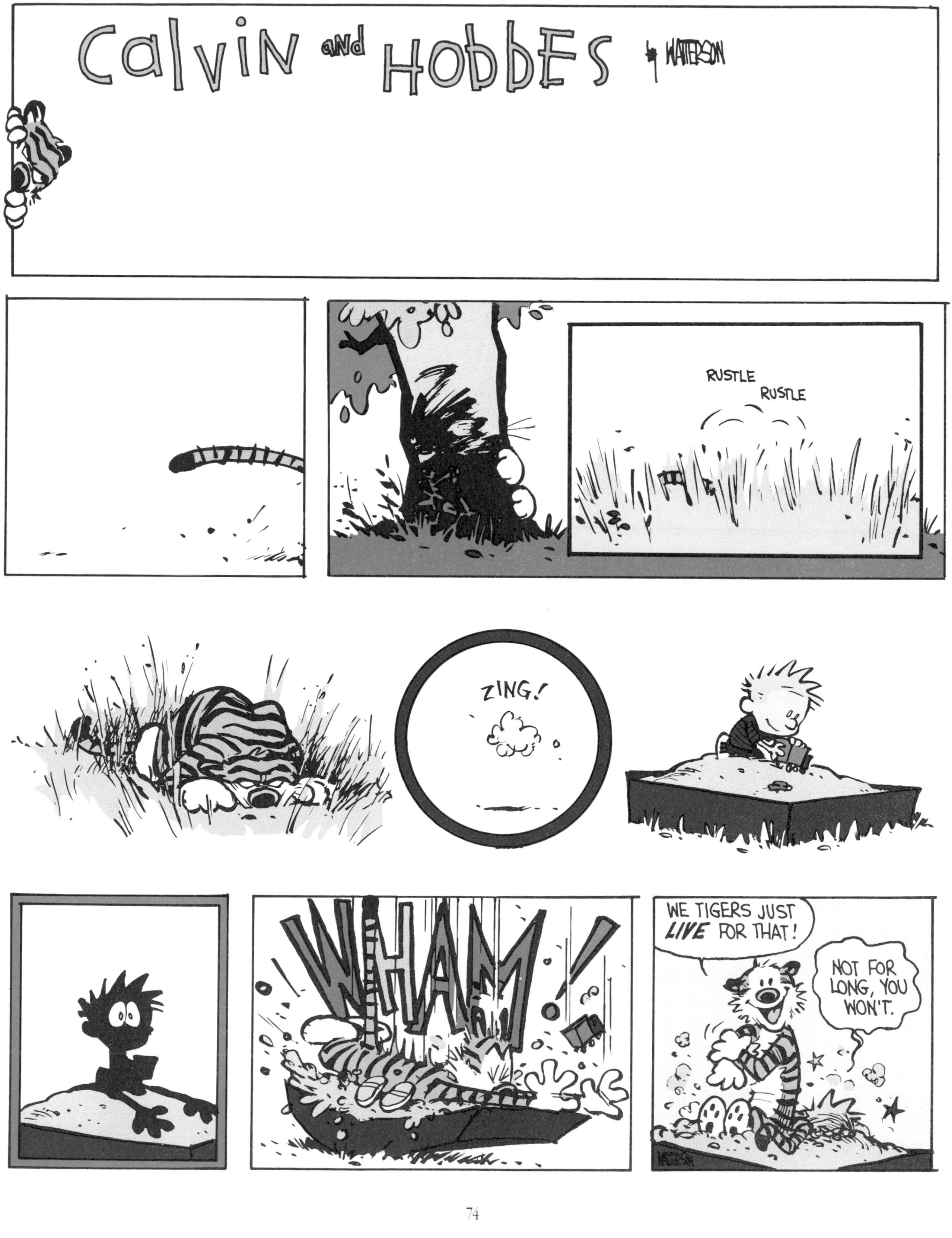
Calvin and HOBBES
by WATTERSON
RUSTLE
RUSTLE
ZING!
WHAM!
WE TIGERS JUST LIVE FOR THAT!
NOT FOR LONG, YOU WON'T.

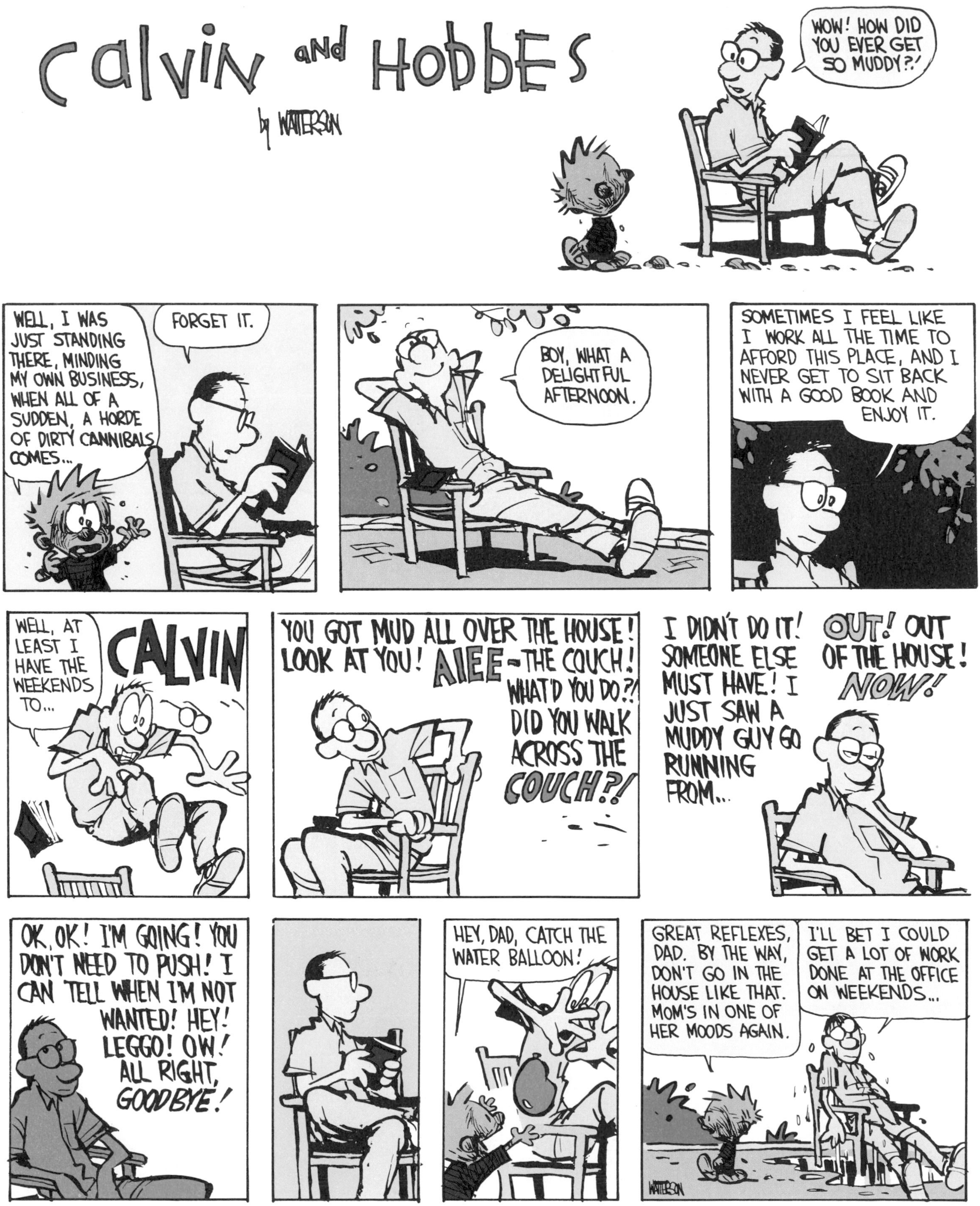

Calvin and Hobbes
by WATTERSON
WOW! HOW DID YOU EVER GET SO MUDDY?!
WELL, I WAS JUST STANDING THERE, MINDING MY OWN BUSINESS, WHEN ALL OF A SUDDEN, A HORDE OF DIRTY CANNIBALS COMES...
FORGET IT.
BOY, WHAT A DELIGHTFUL AFTERNOON.
SOMETIMES I FEEL LIKE I WORK ALL THE TIME TO AFFORD THIS PLACE, AND I NEVER GET TO SIT BACK WITH A GOOD BOOK AND ENJOY IT.
WELL, AT LEAST I HAVE THE WEEKENDS TO...
CALVIN
YOU GOT MUD ALL OVER THE HOUSE! LOOK AT YOU! AIEE - THE COUCH! WHAT'D YOU DO?! DID YOU WALK ACROSS THE COUCH?!
I DIDN'T DO IT! SOMEONE ELSE MUST HAVE! I JUST SAW A MUDDY GUY GO RUNNING FROM...
OUT! OUT OF THE HOUSE! NOW!
OK, OK! I'M GOING! YOU DON'T NEED TO PUSH! I CAN TELL WHEN I'M NOT WANTED! HEY! LEGGO! OW! ALL RIGHT, GOODBYE!
HEY, DAD, CATCH THE WATER BALLOON!
GREAT REFLEXES, DAD. BY THE WAY, DON'T GO IN THE HOUSE LIKE THAT. MOM'S IN ONE OF HER MOODS AGAIN.
I'LL BET I COULD GET A LOT OF WORK DONE AT THE OFFICE ON WEEKENDS...
WATTERSON

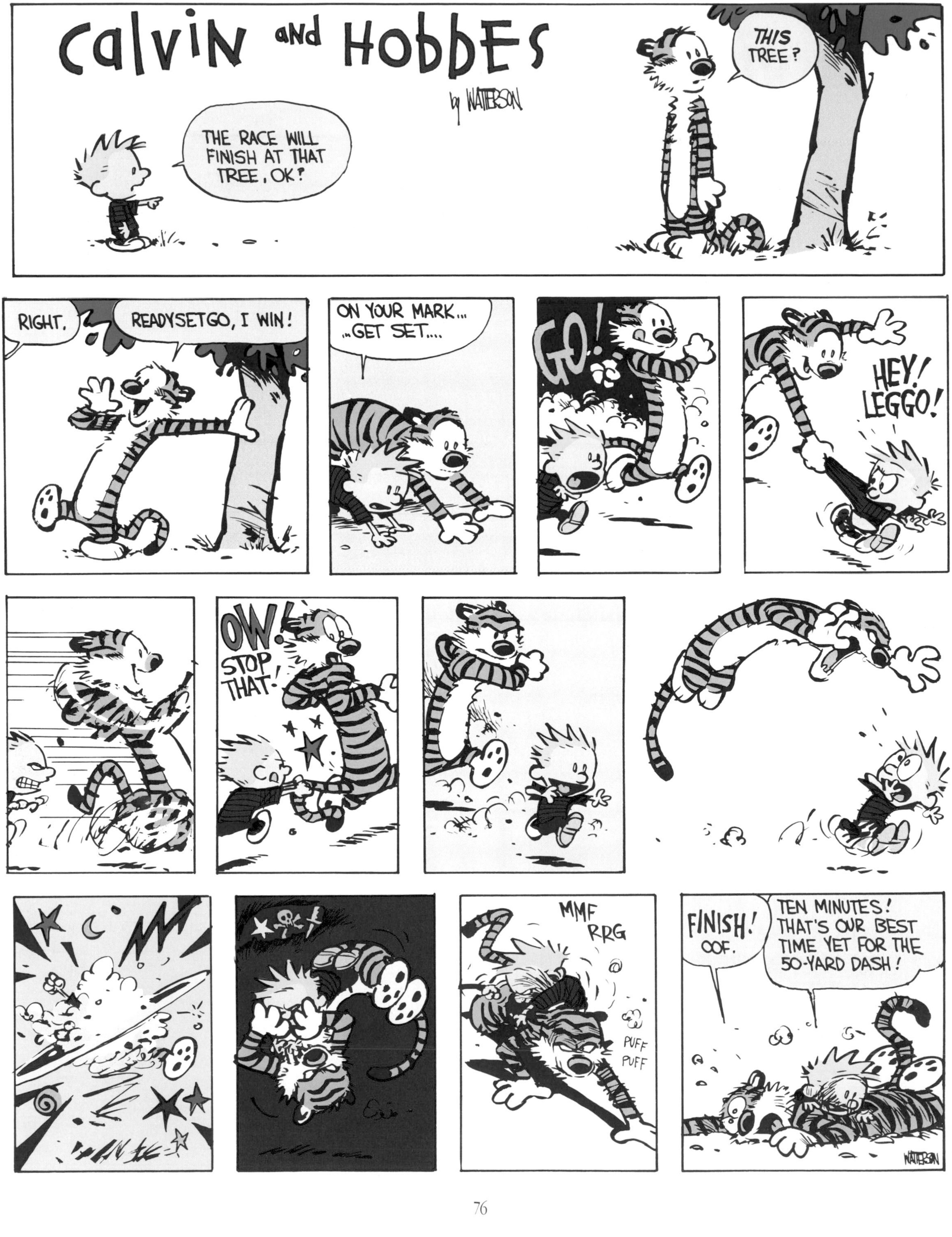
Calvin and HOBBES
by WATTERSON
THE RACE WILL FINISH AT THAT TREE, OK?
THIS TREE?
RIGHT.
READYSETGO, I WIN!
ON YOUR MARK...
...GET SET....
GO!
HEY! LEGGO!
OW!
STOP THAT!
MMF
RRG
PUFF
PUFF
FINISH!
OOF.
TEN MINUTES! THAT'S OUR BEST TIME YET FOR THE 50-YARD DASH!
WATTERSON

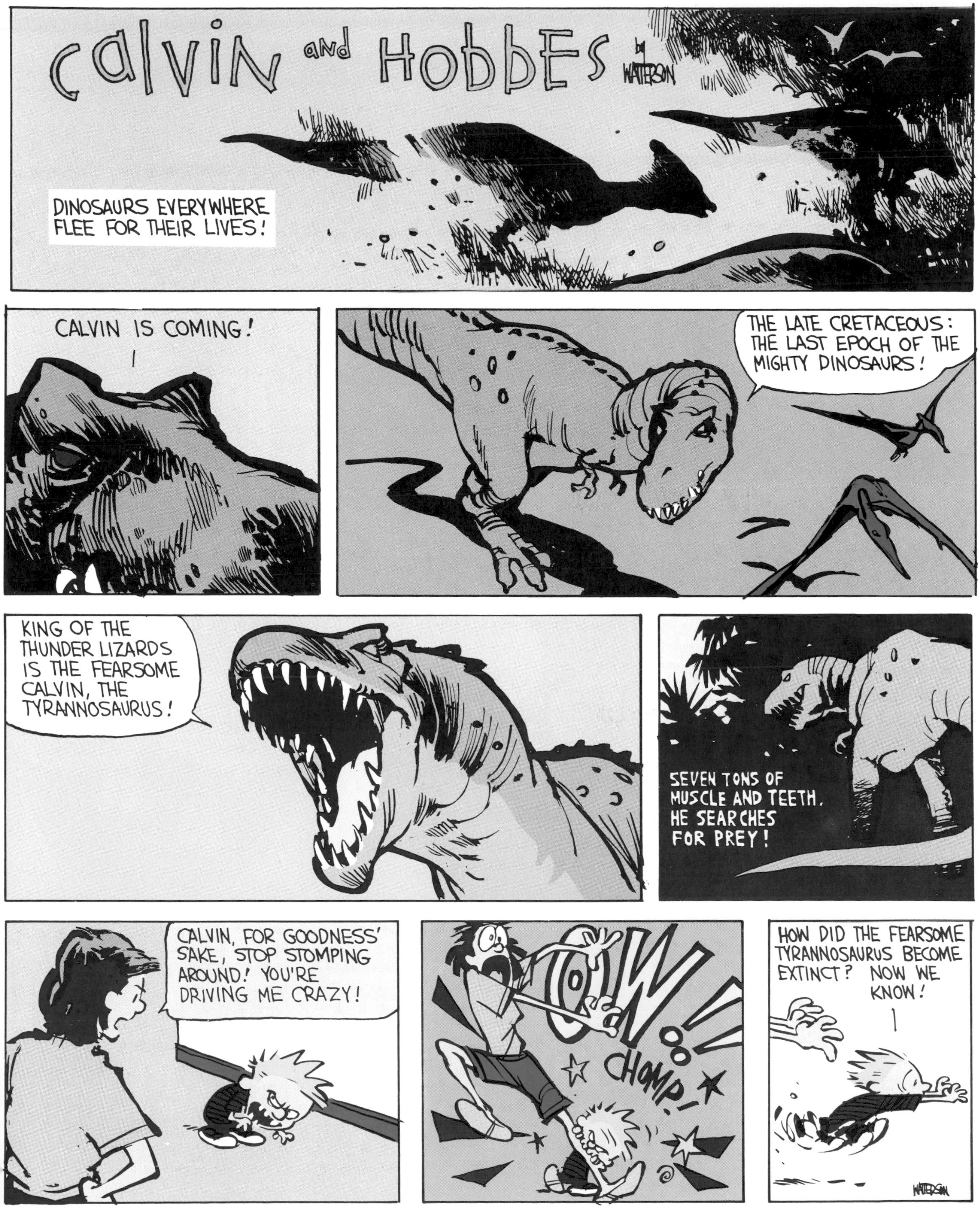
Calvin and HobbEs by WATTERSON
DINOSAURS EVERYWHERE FLEE FOR THEIR LIVES!
CALVIN IS COMING!
THE LATE CRETACEOUS: THE LAST EPOCH OF THE MIGHTY DINOSAURS!
KING OF THE THUNDER LIZARDS IS THE FEARSOME CALVIN, THE TYRANNOSAURUS!
SEVEN TONS OF MUSCLE AND TEETH, HE SEARCHES FOR PREY!
CALVIN, FOR GOODNESS' SAKE, STOP STOMPING AROUND! YOU'RE DRIVING ME CRAZY!
OOW!!
CHOMP!
HOW DID THE FEARSOME TYRANNOSAURUS BECOME EXTINCT? NOW WE KNOW!
WATTERSON

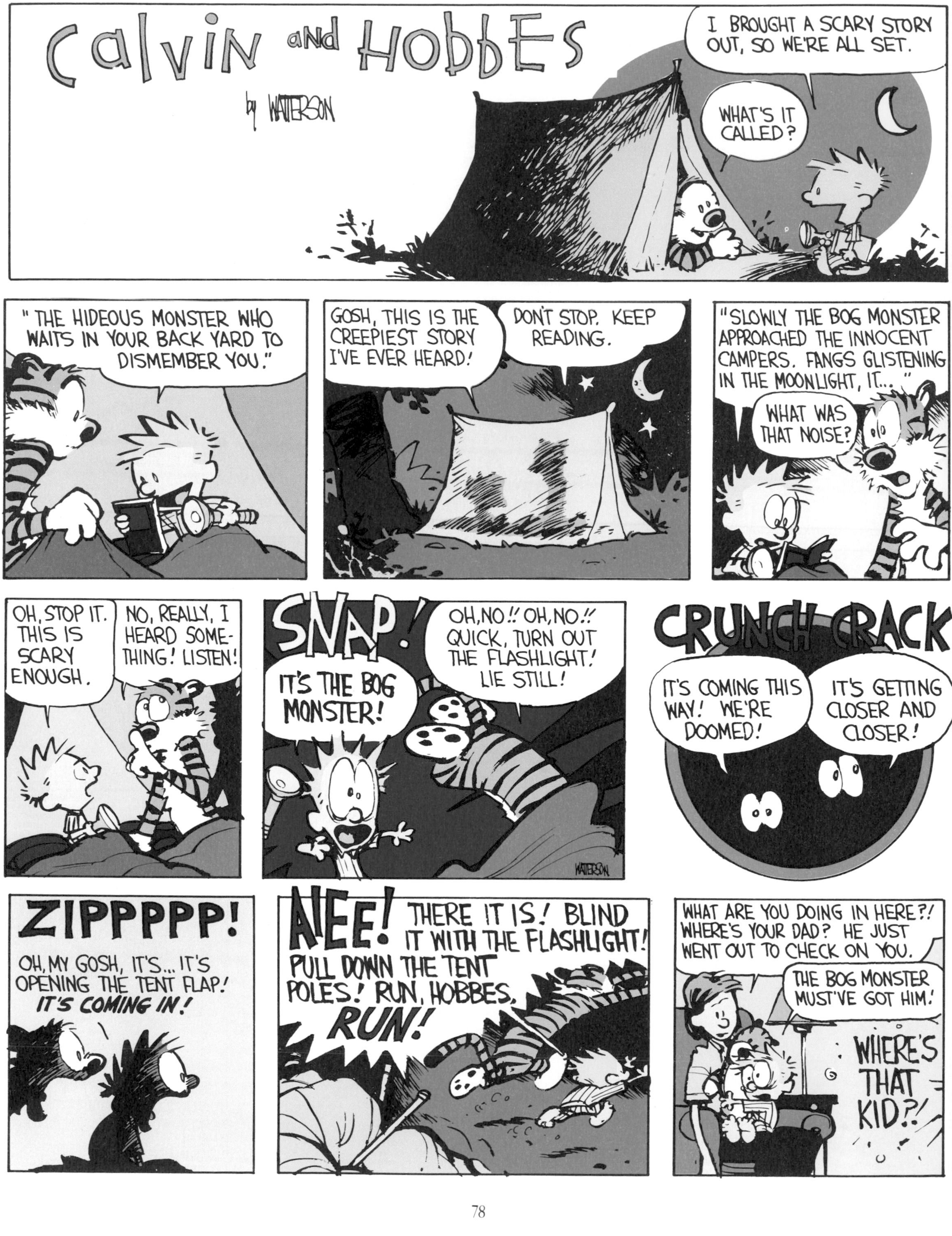
Calvin and HOBBES
by WATTERSON
I BROUGHT A SCARY STORY OUT, SO WE'RE ALL SET.
WHAT'S IT CALLED?
" THE HIDEOUS MONSTER WHO WAITS IN YOUR BACK YARD TO DISMEMBER YOU."
GOSH, THIS IS THE CREEPIEST STORY I'VE EVER HEARD!
DON'T STOP. KEEP READING.
"SLOWLY THE BOG MONSTER APPROACHED THE INNOCENT CAMPERS. FANGS GLISTENING IN THE MOONLIGHT, IT... "
WHAT WAS THAT NOISE?
OH, STOP IT. THIS IS SCARY ENOUGH.
NO, REALLY, I HEARD SOMETHING! LISTEN!
SNAP!
IT'S THE BOG MONSTER!
OH, NO!! OH, NO!! QUICK, TURN OUT THE FLASHLIGHT! LIE STILL!
WATTERSON
CRUNCH CRACK
IT'S COMING THIS WAY! WE'RE DOOMED!
IT'S GETTING CLOSER AND CLOSER!
ZIPPPPPP!
OH, MY GOSH, IT'S... IT'S OPENING THE TENT FLAP! IT'S COMING IN!
AIEE!
THERE IT IS! BLIND IT WITH THE FLASHLIGHT! PULL DOWN THE TENT POLES! RUN, HOBBES, RUN!
WHAT ARE YOU DOING IN HERE?! WHERE'S YOUR DAD? HE JUST WENT OUT TO CHECK ON YOU.
THE BOG MONSTER MUST'VE GOT HIM!
WHERE'S THAT KID?!

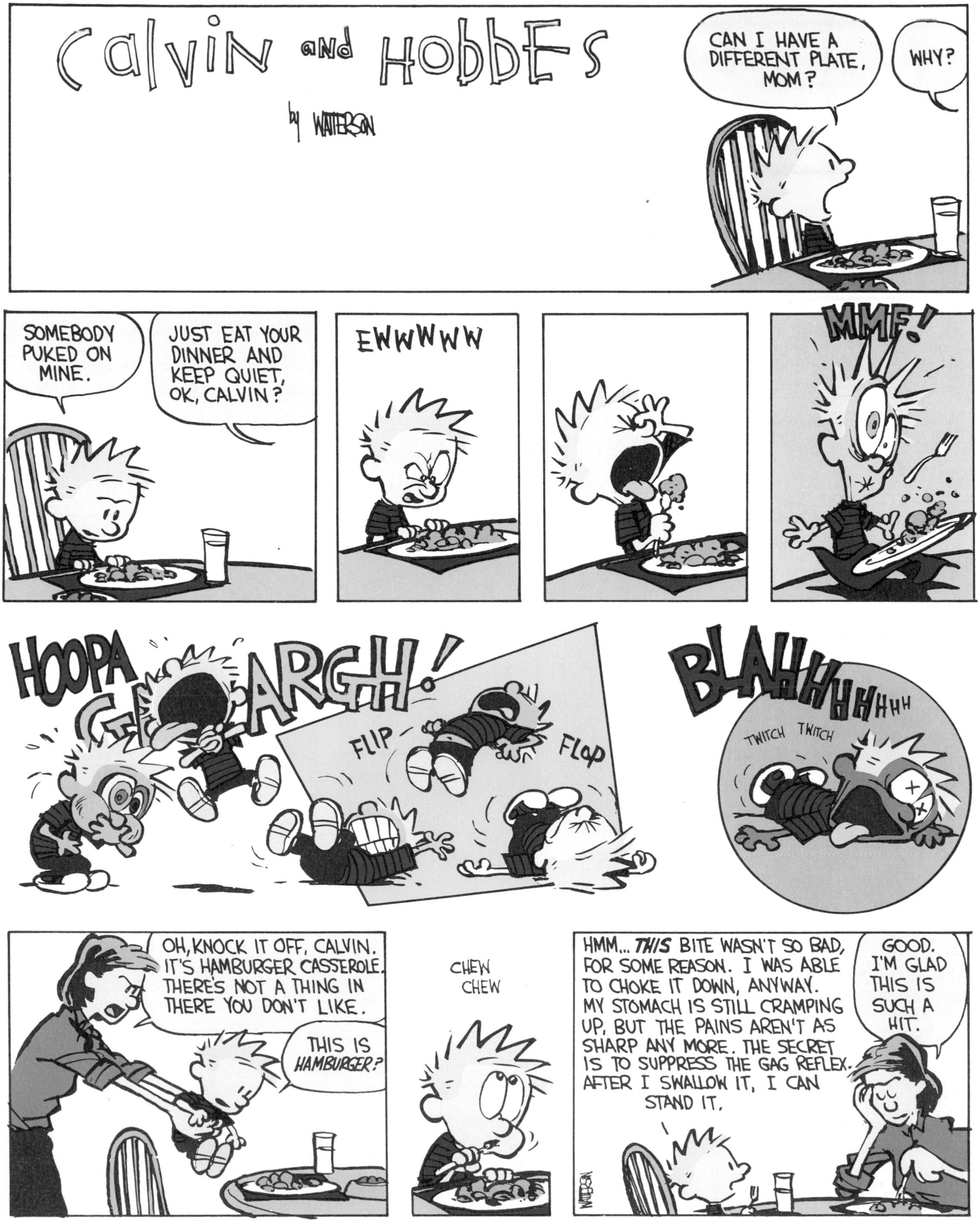
Calvin and HOBBES
by WATTERSON
CAN I HAVE A DIFFERENT PLATE, MOM?
WHY?
SOMEBODY PUKED ON MINE.
JUST EAT YOUR DINNER AND KEEP QUIET, OK, CALVIN?
EWWWWW
MMF!
HOOPA
ARGH!
FLIP
FLOP
BLAHHHHHHH
TWITCH TWITCH
OH, KNOCK IT OFF, CALVIN. IT'S HAMBURGER CASSEROLE. THERE'S NOT A THING IN THERE YOU DON'T LIKE.
THIS IS HAMBURGER?
CHEW CHEW
HMM... THIS BITE WASN'T SO BAD, FOR SOME REASON. I WAS ABLE TO CHOKE IT DOWN, ANYWAY. MY STOMACH IS STILL CRAMPING UP, BUT THE PAINS AREN'T AS SHARP ANY MORE. THE SECRET IS TO SUPPRESS THE GAG REFLEX. AFTER I SWALLOW IT, I CAN STAND IT.
GOOD. I'M GLAD THIS IS SUCH A HIT.
WATTERSON

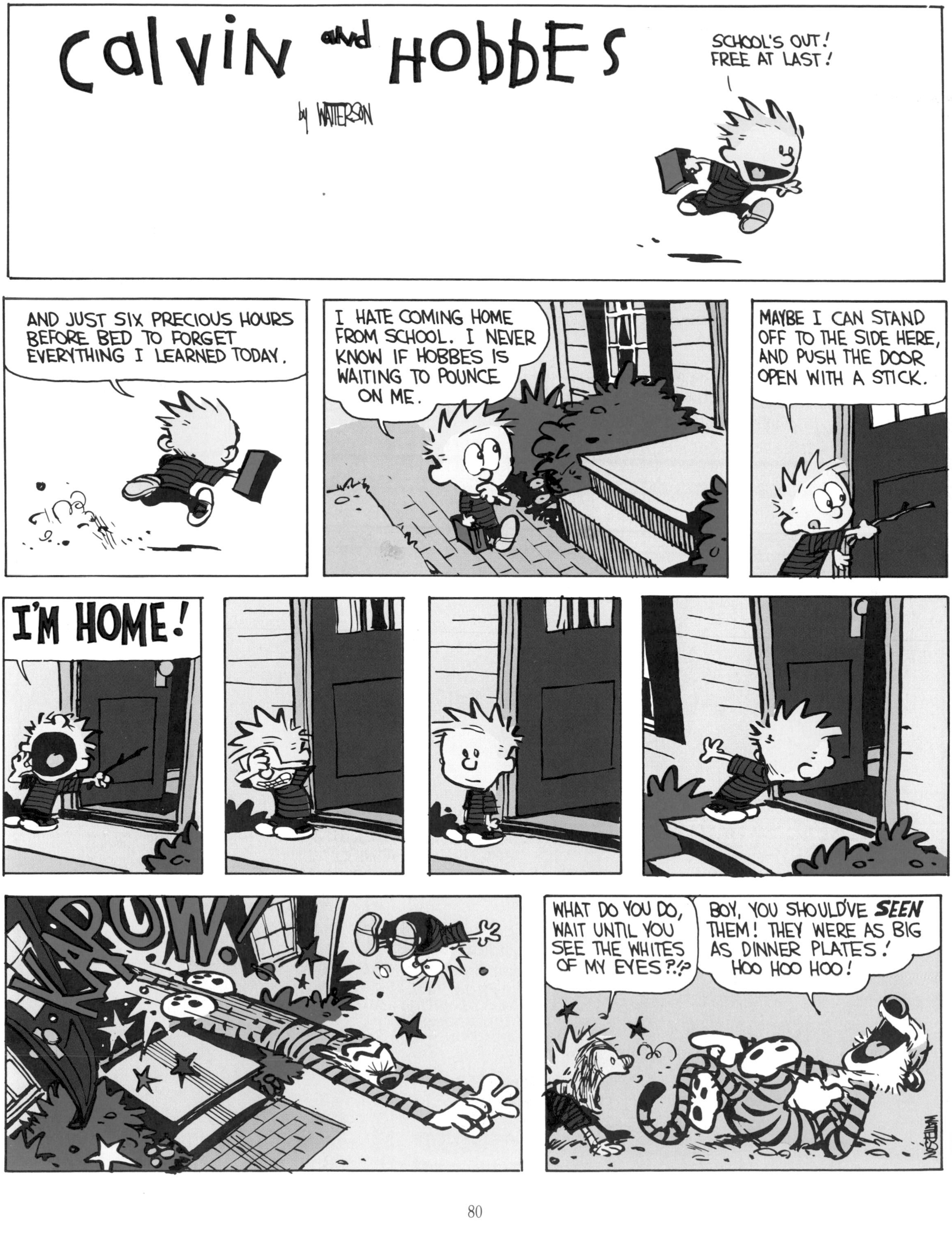

Calvin and HOBBES
by WATTERSON
SCHOOL'S OUT! FREE AT LAST!
AND JUST SIX PRECIOUS HOURS BEFORE BED TO FORGET EVERYTHING I LEARNED TODAY.
I HATE COMING HOME FROM SCHOOL. I NEVER KNOW IF HOBBES IS WAITING TO POUNCE ON ME.
MAYBE I CAN STAND OFF TO THE SIDE HERE, AND PUSH THE DOOR OPEN WITH A STICK.
I'M HOME!
KAPOW!
WHAT DO YOU DO, WAIT UNTIL YOU SEE THE WHITES OF MY EYES?!?
BOY, YOU SHOULD'VE SEEN THEM! THEY WERE AS BIG AS DINNER PLATES! HOO HOO HOO!
WATTERSON

Calvin and HOBBES
by WATTERSON
CALL IT.
TAILS.
OK, BEST TWO OUT OF THREE.
OOOMPH
LET'S CHANGE THIS TO **TOUCH** FOOTBALL, OK?
WATTERSON

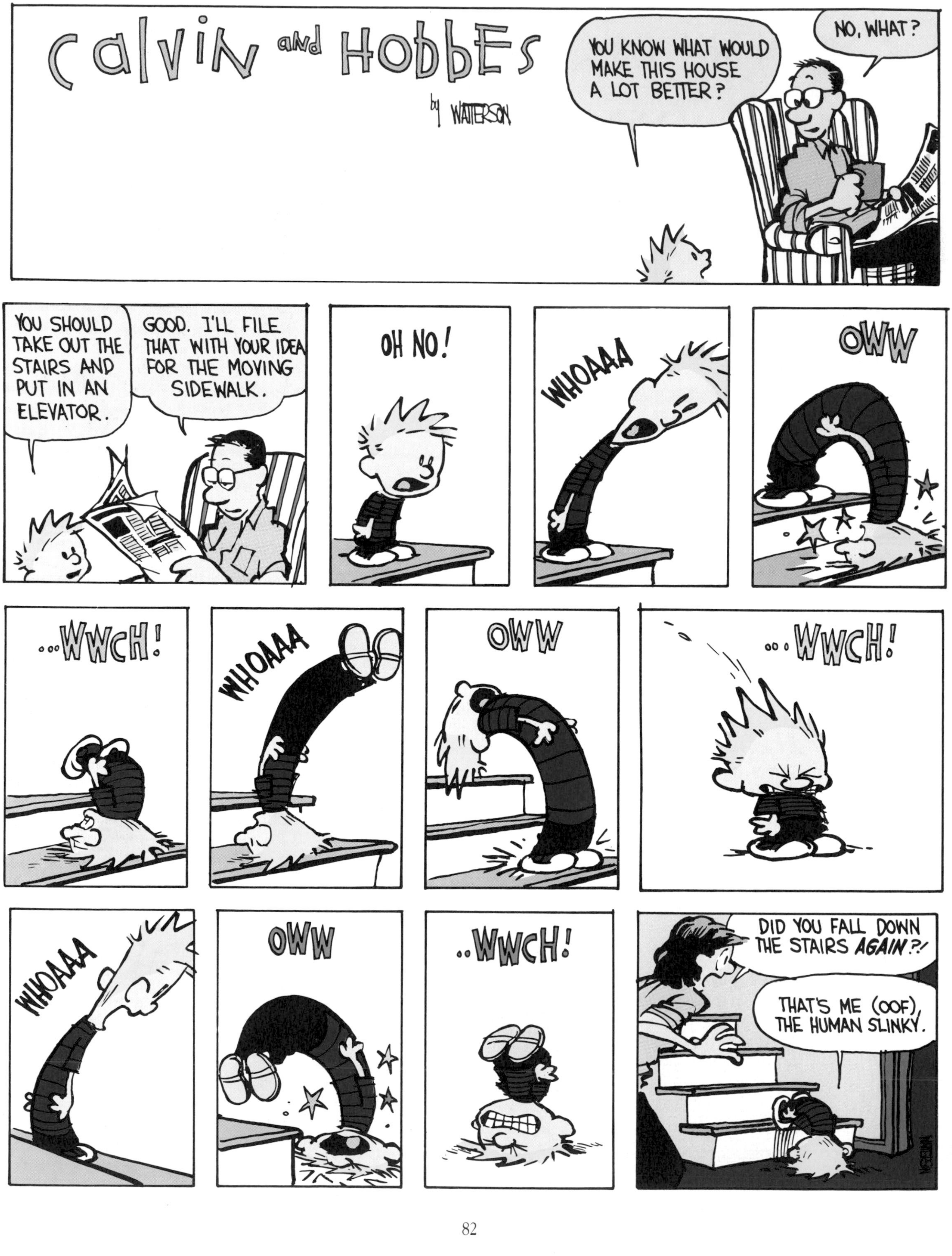
Calvin and Hobbes
by WATTERSON
YOU KNOW WHAT WOULD MAKE THIS HOUSE A LOT BETTER?
NO, WHAT?
YOU SHOULD TAKE OUT THE STAIRS AND PUT IN AN ELEVATOR.
GOOD. I'LL FILE THAT WITH YOUR IDEA FOR THE MOVING SIDEWALK.
OH NO!
WHOAAA
OWW
...WWCH!
WHOAAA
OWW
...WWCH!
WHOAAA
OWW
..WWCH!
DID YOU FALL DOWN THE STAIRS AGAIN?!
THAT'S ME (OOF), THE HUMAN SLINKY.

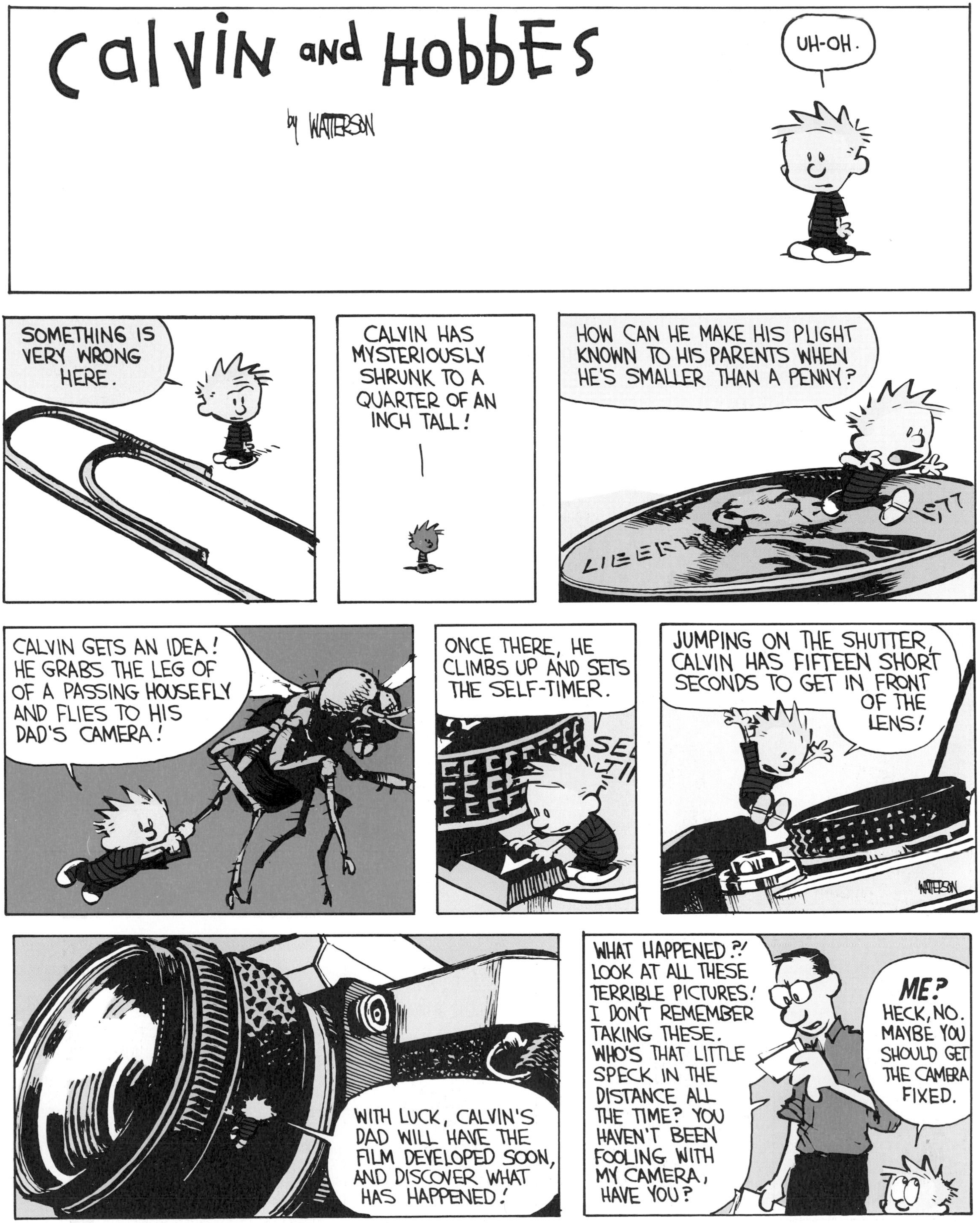

Calvin and Hobbes
by WATTERSON
UH-OH.
SOMETHING IS VERY WRONG HERE.
CALVIN HAS MYSTERIOUSLY SHRUNK TO A QUARTER OF AN INCH TALL!
HOW CAN HE MAKE HIS PLIGHT KNOWN TO HIS PARENTS WHEN HE'S SMALLER THAN A PENNY?
LIBERTY
1977
CALVIN GETS AN IDEA! HE GRABS THE LEG OF OF A PASSING HOUSEFLY AND FLIES TO HIS DAD'S CAMERA!
ONCE THERE, HE CLIMBS UP AND SETS THE SELF-TIMER.
JUMPING ON THE SHUTTER, CALVIN HAS FIFTEEN SHORT SECONDS TO GET IN FRONT OF THE LENS!
WATTERSON
WITH LUCK, CALVIN'S DAD WILL HAVE THE FILM DEVELOPED SOON, AND DISCOVER WHAT HAS HAPPENED!
WHAT HAPPENED?! LOOK AT ALL THESE TERRIBLE PICTURES! I DON'T REMEMBER TAKING THESE. WHO'S THAT LITTLE SPECK IN THE DISTANCE ALL THE TIME? YOU HAVEN'T BEEN FOOLING WITH MY CAMERA, HAVE YOU?
ME? HECK, NO. MAYBE YOU SHOULD GET THE CAMERA FIXED.

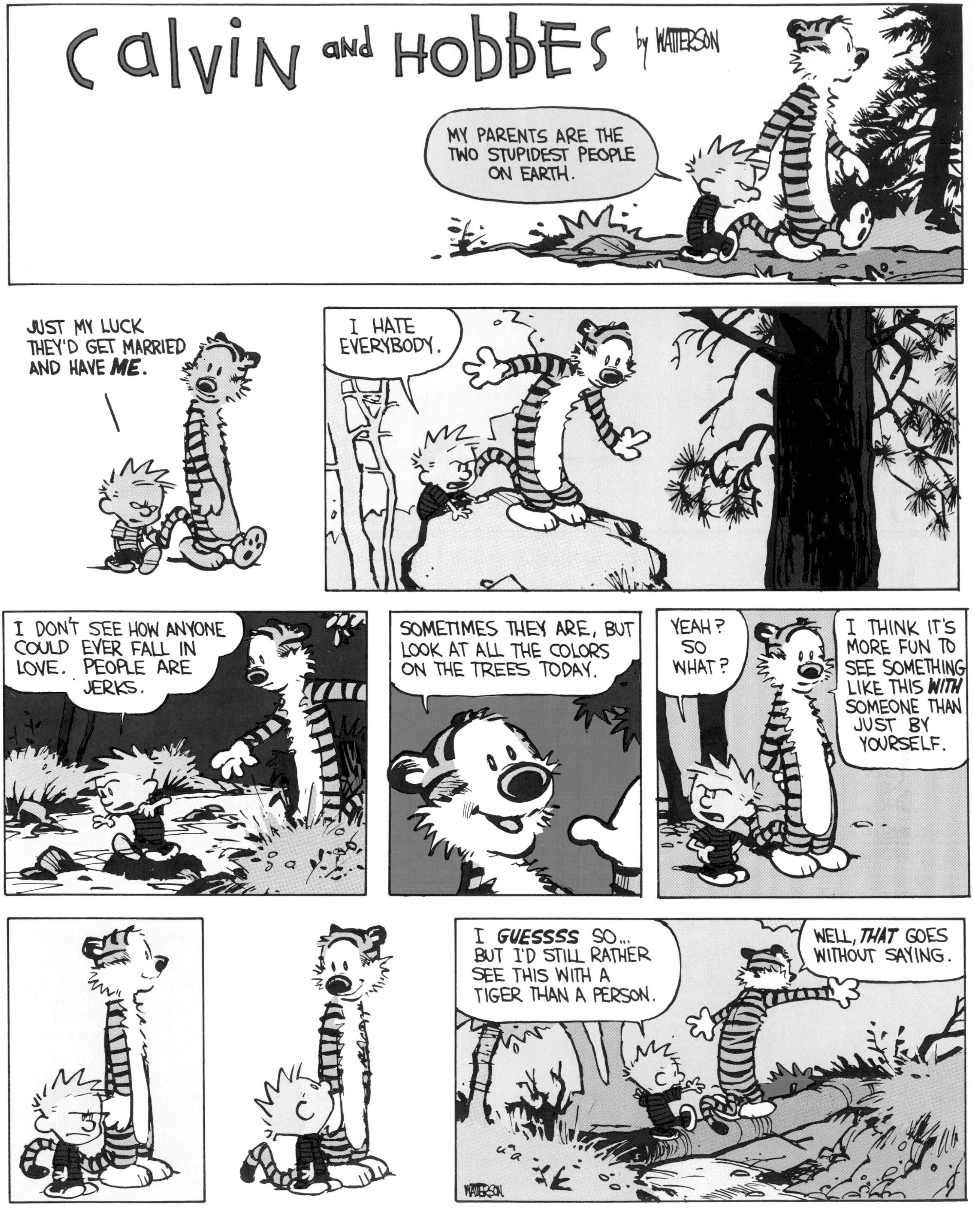
Calvin and HobbEs by WATTERSON
MY PARENTS ARE THE TWO STUPIDEST PEOPLE ON EARTH.
JUST MY LUCK THEY'D GET MARRIED AND HAVE ME.
I HATE EVERYBODY.
I DON'T SEE HOW ANYONE COULD EVER FALL IN LOVE. PEOPLE ARE JERKS.
SOMETIMES THEY ARE, BUT LOOK AT ALL THE COLORS ON THE TREES TODAY.
YEAH? SO WHAT?
I THINK IT'S MORE FUN TO SEE SOMETHING LIKE THIS WITH SOMEONE THAN JUST BY YOURSELF.
I GUESSSS SO... BUT I'D STILL RATHER SEE THIS WITH A TIGER THAN A PERSON.
WELL, THAT GOES WITHOUT SAYING.
WATTERSON

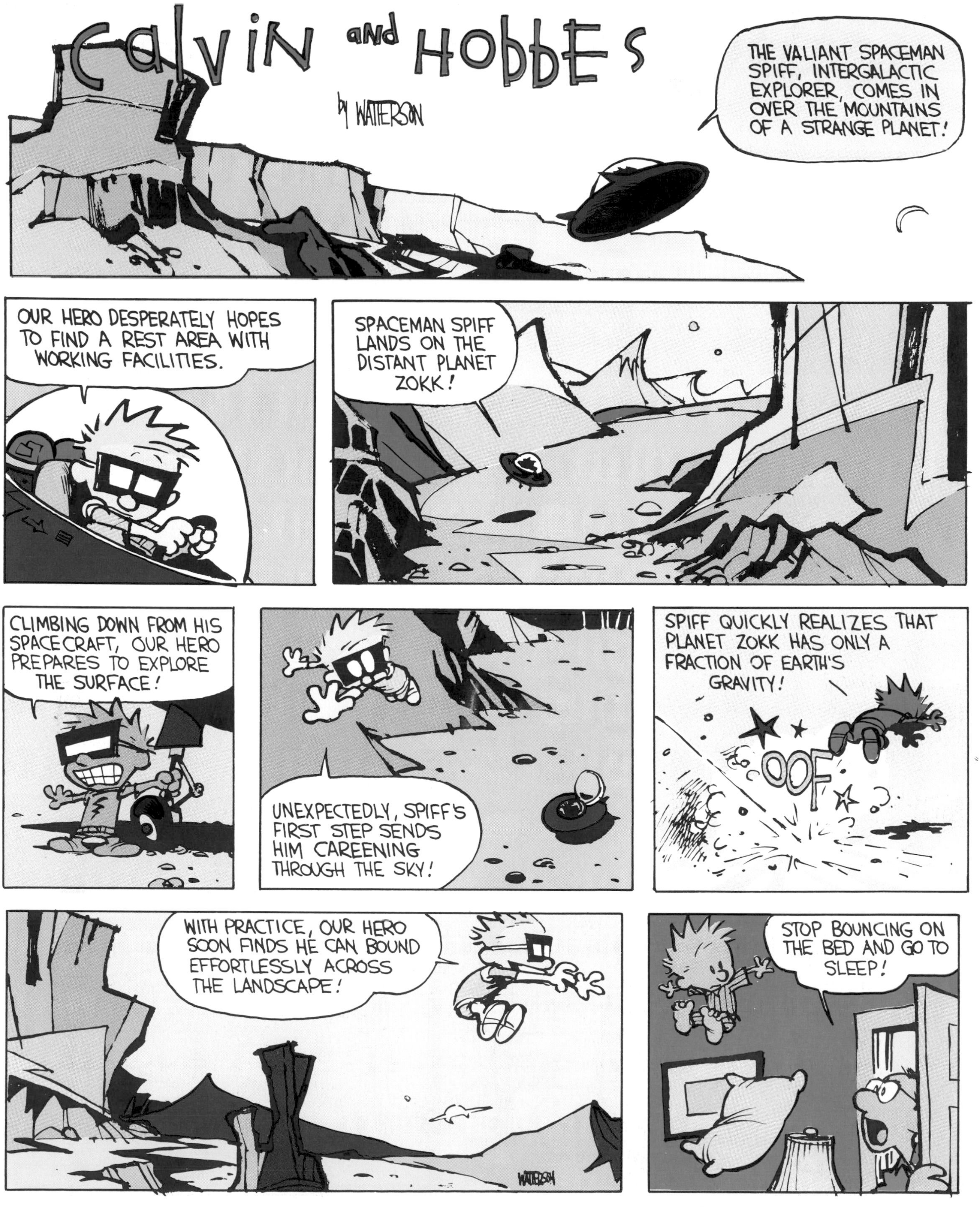
Calvin and Hobbes
by WATTERSON
THE VALIANT SPACEMAN SPIFF, INTERGALACTIC EXPLORER, COMES IN OVER THE MOUNTAINS OF A STRANGE PLANET!
OUR HERO DESPERATELY HOPES TO FIND A REST AREA WITH WORKING FACILITIES.
SPACEMAN SPIFF LANDS ON THE DISTANT PLANET ZOKK!
CLIMBING DOWN FROM HIS SPACECRAFT, OUR HERO PREPARES TO EXPLORE THE SURFACE!
UNEXPECTEDLY, SPIFF'S FIRST STEP SENDS HIM CAREENING THROUGH THE SKY!
SPIFF QUICKLY REALIZES THAT PLANET ZOKK HAS ONLY A FRACTION OF EARTH'S GRAVITY!
OOF
WITH PRACTICE, OUR HERO SOON FINDS HE CAN BOUND EFFORTLESSLY ACROSS THE LANDSCAPE!
WATTERSON
STOP BOUNCING ON THE BED AND GO TO SLEEP!

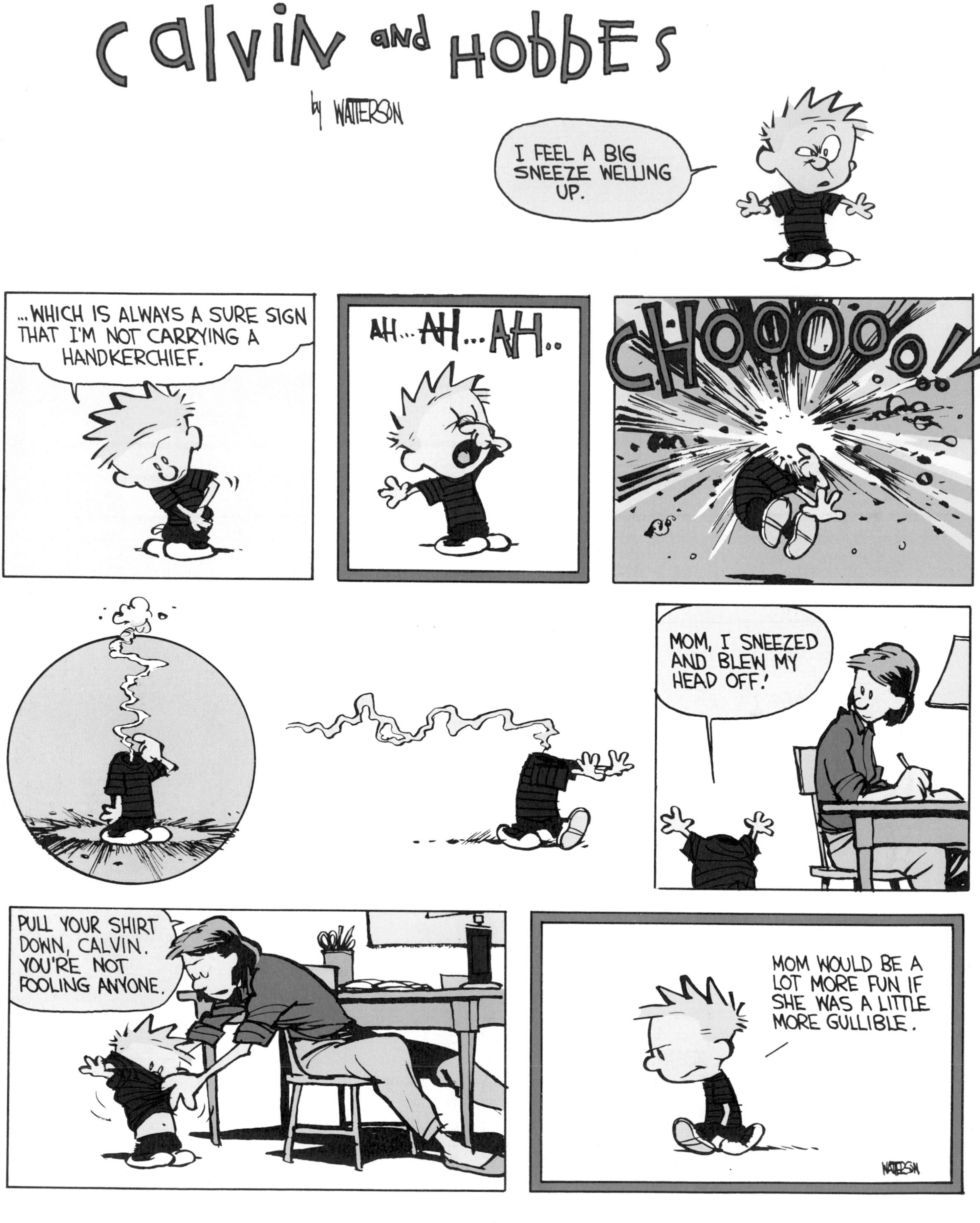

Calvin and Hobbes
by WATTERSON
I FEEL A BIG SNEEZE WELLING UP.
...WHICH IS ALWAYS A SURE SIGN THAT I'M NOT CARRYING A HANDKERCHIEF.
AH... AH... AH..
CHOOOOOO!!
MOM, I SNEEZED AND BLEW MY HEAD OFF!
PULL YOUR SHIRT DOWN, CALVIN. YOU'RE NOT FOOLING ANYONE.
MOM WOULD BE A LOT MORE FUN IF SHE WAS A LITTLE MORE GULLIBLE.
WATTERSON

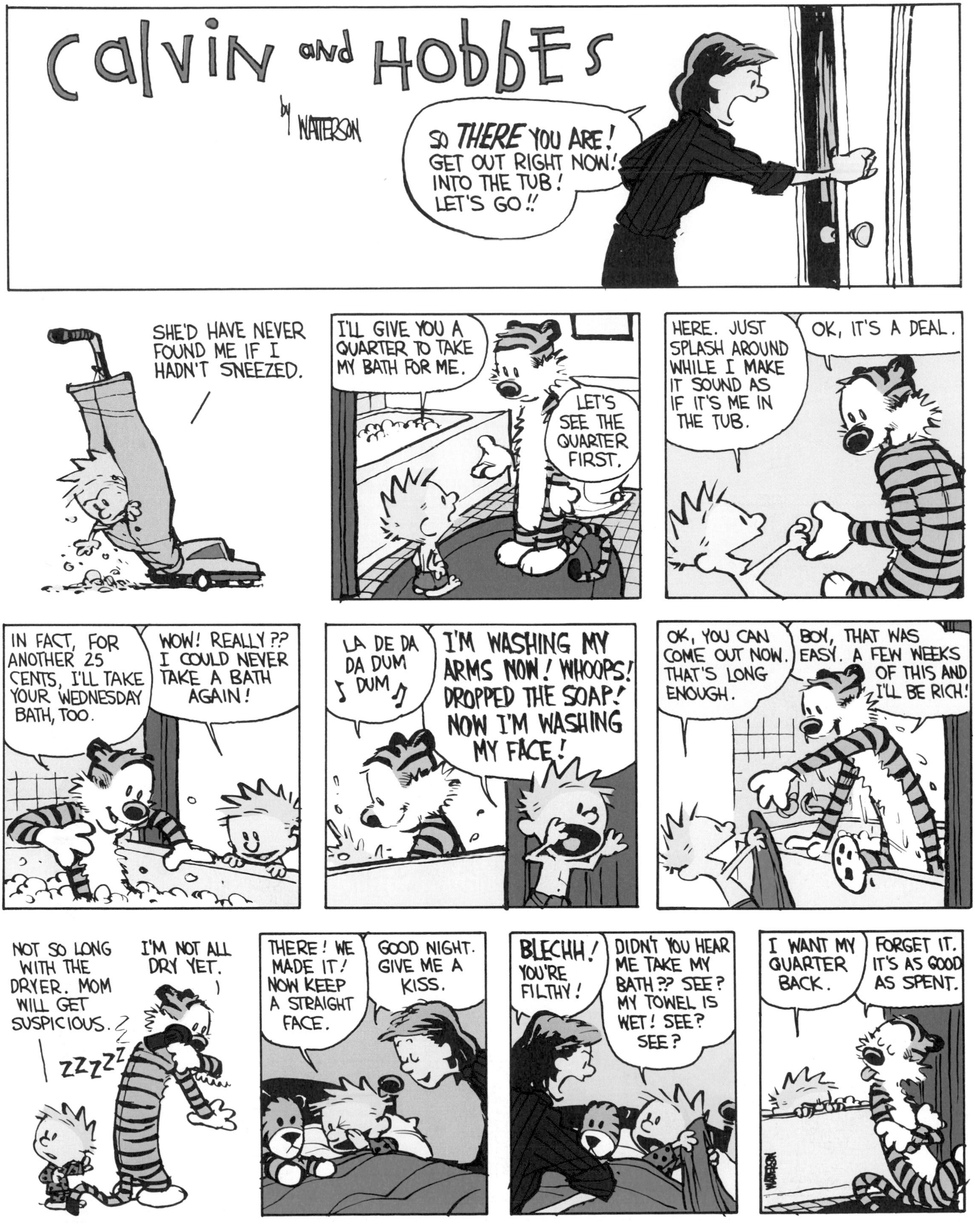
Calvin and HOBBES
by WATTERSON
SO THERE YOU ARE! GET OUT RIGHT NOW! INTO THE TUB! LET'S GO!!
SHE'D HAVE NEVER FOUND ME IF I HADN'T SNEEZED.
I'LL GIVE YOU A QUARTER TO TAKE MY BATH FOR ME.
LET'S SEE THE QUARTER FIRST.
HERE. JUST SPLASH AROUND WHILE I MAKE IT SOUND AS IF IT'S ME IN THE TUB.
OK, IT'S A DEAL.
IN FACT, FOR ANOTHER 25 CENTS, I'LL TAKE YOUR WEDNESDAY BATH, TOO.
WOW! REALLY?? I COULD NEVER TAKE A BATH AGAIN!
LA DE DA DA DUM DUM
I'M WASHING MY ARMS NOW! WHOOPS! DROPPED THE SOAP! NOW I'M WASHING MY FACE!
OK, YOU CAN COME OUT NOW. THAT'S LONG ENOUGH.
BOY, THAT WAS EASY. A FEW WEEKS OF THIS AND I'LL BE RICH!
NOT SO LONG WITH THE DRYER. MOM WILL GET SUSPICIOUS.
I'M NOT ALL DRY YET.
ZZZZZ
THERE! WE MADE IT! NOW KEEP A STRAIGHT FACE.
GOOD NIGHT. GIVE ME A KISS.
BLECHH! YOU'RE FILTHY!
DIDN'T YOU HEAR ME TAKE MY BATH?? SEE? MY TOWEL IS WET! SEE? SEE?
I WANT MY QUARTER BACK.
FORGET IT. IT'S AS GOOD AS SPENT.
WATTERSON

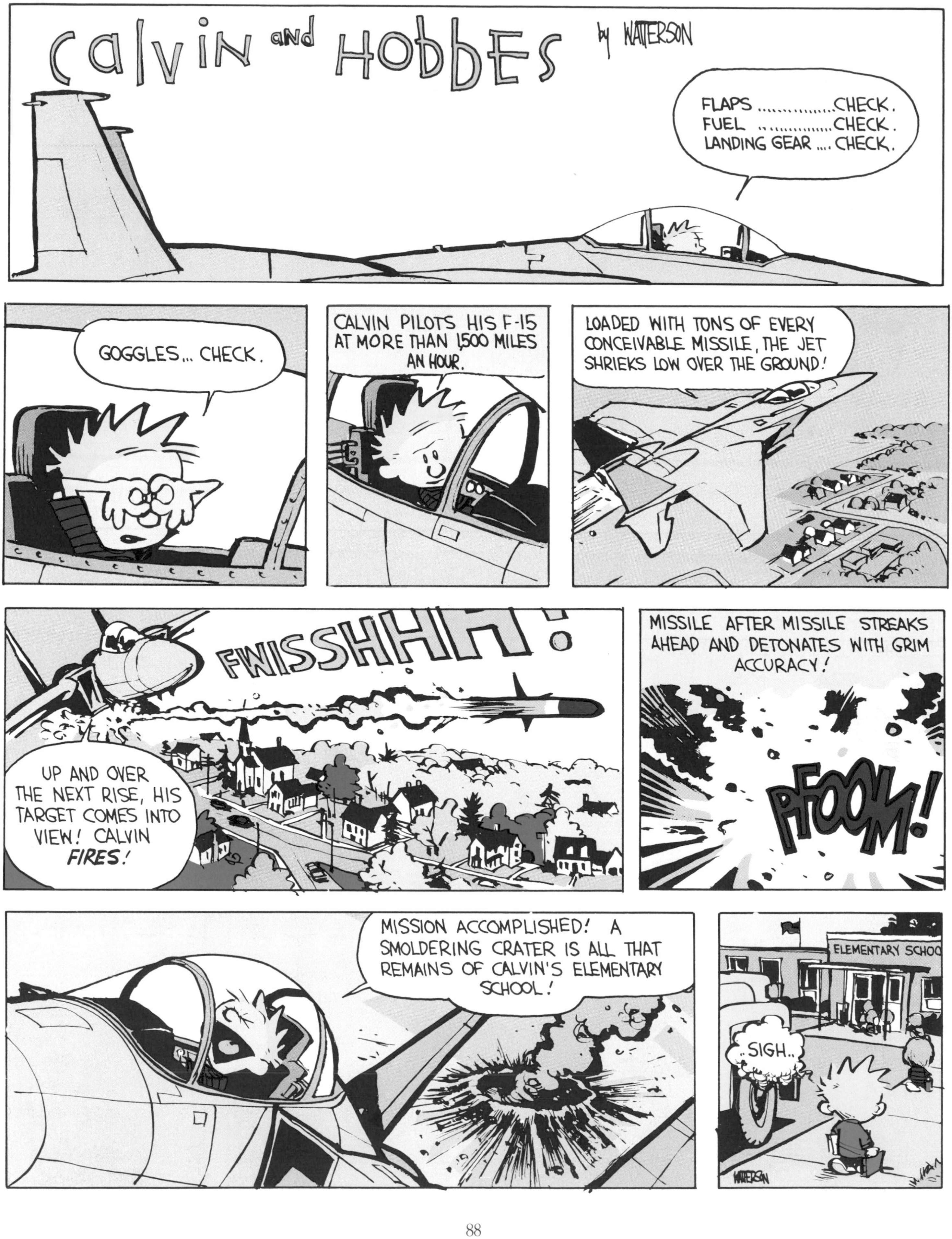
Calvin and HOBBES by WATTERSON
FLAPS ....CHECK. FUEL ....CHECK. LANDING GEAR .... CHECK.
GOGGLES... CHECK.
CALVIN PILOTS HIS F-15 AT MORE THAN 1,500 MILES AN HOUR.
LOADED WITH TONS OF EVERY CONCEIVABLE MISSILE, THE JET SHRIEKS LOW OVER THE GROUND!
FWISSHHH!
UP AND OVER THE NEXT RISE, HIS TARGET COMES INTO VIEW! CALVIN FIRES!
MISSILE AFTER MISSILE STREAKS AHEAD AND DETONATES WITH GRIM ACCURACY!
PFOOM!
MISSION ACCOMPLISHED! A SMOLDERING CRATER IS ALL THAT REMAINS OF CALVIN'S ELEMENTARY SCHOOL!
ELEMENTARY SCHO
..SIGH..
WATTERSON

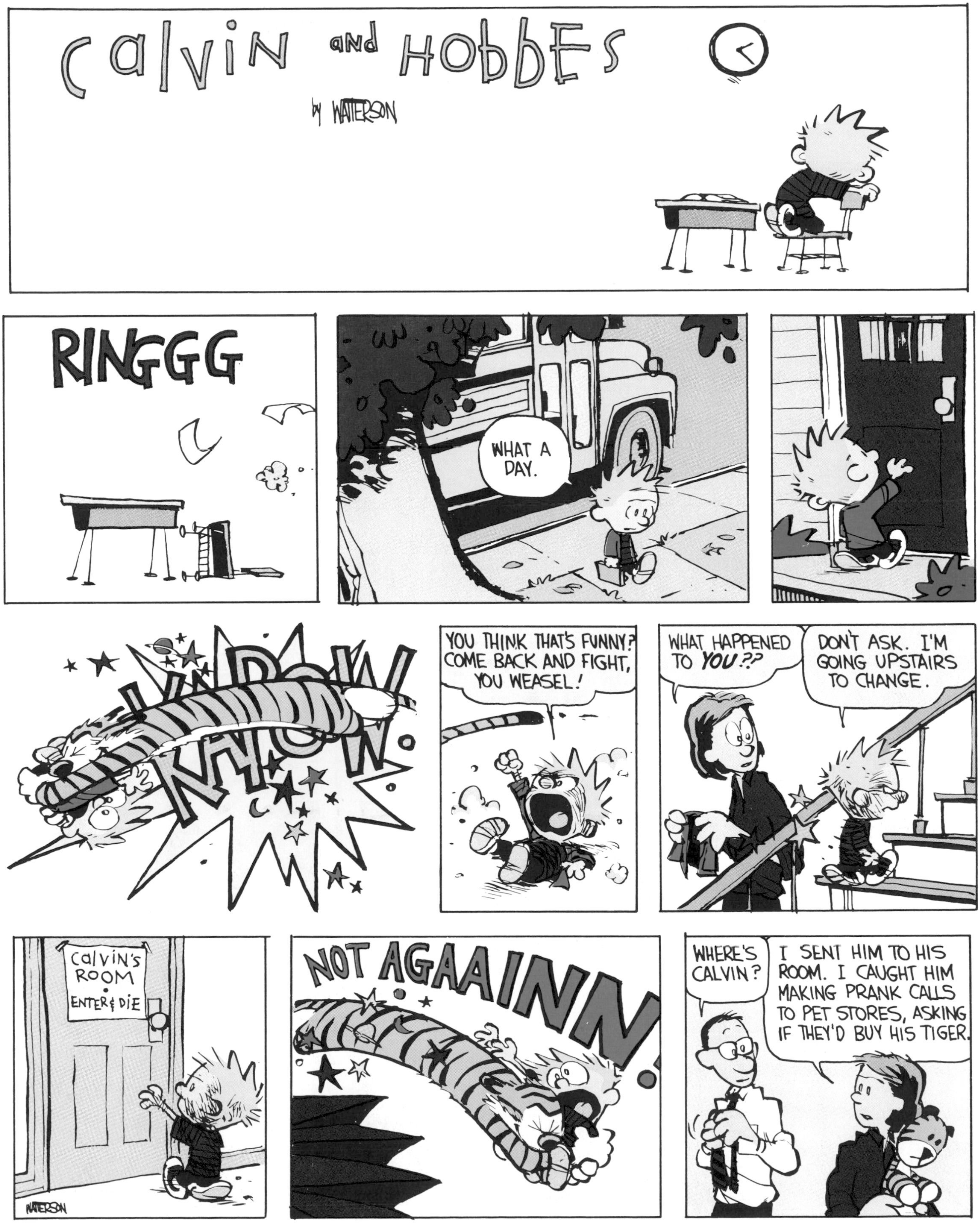
Calvin and HOBBES
by WATTERSON
RINGGG
WHAT A DAY.
KAPOW
YOU THINK THAT'S FUNNY? COME BACK AND FIGHT, YOU WEASEL!
WHAT HAPPENED TO *YOU* ??
DON'T ASK. I'M GOING UPSTAIRS TO CHANGE.
Calvin's ROOM • ENTER & DIE
WATTERSON
NOT AGAAINN!
WHERE'S CALVIN?
I SENT HIM TO HIS ROOM. I CAUGHT HIM MAKING PRANK CALLS TO PET STORES, ASKING IF THEY'D BUY HIS TIGER.

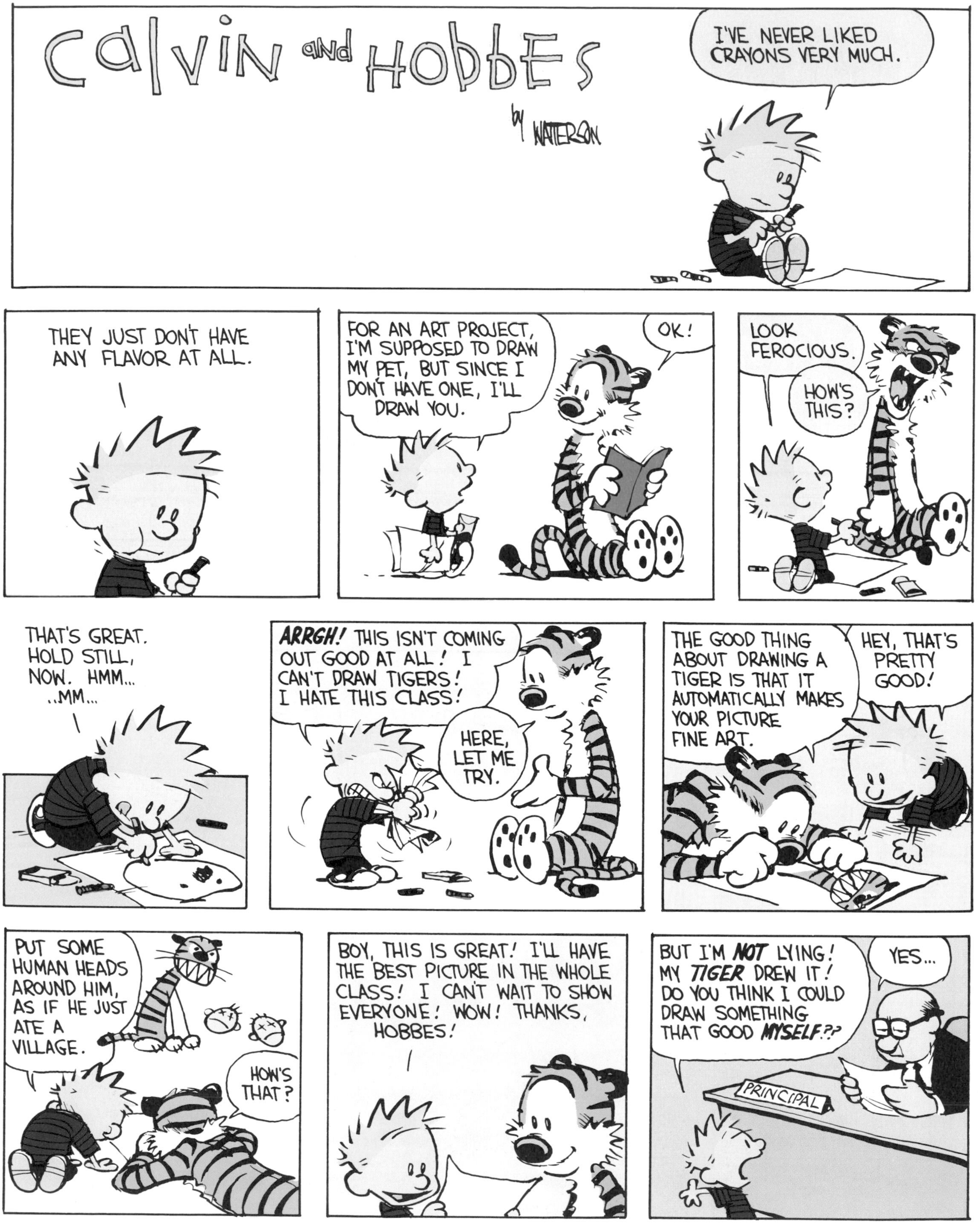
Calvin and Hobbes
by WATTERSON
I'VE NEVER LIKED CRAYONS VERY MUCH.
THEY JUST DON'T HAVE ANY FLAVOR AT ALL.
FOR AN ART PROJECT, I'M SUPPOSED TO DRAW MY PET, BUT SINCE I DON'T HAVE ONE, I'LL DRAW YOU.
OK!
LOOK FEROCIOUS.
HOW'S THIS?
THAT'S GREAT. HOLD STILL, NOW. HMM... ..MM...
ARRGH! THIS ISN'T COMING OUT GOOD AT ALL! I CAN'T DRAW TIGERS! I HATE THIS CLASS!
HERE, LET ME TRY.
THE GOOD THING ABOUT DRAWING A TIGER IS THAT IT AUTOMATICALLY MAKES YOUR PICTURE FINE ART.
HEY, THAT'S PRETTY GOOD!
PUT SOME HUMAN HEADS AROUND HIM, AS IF HE JUST ATE A VILLAGE.
HOW'S THAT?
BOY, THIS IS GREAT! I'LL HAVE THE BEST PICTURE IN THE WHOLE CLASS! I CAN'T WAIT TO SHOW EVERYONE! WOW! THANKS, HOBBES!
BUT I'M NOT LYING! MY TIGER DREW IT! DO YOU THINK I COULD DRAW SOMETHING THAT GOOD MYSELF??
YES...
PRINCIPAL

CALVIN AND HOBBES

by WATTERSON

IF *I* WAS IN CHARGE, WE'D NEVER SEE GRASS BETWEEN OCTOBER AND MAY.

ON "THREE", READY? ONE... TWO... THREE!

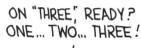

SNOW!

I SAID SNOW! C'MON! SNOW!

SNOW!

OK THEN, *DON'T* SNOW! SEE WHAT *I* CARE! I *LIKE* THIS WEATHER! LET'S HAVE IT FOREVER!

PLEEAASE SNOW! PLEASE?? JUST A FOOT! OK, EIGHT INCHES! THAT'S ALL! C'MON! SIX INCHES, EVEN! HOW ABOUT JUST SIX??

I'M *WAAIIITING...*

RRRRGGHHH

DO YOU WANT ME TO BECOME AN ATHEIST?

91

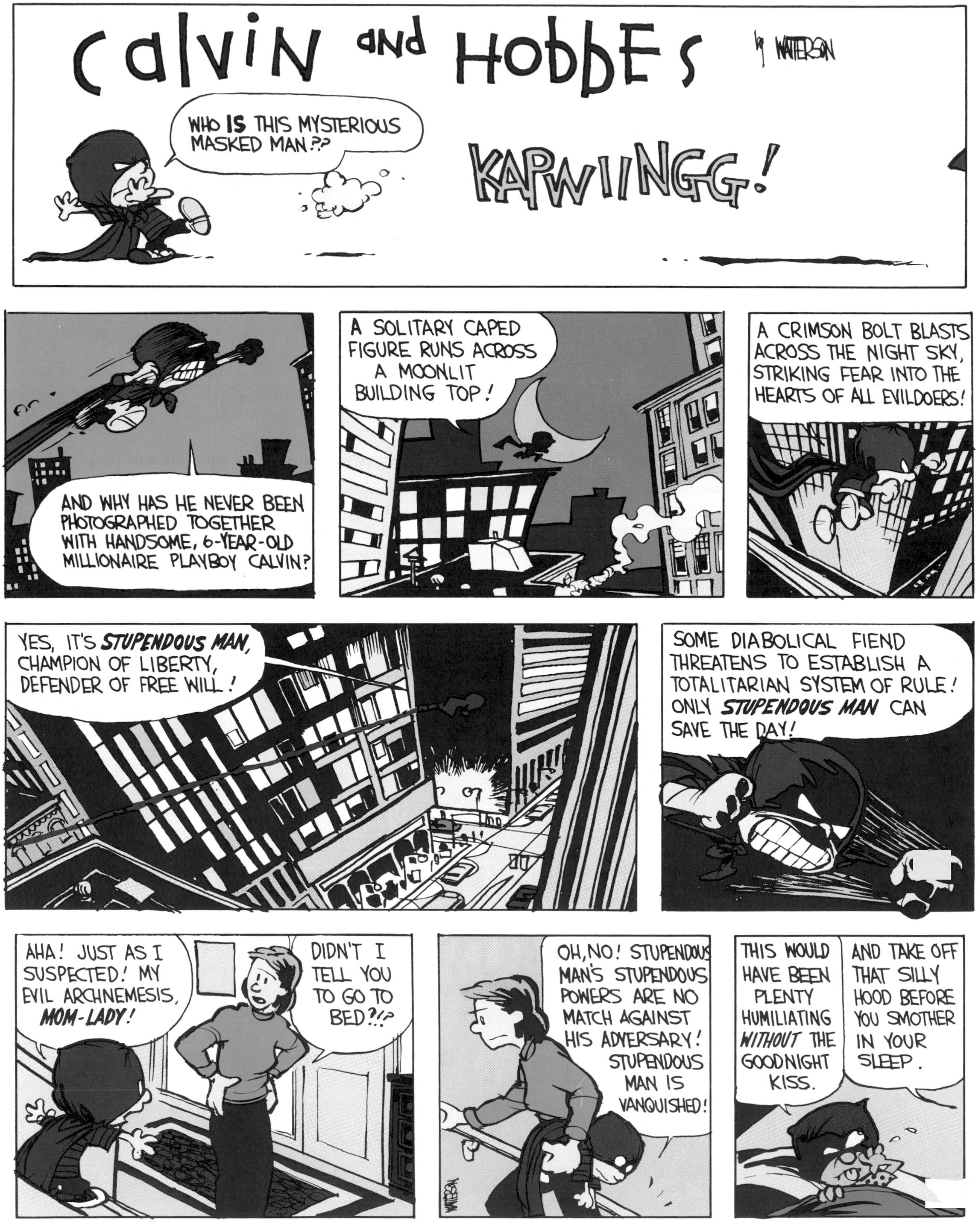
Calvin and Hobbes
by WATTERSON
WHO IS THIS MYSTERIOUS MASKED MAN ??
KAPWIINGG!
AND WHY HAS HE NEVER BEEN PHOTOGRAPHED TOGETHER WITH HANDSOME, 6-YEAR-OLD MILLIONAIRE PLAYBOY CALVIN?
A SOLITARY CAPED FIGURE RUNS ACROSS A MOONLIT BUILDING TOP!
A CRIMSON BOLT BLASTS ACROSS THE NIGHT SKY, STRIKING FEAR INTO THE HEARTS OF ALL EVILDOERS!
YES, IT'S STUPENDOUS MAN, CHAMPION OF LIBERTY, DEFENDER OF FREE WILL!
SOME DIABOLICAL FIEND THREATENS TO ESTABLISH A TOTALITARIAN SYSTEM OF RULE! ONLY STUPENDOUS MAN CAN SAVE THE DAY!
AHA! JUST AS I SUSPECTED! MY EVIL ARCHNEMESIS, MOM-LADY!
DIDN'T I TELL YOU TO GO TO BED?!?
OH, NO! STUPENDOUS MAN'S STUPENDOUS POWERS ARE NO MATCH AGAINST HIS ADVERSARY! STUPENDOUS MAN IS VANQUISHED!
WATTERSON
THIS WOULD HAVE BEEN PLENTY HUMILIATING WITHOUT THE GOODNIGHT KISS.
AND TAKE OFF THAT SILLY HOOD BEFORE YOU SMOTHER IN YOUR SLEEP.

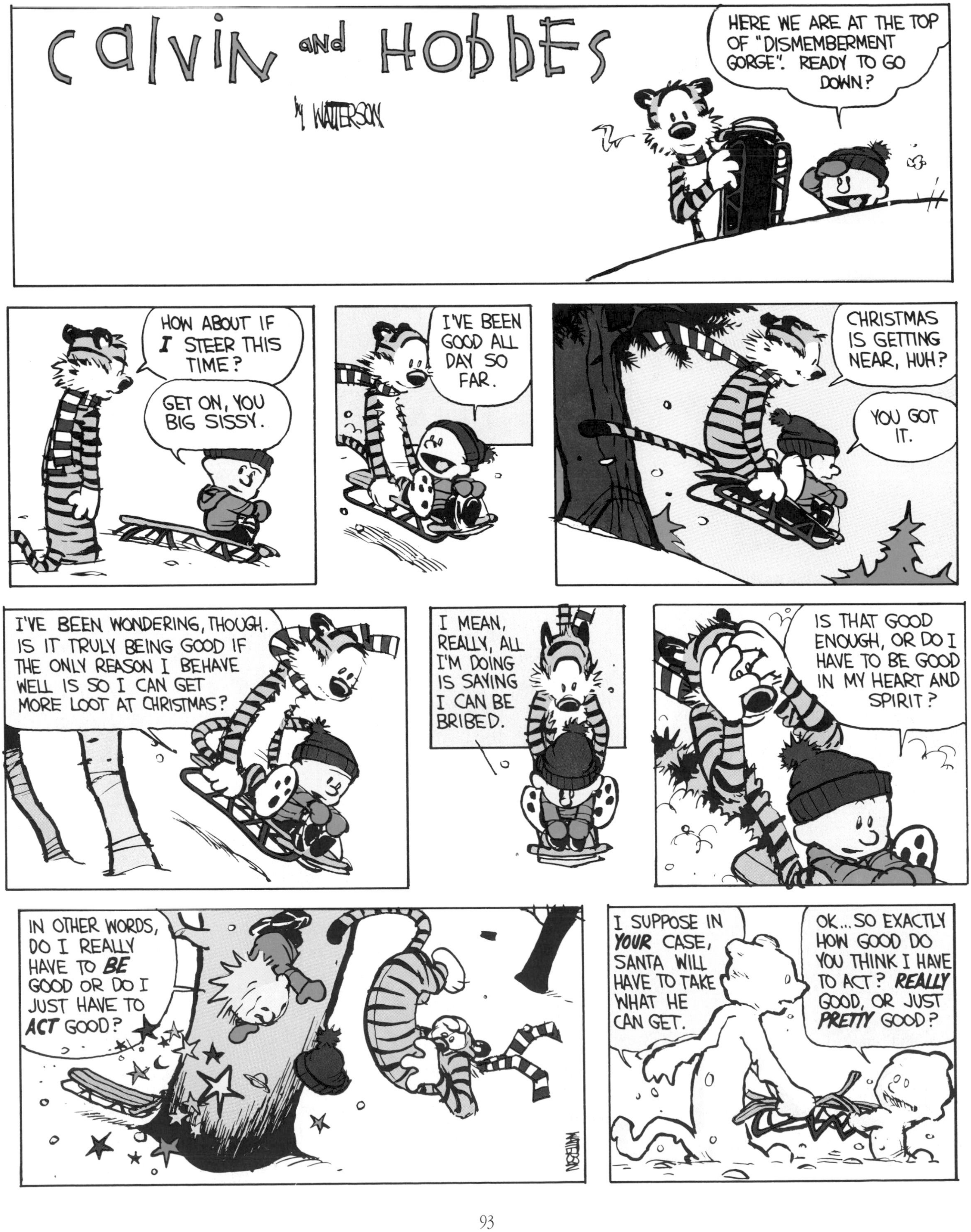
Calvin and Hobbes
by WATTERSON
HERE WE ARE AT THE TOP OF "DISMEMBERMENT GORGE". READY TO GO DOWN?
HOW ABOUT IF *I* STEER THIS TIME?
GET ON, YOU BIG SISSY.
I'VE BEEN GOOD ALL DAY SO FAR.
CHRISTMAS IS GETTING NEAR, HUH?
YOU GOT IT.
I'VE BEEN WONDERING, THOUGH. IS IT TRULY BEING GOOD IF THE ONLY REASON I BEHAVE WELL IS SO I CAN GET MORE LOOT AT CHRISTMAS?
I MEAN, REALLY, ALL I'M DOING IS SAYING I CAN BE BRIBED.
IS THAT GOOD ENOUGH, OR DO I HAVE TO BE GOOD IN MY HEART AND SPIRIT?
IN OTHER WORDS, DO I REALLY HAVE TO ***BE*** GOOD OR DO I JUST HAVE TO ***ACT*** GOOD?
WATTERSON
I SUPPOSE IN ***YOUR*** CASE, SANTA WILL HAVE TO TAKE WHAT HE CAN GET.
OK... SO EXACTLY HOW GOOD DO YOU THINK I HAVE TO ACT? ***REALLY*** GOOD, OR JUST ***PRETTY*** GOOD?

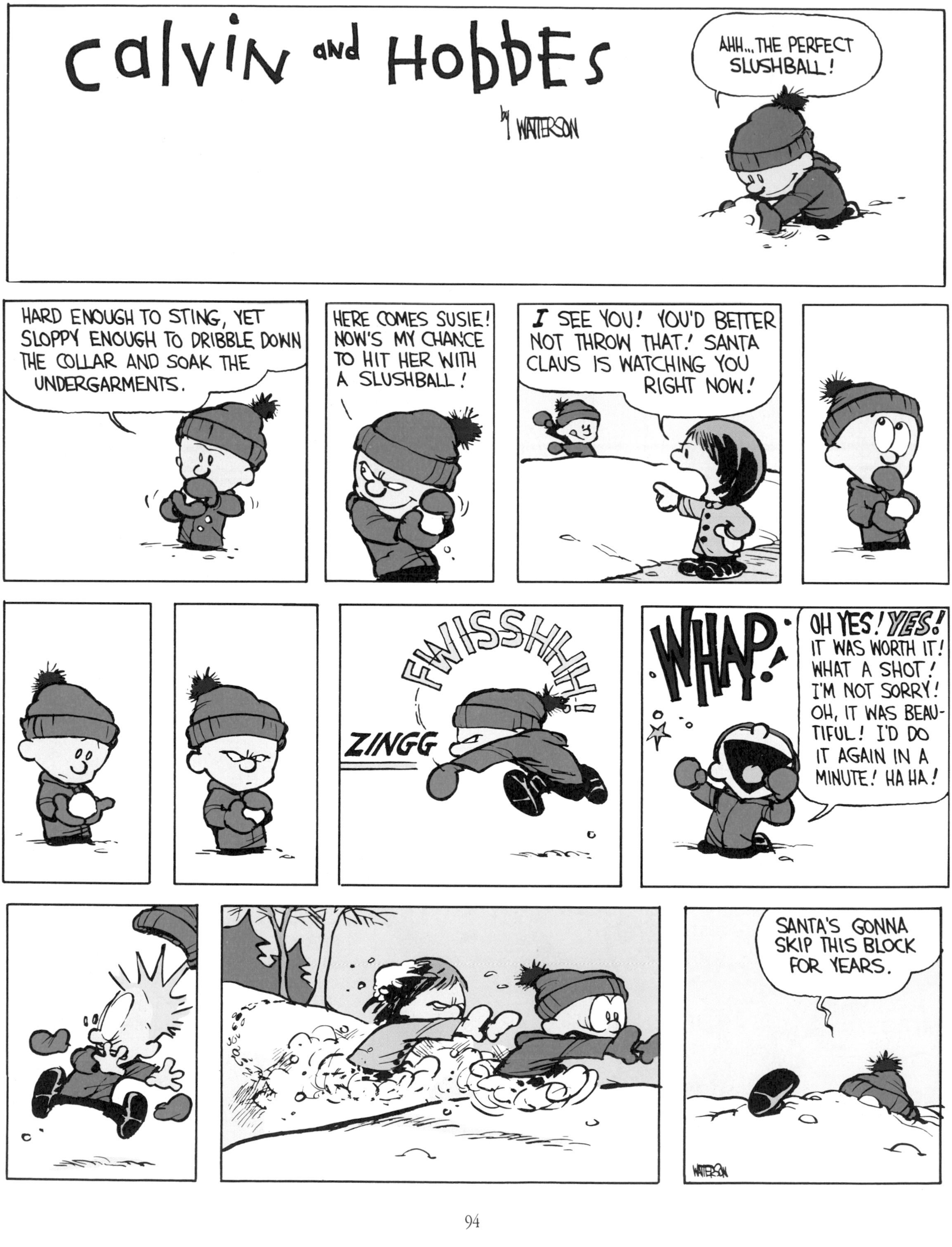
Calvin and Hobbes
by WATTERSON
AHH... THE PERFECT SLUSHBALL!
HARD ENOUGH TO STING, YET SLOPPY ENOUGH TO DRIBBLE DOWN THE COLLAR AND SOAK THE UNDERGARMENTS.
HERE COMES SUSIE! NOW'S MY CHANCE TO HIT HER WITH A SLUSHBALL!
I SEE YOU! YOU'D BETTER NOT THROW THAT! SANTA CLAUS IS WATCHING YOU RIGHT NOW!
FWISSHHH!
ZINGG
WHAP!
OH YES! YES! IT WAS WORTH IT! WHAT A SHOT! I'M NOT SORRY! OH, IT WAS BEAUTIFUL! I'D DO IT AGAIN IN A MINUTE! HA HA!
SANTA'S GONNA SKIP THIS BLOCK FOR YEARS.
WATTERSON

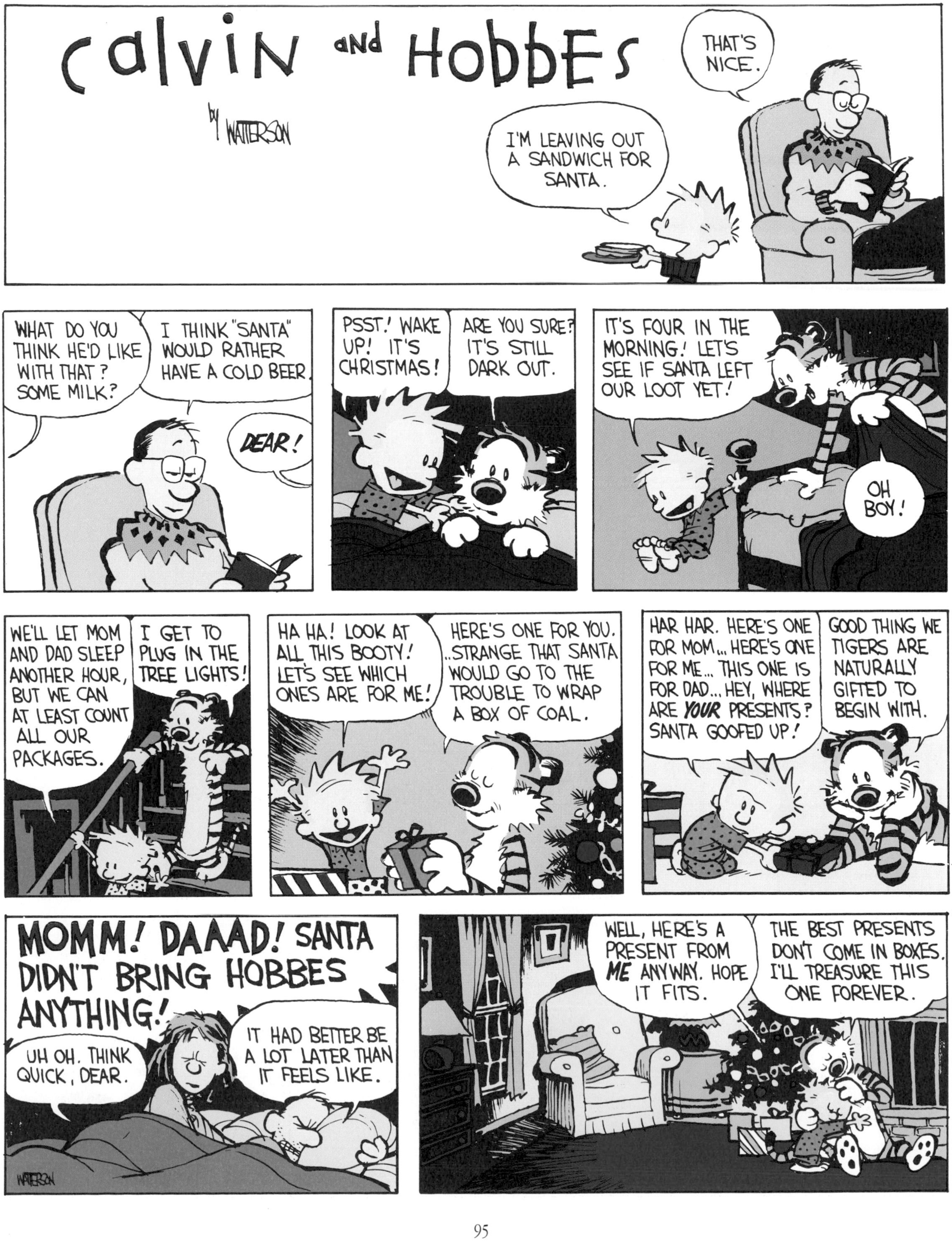
Calvin and HOBBES
by WATTERSON
THAT'S NICE.
I'M LEAVING OUT A SANDWICH FOR SANTA.
WHAT DO YOU THINK HE'D LIKE WITH THAT? SOME MILK?
I THINK "SANTA" WOULD RATHER HAVE A COLD BEER.
DEAR!
PSST! WAKE UP! IT'S CHRISTMAS!
ARE YOU SURE? IT'S STILL DARK OUT.
IT'S FOUR IN THE MORNING! LET'S SEE IF SANTA LEFT OUR LOOT YET!
OH BOY!
WE'LL LET MOM AND DAD SLEEP ANOTHER HOUR, BUT WE CAN AT LEAST COUNT ALL OUR PACKAGES.
I GET TO PLUG IN THE TREE LIGHTS!
HA HA! LOOK AT ALL THIS BOOTY! LET'S SEE WHICH ONES ARE FOR ME!
HERE'S ONE FOR YOU. ..STRANGE THAT SANTA WOULD GO TO THE TROUBLE TO WRAP A BOX OF COAL.
HAR HAR. HERE'S ONE FOR MOM... HERE'S ONE FOR ME... THIS ONE IS FOR DAD... HEY, WHERE ARE YOUR PRESENTS? SANTA GOOFED UP!
GOOD THING WE TIGERS ARE NATURALLY GIFTED TO BEGIN WITH.
MOMM! DAAAD! SANTA DIDN'T BRING HOBBES ANYTHING!
UH OH. THINK QUICK, DEAR.
IT HAD BETTER BE A LOT LATER THAN IT FEELS LIKE.
WATTERSON
WELL, HERE'S A PRESENT FROM ME ANYWAY. HOPE IT FITS.
THE BEST PRESENTS DON'T COME IN BOXES. I'LL TREASURE THIS ONE FOREVER.

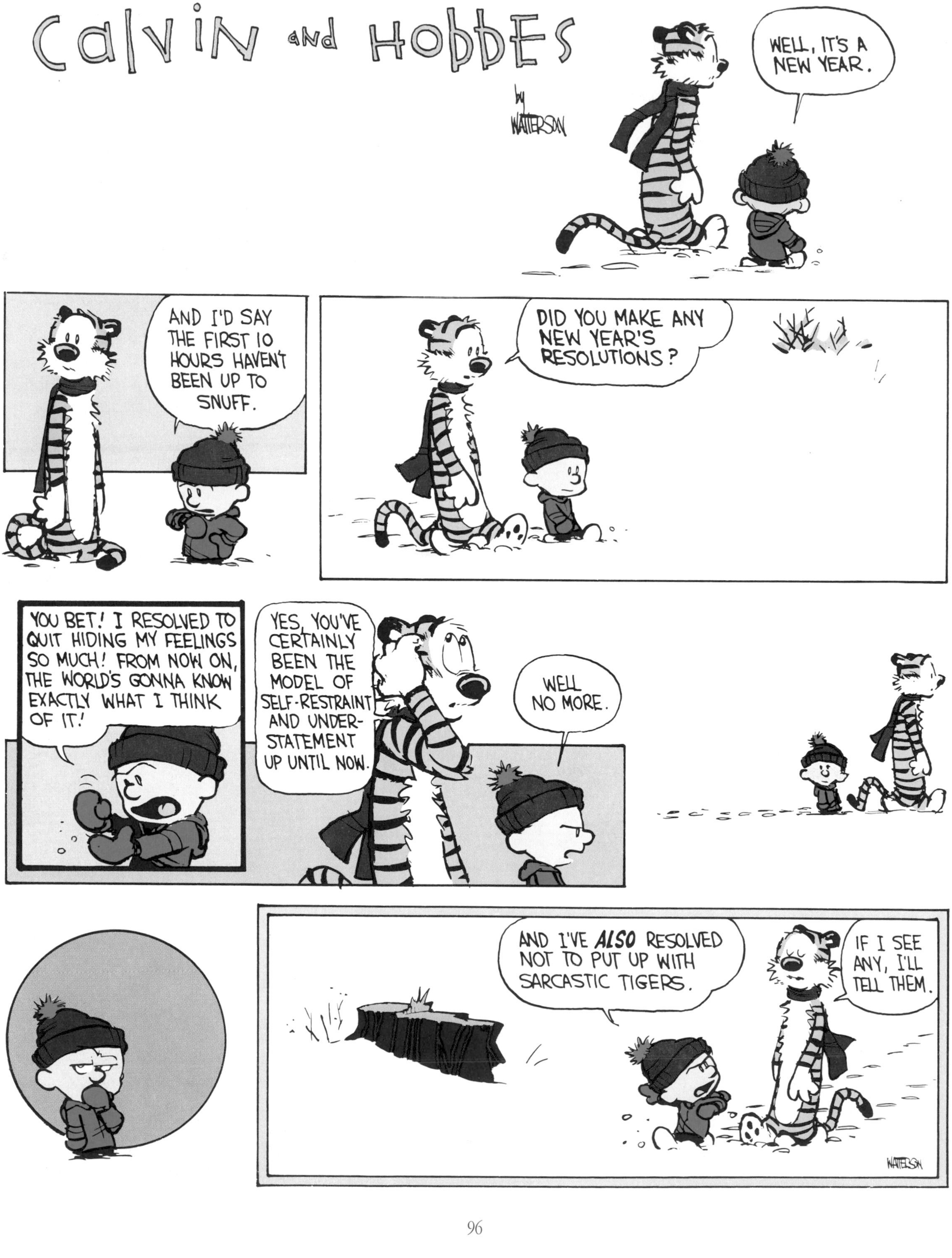
Calvin and Hobbes
by WATTERSON
WELL, IT'S A NEW YEAR.
AND I'D SAY THE FIRST 10 HOURS HAVEN'T BEEN UP TO SNUFF.
DID YOU MAKE ANY NEW YEAR'S RESOLUTIONS?
YOU BET! I RESOLVED TO QUIT HIDING MY FEELINGS SO MUCH! FROM NOW ON, THE WORLD'S GONNA KNOW EXACTLY WHAT I THINK OF IT!
YES, YOU'VE CERTAINLY BEEN THE MODEL OF SELF-RESTRAINT AND UNDER-STATEMENT UP UNTIL NOW.
WELL NO MORE.
AND I'VE ALSO RESOLVED NOT TO PUT UP WITH SARCASTIC TIGERS.
IF I SEE ANY, I'LL TELL THEM.
WATTERSON

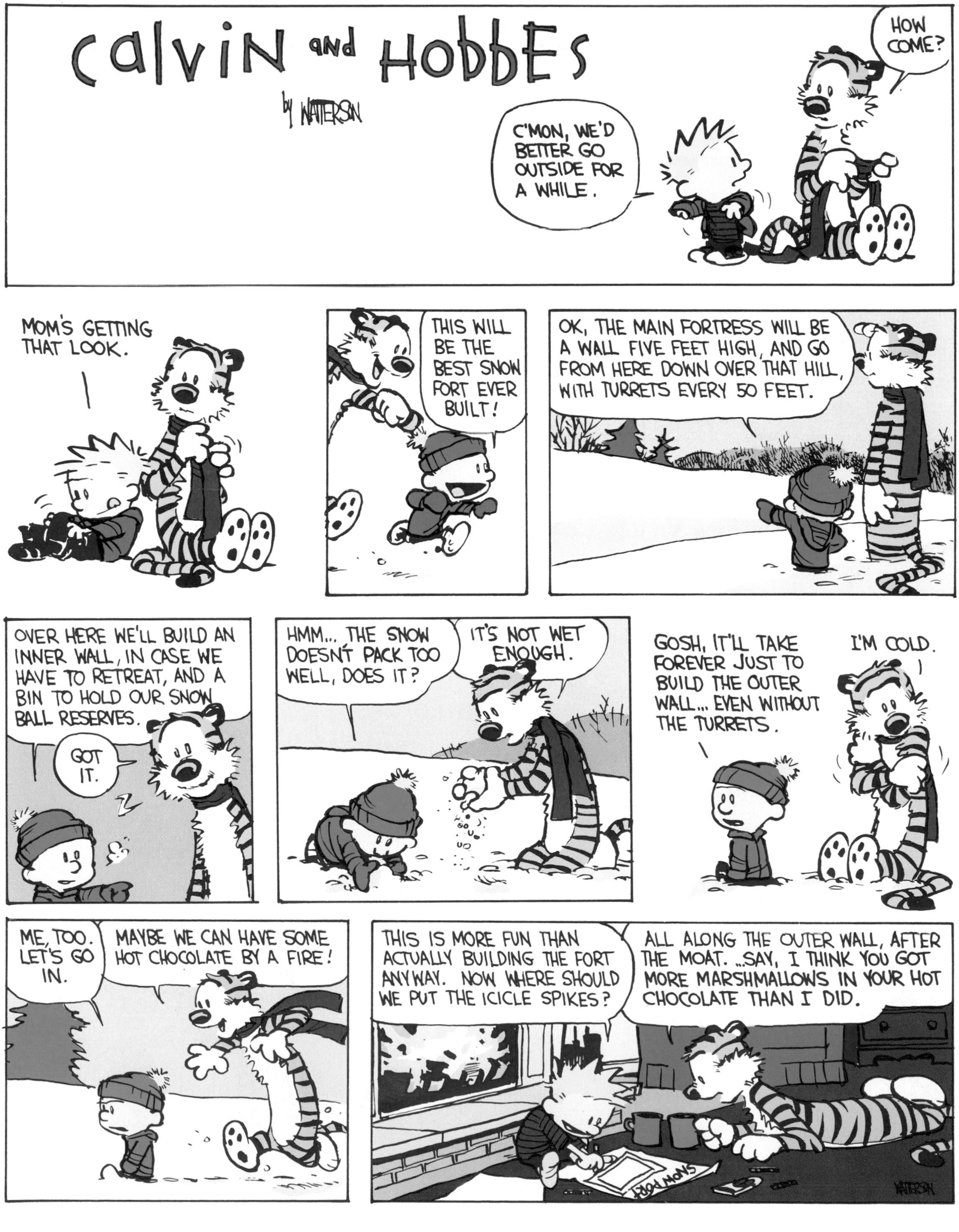
Calvin and HOBBES
by WATTERSON
C'MON, WE'D BETTER GO OUTSIDE FOR A WHILE.
HOW COME?
MOM'S GETTING THAT LOOK.
THIS WILL BE THE BEST SNOW FORT EVER BUILT!
OK, THE MAIN FORTRESS WILL BE A WALL FIVE FEET HIGH, AND GO FROM HERE DOWN OVER THAT HILL, WITH TURRETS EVERY 50 FEET.
OVER HERE WE'LL BUILD AN INNER WALL, IN CASE WE HAVE TO RETREAT, AND A BIN TO HOLD OUR SNOW BALL RESERVES.
GOT IT.
HMM... THE SNOW DOESN'T PACK TOO WELL, DOES IT?
IT'S NOT WET ENOUGH.
GOSH, IT'LL TAKE FOREVER JUST TO BUILD THE OUTER WALL... EVEN WITHOUT THE TURRETS.
I'M COLD.
ME, TOO. LET'S GO IN.
MAYBE WE CAN HAVE SOME HOT CHOCOLATE BY A FIRE!
THIS IS MORE FUN THAN ACTUALLY BUILDING THE FORT ANYWAY. NOW WHERE SHOULD WE PUT THE ICICLE SPIKES?
ALL ALONG THE OUTER WALL, AFTER THE MOAT. ...SAY, I THINK YOU GOT MORE MARSHMALLOWS IN YOUR HOT CHOCOLATE THAN I DID.
SNOW FORT
WATTERSON

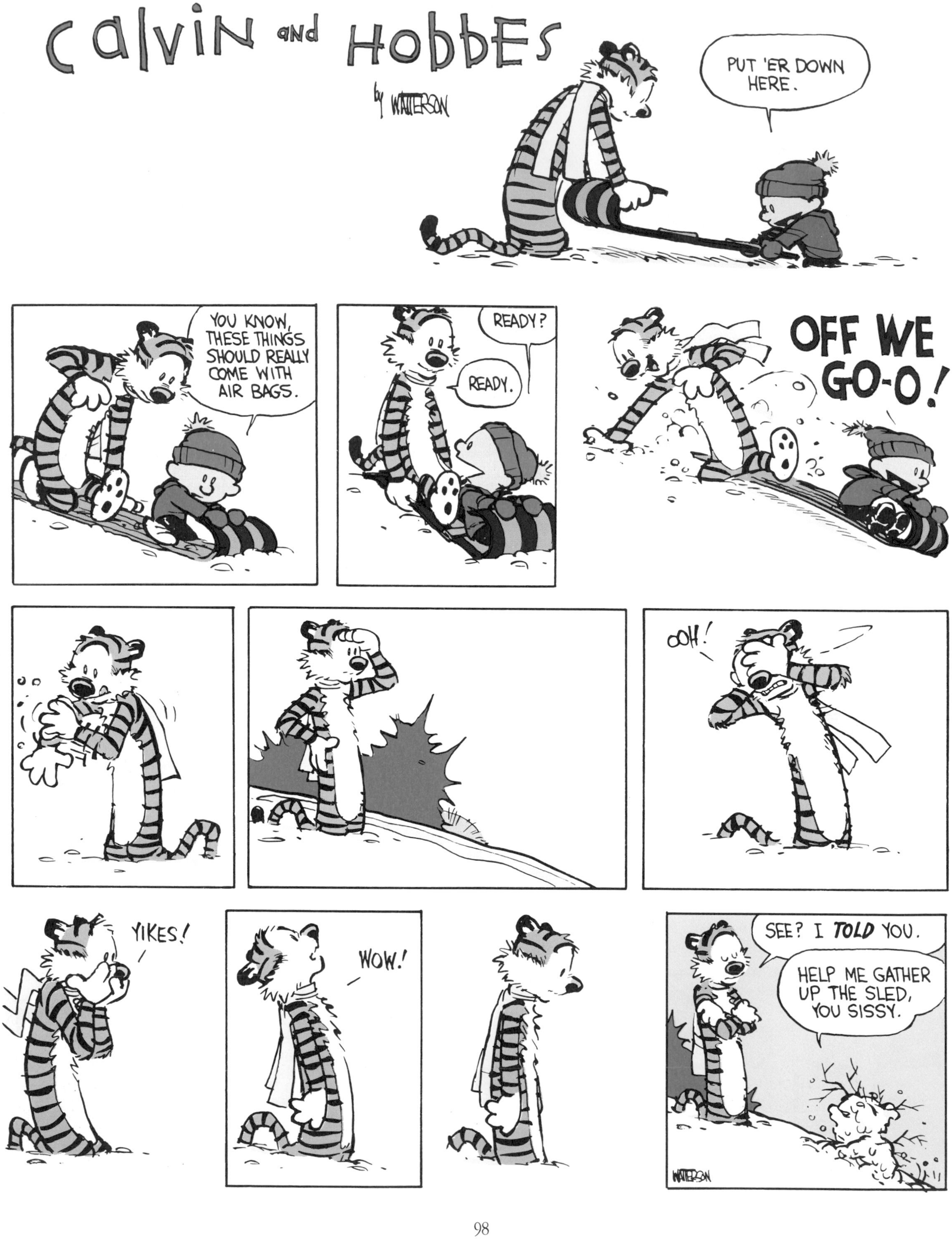
Calvin and Hobbes
by WATTERSON
PUT 'ER DOWN HERE.
YOU KNOW, THESE THINGS SHOULD REALLY COME WITH AIR BAGS.
READY?
READY.
OFF WE GO-O!
OOH!
YIKES!
WOW!
SEE? I TOLD YOU.
HELP ME GATHER UP THE SLED, YOU SISSY.
WATTERSON

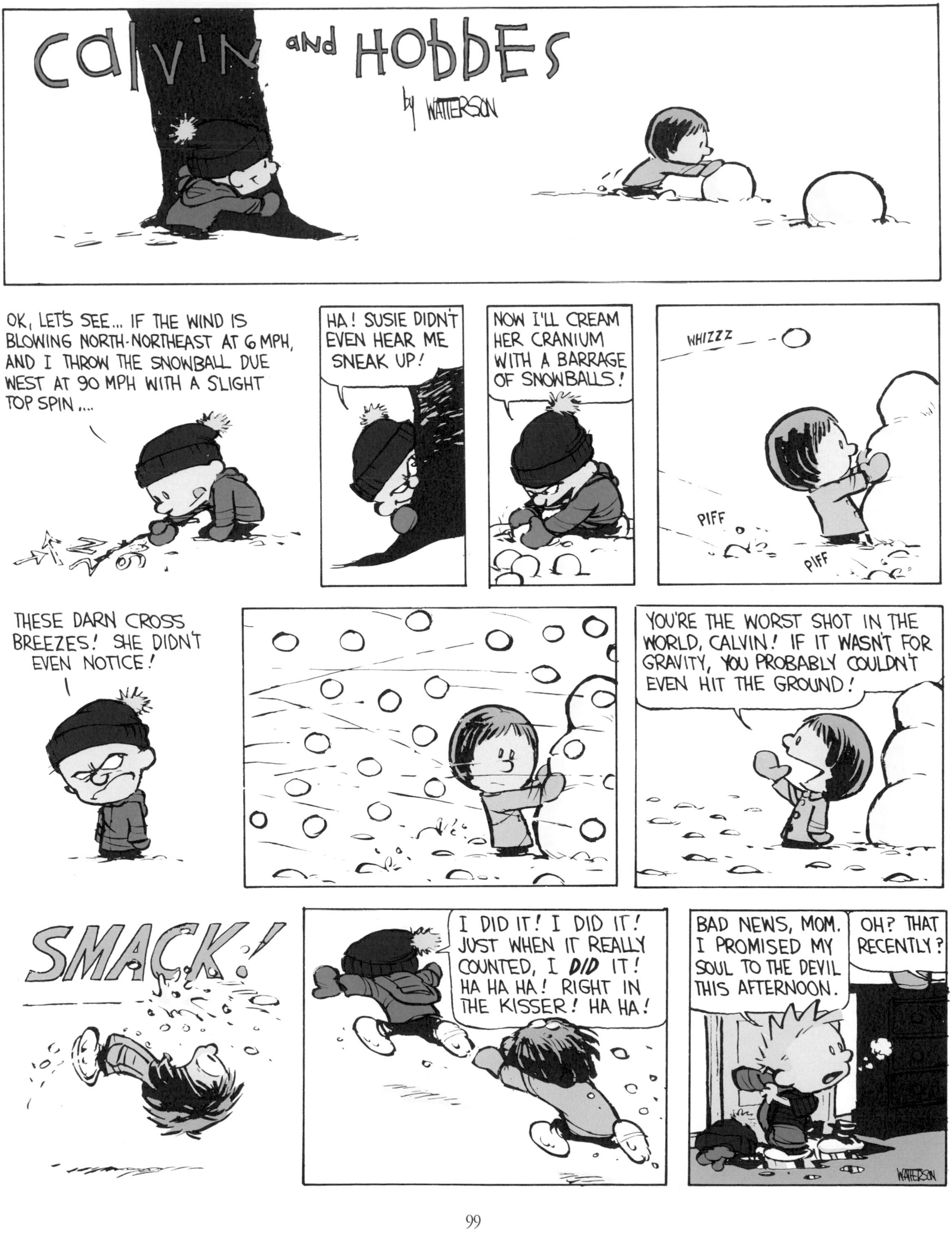
Calvin and HOBBES
by WATTERSON
OK, LET'S SEE... IF THE WIND IS BLOWING NORTH-NORTHEAST AT 6 MPH, AND I THROW THE SNOWBALL DUE WEST AT 90 MPH WITH A SLIGHT TOP SPIN....
N
HA! SUSIE DIDN'T EVEN HEAR ME SNEAK UP!
NOW I'LL CREAM HER CRANIUM WITH A BARRAGE OF SNOWBALLS!
WHIZZZ
PIFF
PIFF
THESE DARN CROSS BREEZES! SHE DIDN'T EVEN NOTICE!
YOU'RE THE WORST SHOT IN THE WORLD, CALVIN! IF IT WASN'T FOR GRAVITY, YOU PROBABLY COULDN'T EVEN HIT THE GROUND!
SMACK!
I DID IT! I DID IT! JUST WHEN IT REALLY COUNTED, I DID IT! HA HA HA! RIGHT IN THE KISSER! HA HA!
BAD NEWS, MOM. I PROMISED MY SOUL TO THE DEVIL THIS AFTERNOON.
OH? THAT RECENTLY?
WATTERSON

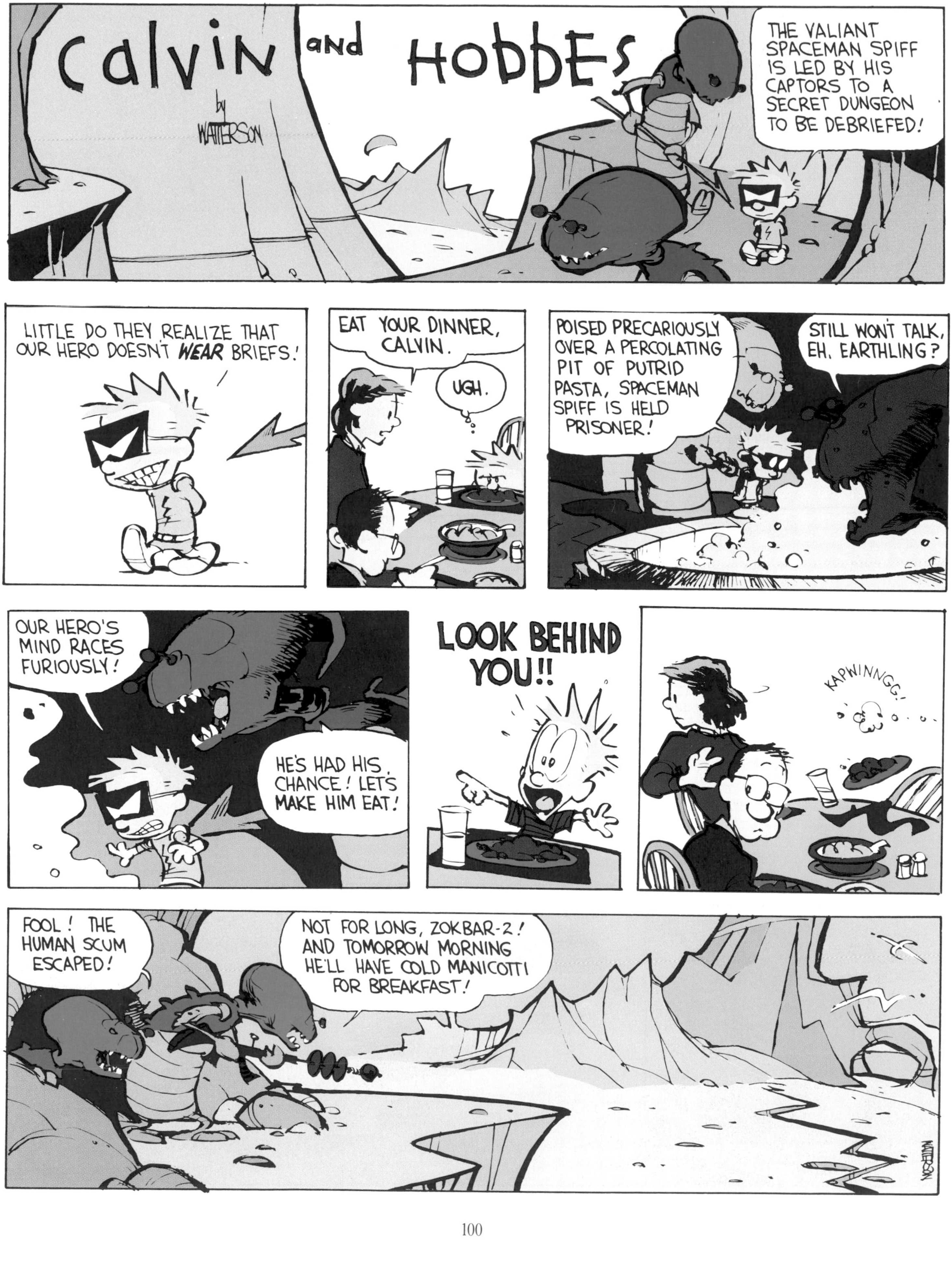
Calvin and HOBBES
by WATTERSON
THE VALIANT SPACEMAN SPIFF IS LED BY HIS CAPTORS TO A SECRET DUNGEON TO BE DEBRIEFED!
LITTLE DO THEY REALIZE THAT OUR HERO DOESN'T WEAR BRIEFS!
EAT YOUR DINNER, CALVIN.
UGH.
POISED PRECARIOUSLY OVER A PERCOLATING PIT OF PUTRID PASTA, SPACEMAN SPIFF IS HELD PRISONER!
STILL WON'T TALK, EH, EARTHLING?
OUR HERO'S MIND RACES FURIOUSLY!
HE'S HAD HIS CHANCE! LET'S MAKE HIM EAT!
LOOK BEHIND YOU!!
KAPWINNGG!
FOOL! THE HUMAN SCUM ESCAPED!
NOT FOR LONG, ZOKBAR-2! AND TOMORROW MORNING HE'LL HAVE COLD MANICOTTI FOR BREAKFAST!
WATTERSON

Calvin and Hobbes

by WATTERSON

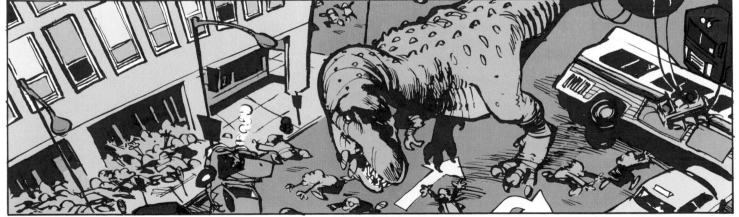

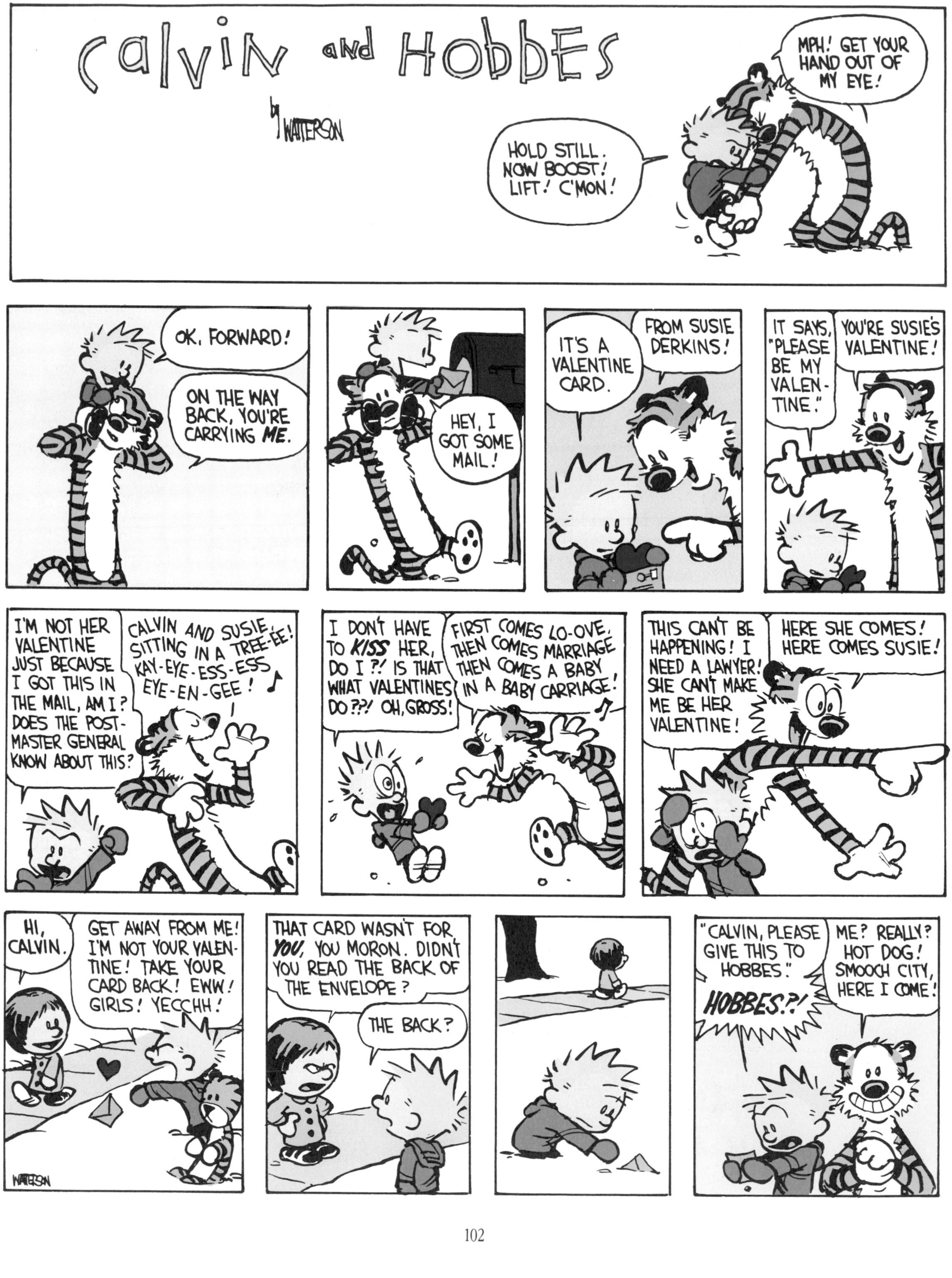
Calvin and Hobbes
by WATTERSON
HOLD STILL. NOW BOOST! LIFT! C'MON!
MPH! GET YOUR HAND OUT OF MY EYE!
OK, FORWARD!
ON THE WAY BACK, YOU'RE CARRYING ME.
HEY, I GOT SOME MAIL!
IT'S A VALENTINE CARD.
FROM SUSIE DERKINS!
IT SAYS, "PLEASE BE MY VALEN-TINE."
YOU'RE SUSIE'S VALENTINE!
I'M NOT HER VALENTINE JUST BECAUSE I GOT THIS IN THE MAIL, AM I? DOES THE POST-MASTER GENERAL KNOW ABOUT THIS?
CALVIN AND SUSIE, SITTING IN A TREE-EE! KAY-EYE-ESS-ESS EYE-EN-GEE!
I DON'T HAVE TO KISS HER, DO I ?! IS THAT WHAT VALENTINES DO ?!?! OH, GROSS!
FIRST COMES LO-OVE, THEN COMES MARRIAGE THEN COMES A BABY IN A BABY CARRIAGE!
THIS CAN'T BE HAPPENING! I NEED A LAWYER! SHE CAN'T MAKE ME BE HER VALENTINE!
HERE SHE COMES! HERE COMES SUSIE!
HI, CALVIN.
GET AWAY FROM ME! I'M NOT YOUR VALEN-TINE! TAKE YOUR CARD BACK! EWW! GIRLS! YECCHH!
WATTERSON
THAT CARD WASN'T FOR YOU, YOU MORON. DIDN'T YOU READ THE BACK OF THE ENVELOPE?
THE BACK?
"CALVIN, PLEASE GIVE THIS TO HOBBES."
HOBBES?!
ME? REALLY? HOT DOG! SMOOCH CITY, HERE I COME!

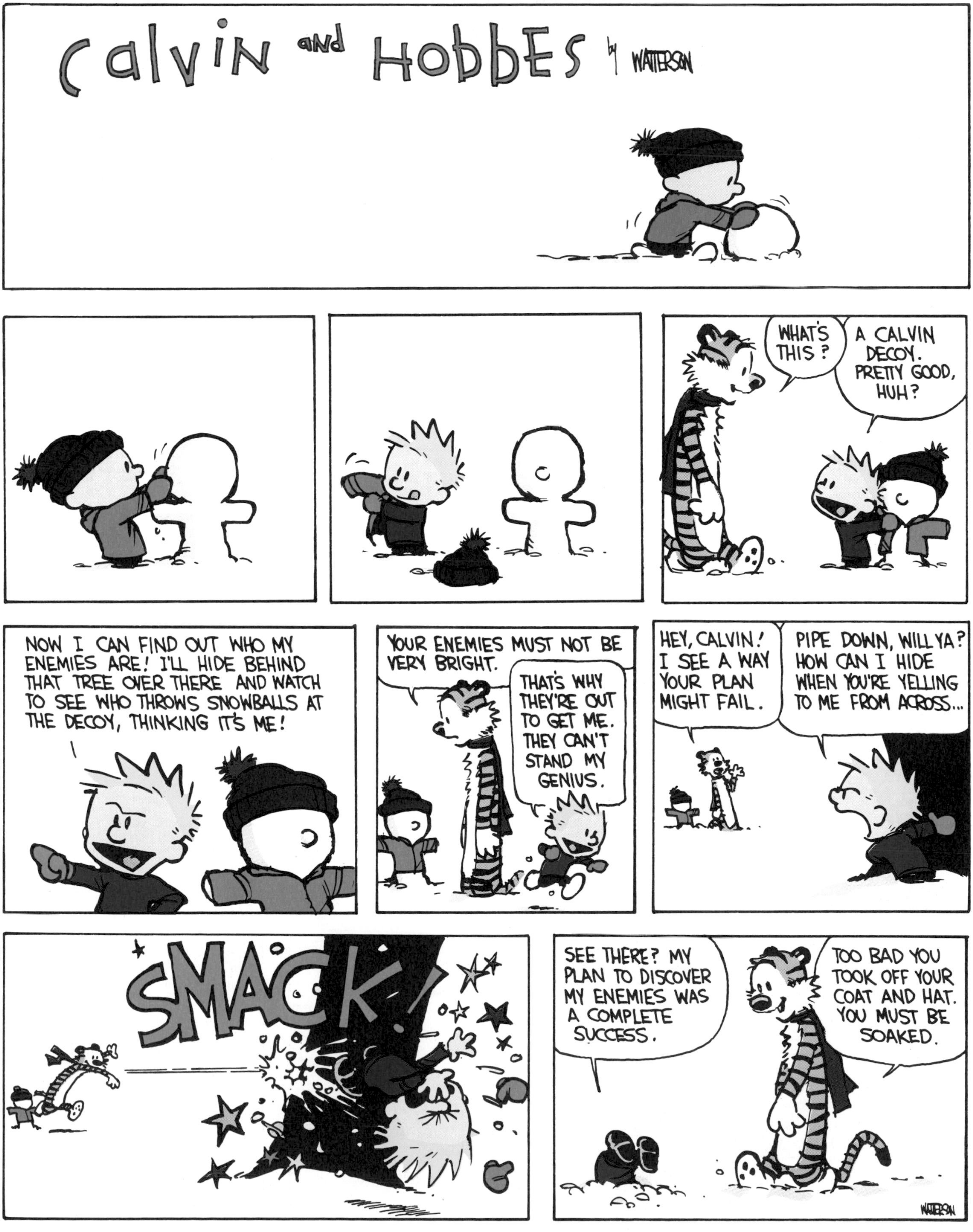
Calvin and Hobbes by WATTERSON
WHAT'S THIS?
A CALVIN DECOY. PRETTY GOOD, HUH?
NOW I CAN FIND OUT WHO MY ENEMIES ARE! I'LL HIDE BEHIND THAT TREE OVER THERE AND WATCH TO SEE WHO THROWS SNOWBALLS AT THE DECOY, THINKING IT'S ME!
YOUR ENEMIES MUST NOT BE VERY BRIGHT.
THAT'S WHY THEY'RE OUT TO GET ME. THEY CAN'T STAND MY GENIUS.
HEY, CALVIN! I SEE A WAY YOUR PLAN MIGHT FAIL.
PIPE DOWN, WILL YA? HOW CAN I HIDE WHEN YOU'RE YELLING TO ME FROM ACROSS...
SMACK!
SEE THERE? MY PLAN TO DISCOVER MY ENEMIES WAS A COMPLETE SUCCESS.
TOO BAD YOU TOOK OFF YOUR COAT AND HAT. YOU MUST BE SOAKED.
WATTERSON

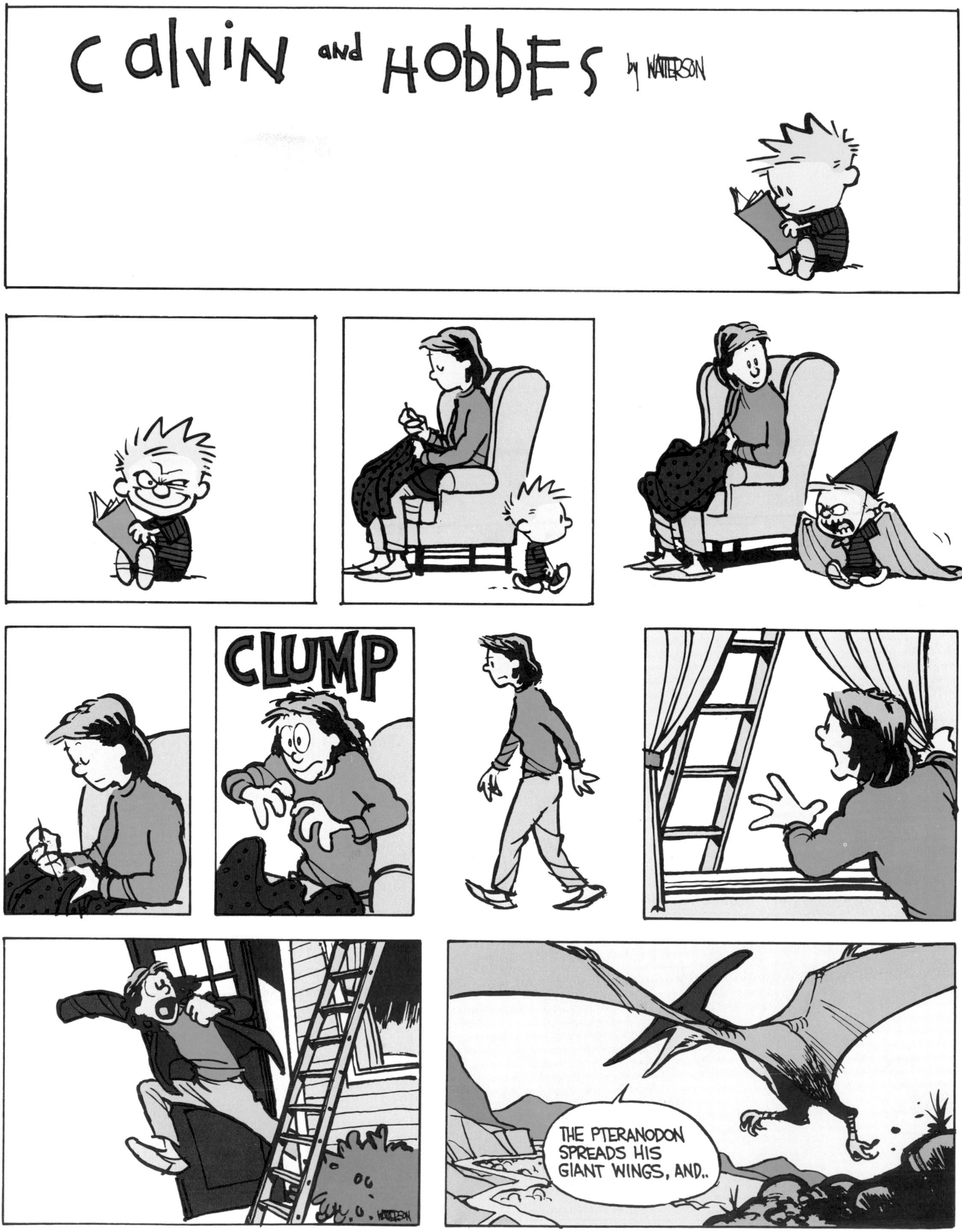
Calvin and HOBBES by WATTERSON
CLUMP
THE PTERANODON SPREADS HIS GIANT WINGS, AND..
WATTERSON

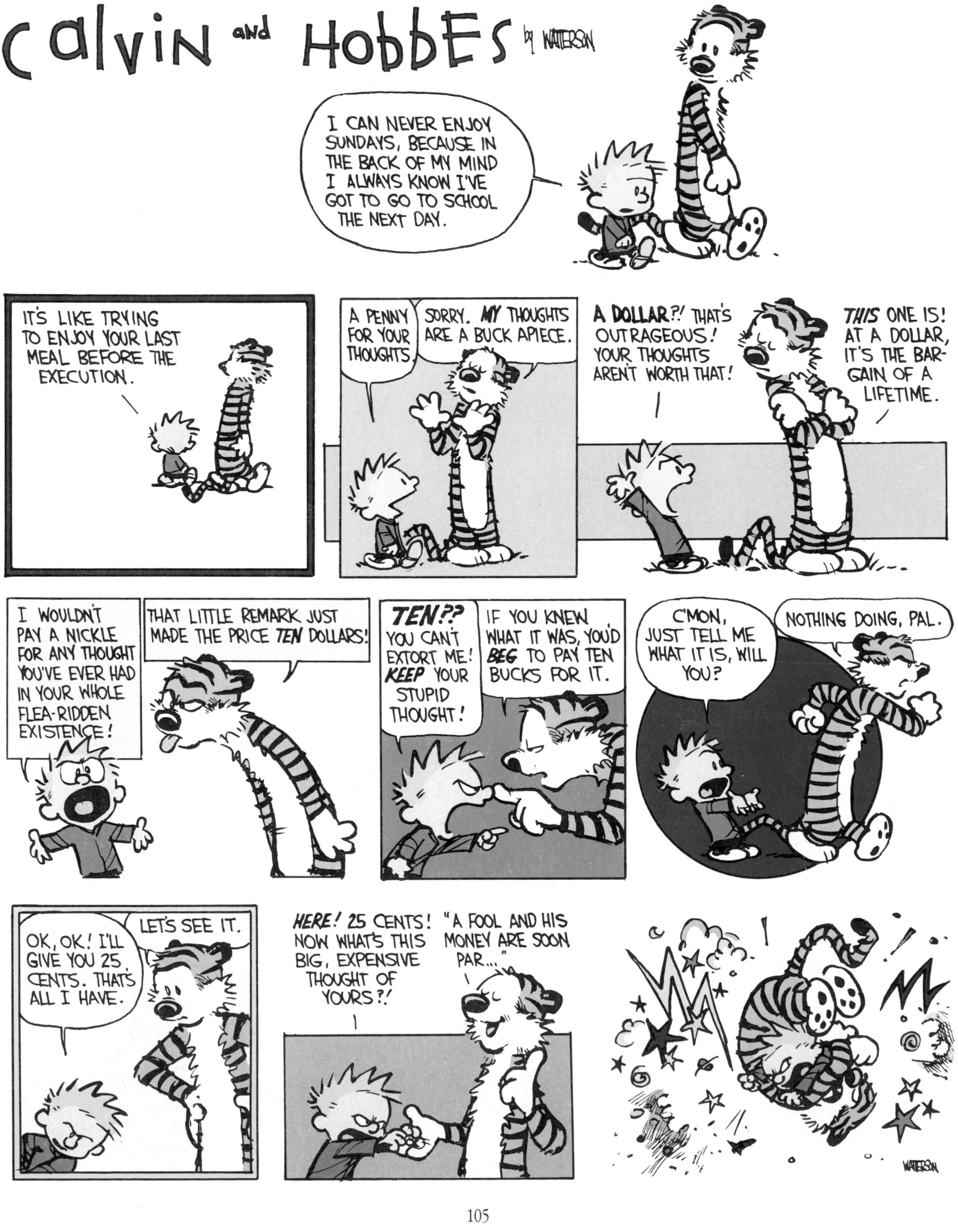
Calvin and Hobbes by WATTERSON
I CAN NEVER ENJOY SUNDAYS, BECAUSE IN THE BACK OF MY MIND I ALWAYS KNOW I'VE GOT TO GO TO SCHOOL THE NEXT DAY.
IT'S LIKE TRYING TO ENJOY YOUR LAST MEAL BEFORE THE EXECUTION.
A PENNY FOR YOUR THOUGHTS.
SORRY. MY THOUGHTS ARE A BUCK APIECE.
A DOLLAR?! THAT'S OUTRAGEOUS! YOUR THOUGHTS AREN'T WORTH THAT!
THIS ONE IS! AT A DOLLAR, IT'S THE BARGAIN OF A LIFETIME.
I WOULDN'T PAY A NICKLE FOR ANY THOUGHT YOU'VE EVER HAD IN YOUR WHOLE FLEA-RIDDEN EXISTENCE!
THAT LITTLE REMARK JUST MADE THE PRICE TEN DOLLARS!
TEN?? YOU CAN'T EXTORT ME! KEEP YOUR STUPID THOUGHT!
IF YOU KNEW WHAT IT WAS, YOU'D BEG TO PAY TEN BUCKS FOR IT.
C'MON, JUST TELL ME WHAT IT IS, WILL YOU?
NOTHING DOING, PAL.
OK, OK! I'LL GIVE YOU 25 CENTS. THAT'S ALL I HAVE.
LET'S SEE IT.
HERE! 25 CENTS! NOW WHAT'S THIS BIG, EXPENSIVE THOUGHT OF YOURS?!
"A FOOL AND HIS MONEY ARE SOON PAR..."
WATTERSON

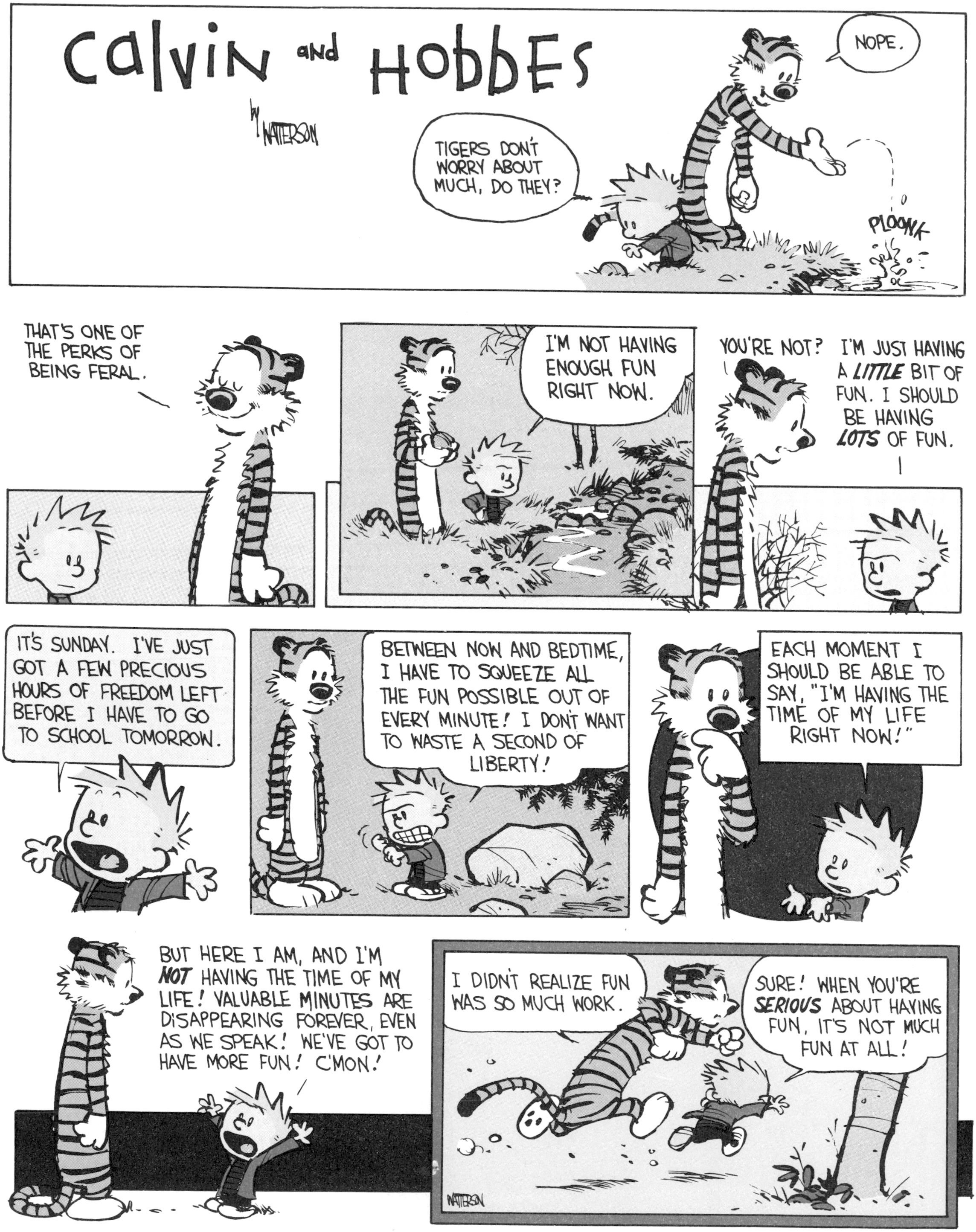

Calvin and HOBBES
by WATTERSON
TIGERS DON'T WORRY ABOUT MUCH, DO THEY?
NOPE.
PLOONK
THAT'S ONE OF THE PERKS OF BEING FERAL.
I'M NOT HAVING ENOUGH FUN RIGHT NOW.
YOU'RE NOT?
I'M JUST HAVING A LITTLE BIT OF FUN. I SHOULD BE HAVING LOTS OF FUN.
IT'S SUNDAY. I'VE JUST GOT A FEW PRECIOUS HOURS OF FREEDOM LEFT BEFORE I HAVE TO GO TO SCHOOL TOMORROW.
BETWEEN NOW AND BEDTIME, I HAVE TO SQUEEZE ALL THE FUN POSSIBLE OUT OF EVERY MINUTE! I DON'T WANT TO WASTE A SECOND OF LIBERTY!
EACH MOMENT I SHOULD BE ABLE TO SAY, "I'M HAVING THE TIME OF MY LIFE RIGHT NOW!"
BUT HERE I AM, AND I'M NOT HAVING THE TIME OF MY LIFE! VALUABLE MINUTES ARE DISAPPEARING FOREVER, EVEN AS WE SPEAK! WE'VE GOT TO HAVE MORE FUN! C'MON!
I DIDN'T REALIZE FUN WAS SO MUCH WORK.
SURE! WHEN YOU'RE SERIOUS ABOUT HAVING FUN, IT'S NOT MUCH FUN AT ALL!
WATTERSON

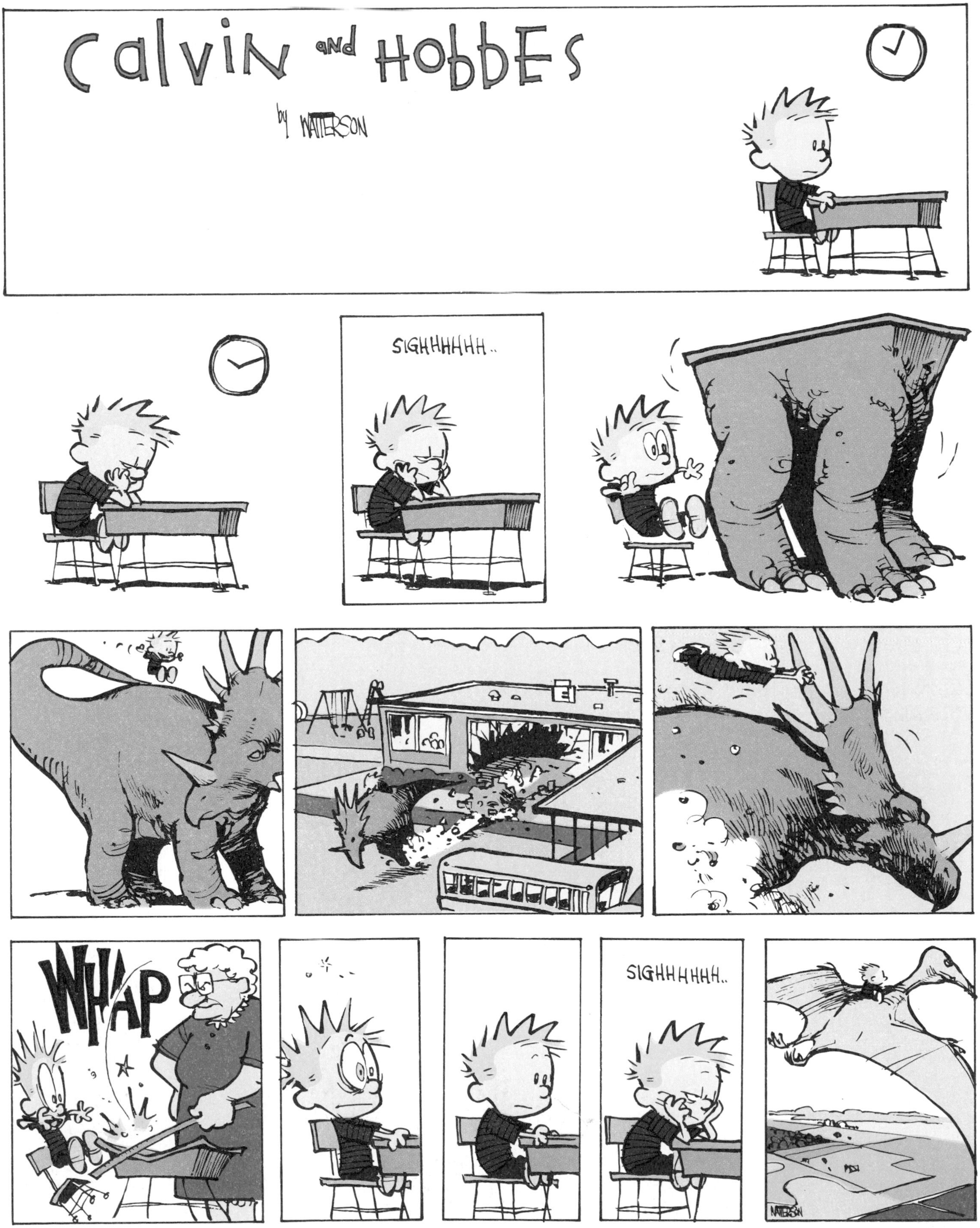
Calvin and Hobbes
by WATTERSON
SIGHHHHHH..
WHAP
SIGHHHHHH..
WATTERSON

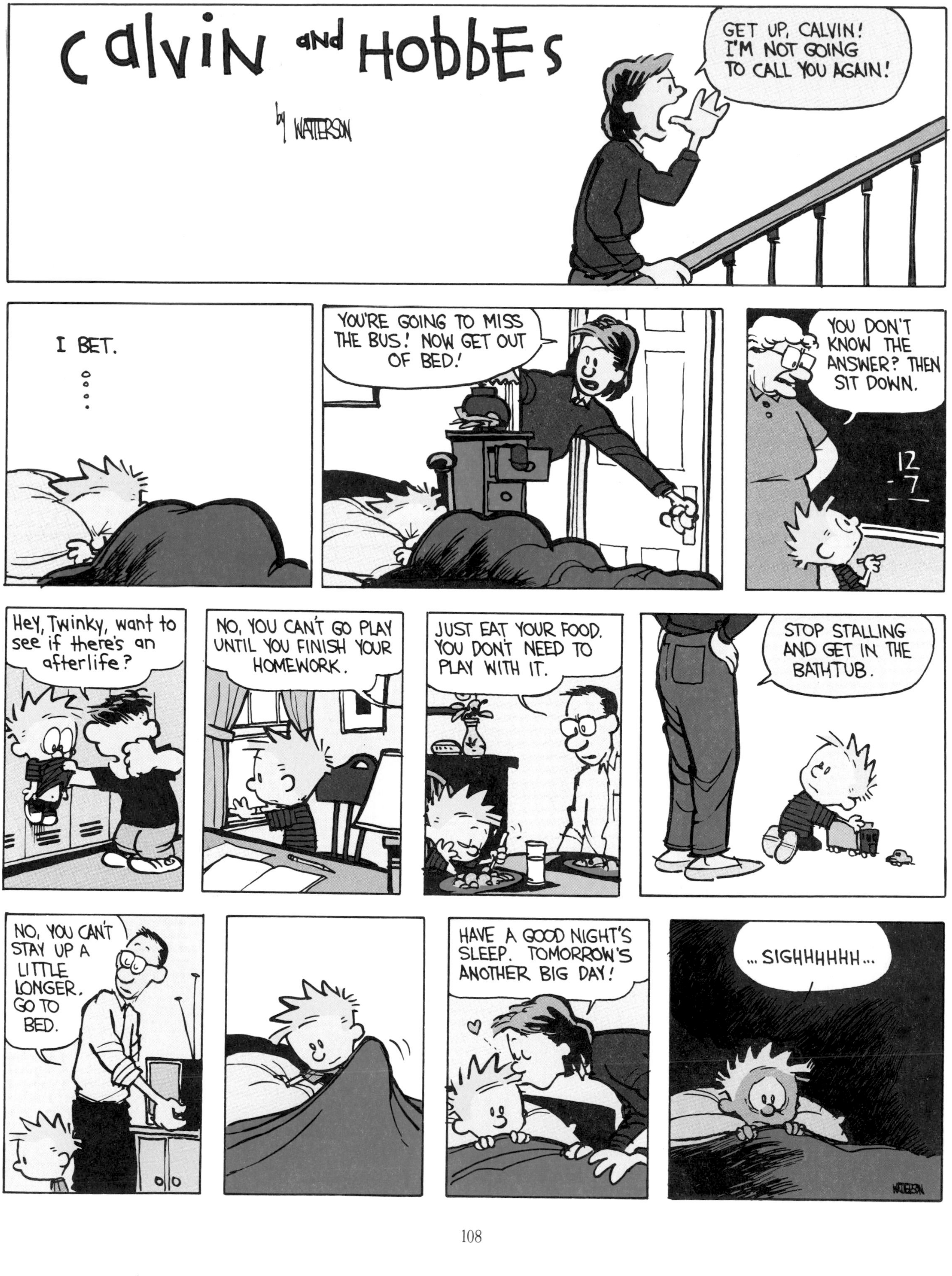
Calvin and Hobbes
by WATTERSON
GET UP, CALVIN! I'M NOT GOING TO CALL YOU AGAIN!
I BET.
YOU'RE GOING TO MISS THE BUS! NOW GET OUT OF BED!
YOU DON'T KNOW THE ANSWER? THEN SIT DOWN.
12
-7
Hey, Twinky, want to see if there's an afterlife?
NO, YOU CAN'T GO PLAY UNTIL YOU FINISH YOUR HOMEWORK.
JUST EAT YOUR FOOD. YOU DON'T NEED TO PLAY WITH IT.
STOP STALLING AND GET IN THE BATHTUB.
NO, YOU CAN'T STAY UP A LITTLE LONGER. GO TO BED.
HAVE A GOOD NIGHT'S SLEEP. TOMORROW'S ANOTHER BIG DAY!
...SIGHHHHHH...
WATTERSON

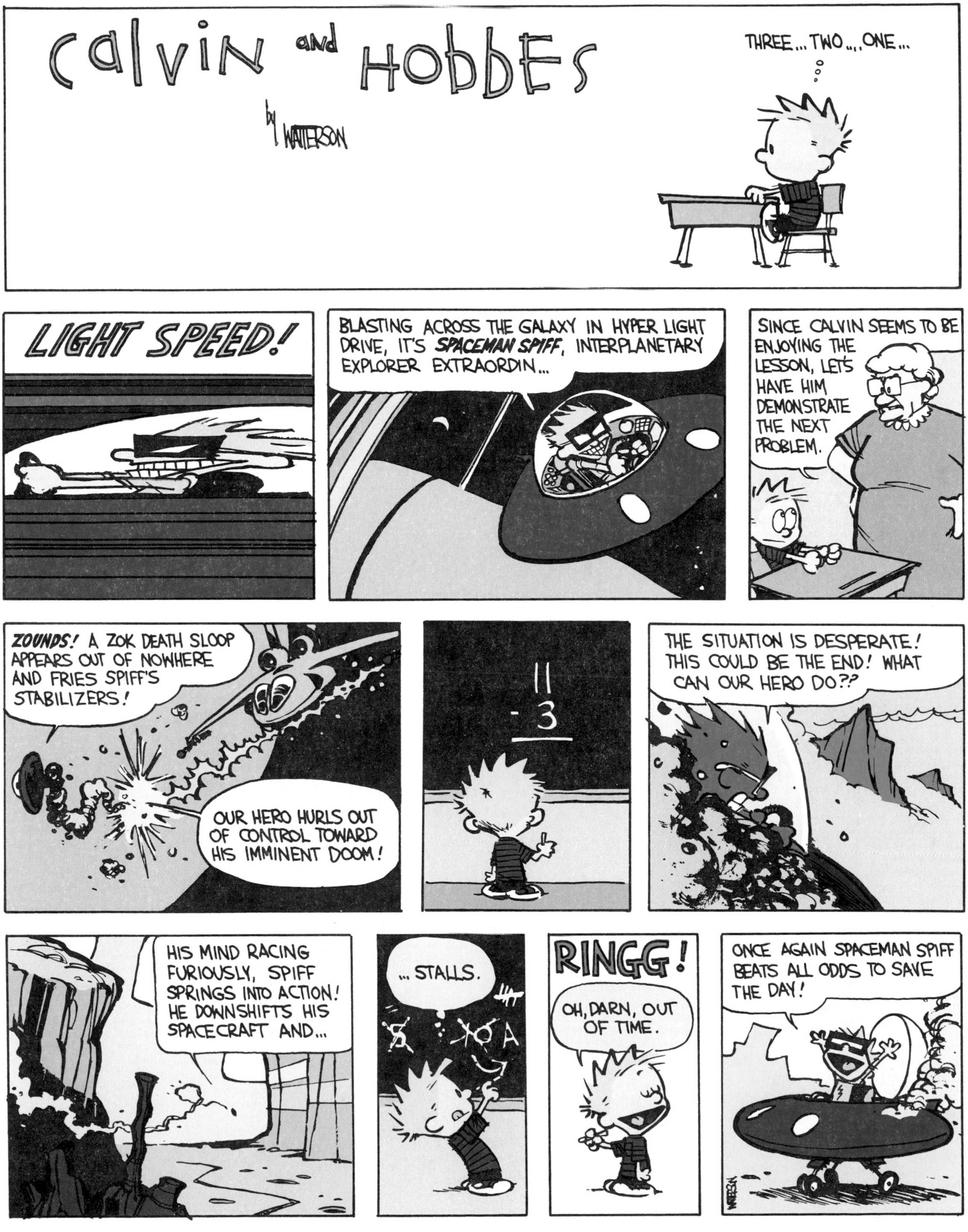
Calvin and Hobbes
by WATTERSON
THREE... TWO..,. ONE...
LIGHT SPEED!
BLASTING ACROSS THE GALAXY IN HYPER LIGHT DRIVE, IT'S SPACEMAN SPIFF, INTERPLANETARY EXPLORER EXTRAORDIN...
SINCE CALVIN SEEMS TO BE ENJOYING THE LESSON, LET'S HAVE HIM DEMONSTRATE THE NEXT PROBLEM.
ZOUNDS! A ZOK DEATH SLOOP APPEARS OUT OF NOWHERE AND FRIES SPIFF'S STABILIZERS!
OUR HERO HURLS OUT OF CONTROL TOWARD HIS IMMINENT DOOM!
11
- 3
THE SITUATION IS DESPERATE! THIS COULD BE THE END! WHAT CAN OUR HERO DO??
HIS MIND RACING FURIOUSLY, SPIFF SPRINGS INTO ACTION! HE DOWNSHIFTS HIS SPACECRAFT AND...
... STALLS.
RINGG!
OH, DARN, OUT OF TIME.
ONCE AGAIN SPACEMAN SPIFF BEATS ALL ODDS TO SAVE THE DAY!

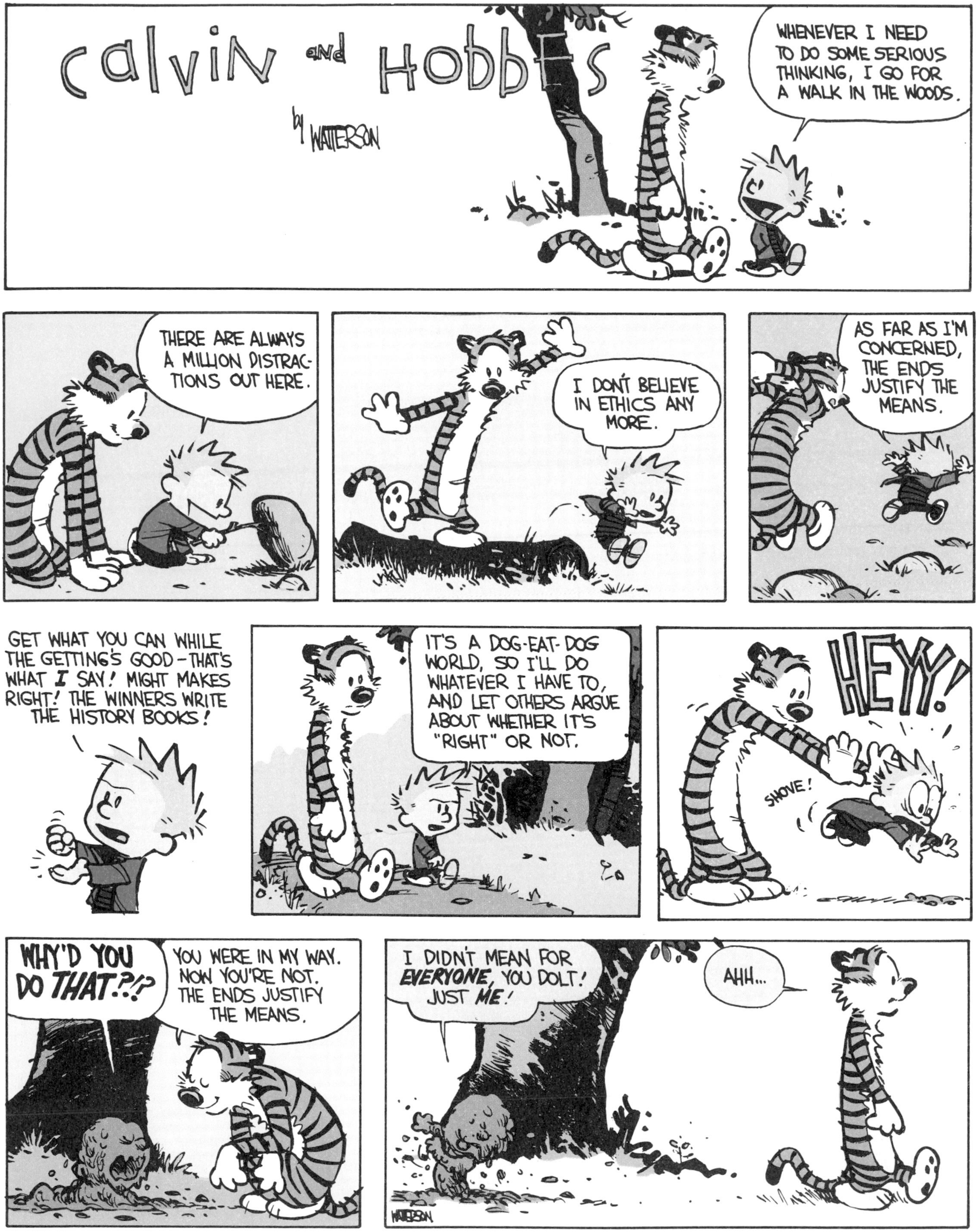

Calvin and HOBBES
by WATTERSON
WHENEVER I NEED TO DO SOME SERIOUS THINKING, I GO FOR A WALK IN THE WOODS.
THERE ARE ALWAYS A MILLION DISTRACTIONS OUT HERE.
I DON'T BELIEVE IN ETHICS ANY MORE.
AS FAR AS I'M CONCERNED, THE ENDS JUSTIFY THE MEANS.
GET WHAT YOU CAN WHILE THE GETTING'S GOOD – THAT'S WHAT I SAY! MIGHT MAKES RIGHT! THE WINNERS WRITE THE HISTORY BOOKS!
IT'S A DOG-EAT-DOG WORLD, SO I'LL DO WHATEVER I HAVE TO, AND LET OTHERS ARGUE ABOUT WHETHER IT'S "RIGHT" OR NOT.
HEYY!
SHOVE!
WHY'D YOU DO THAT?!?
YOU WERE IN MY WAY. NOW YOU'RE NOT. THE ENDS JUSTIFY THE MEANS.
I DIDN'T MEAN FOR EVERYONE, YOU DOLT! JUST ME!
AHH...
WATTERSON

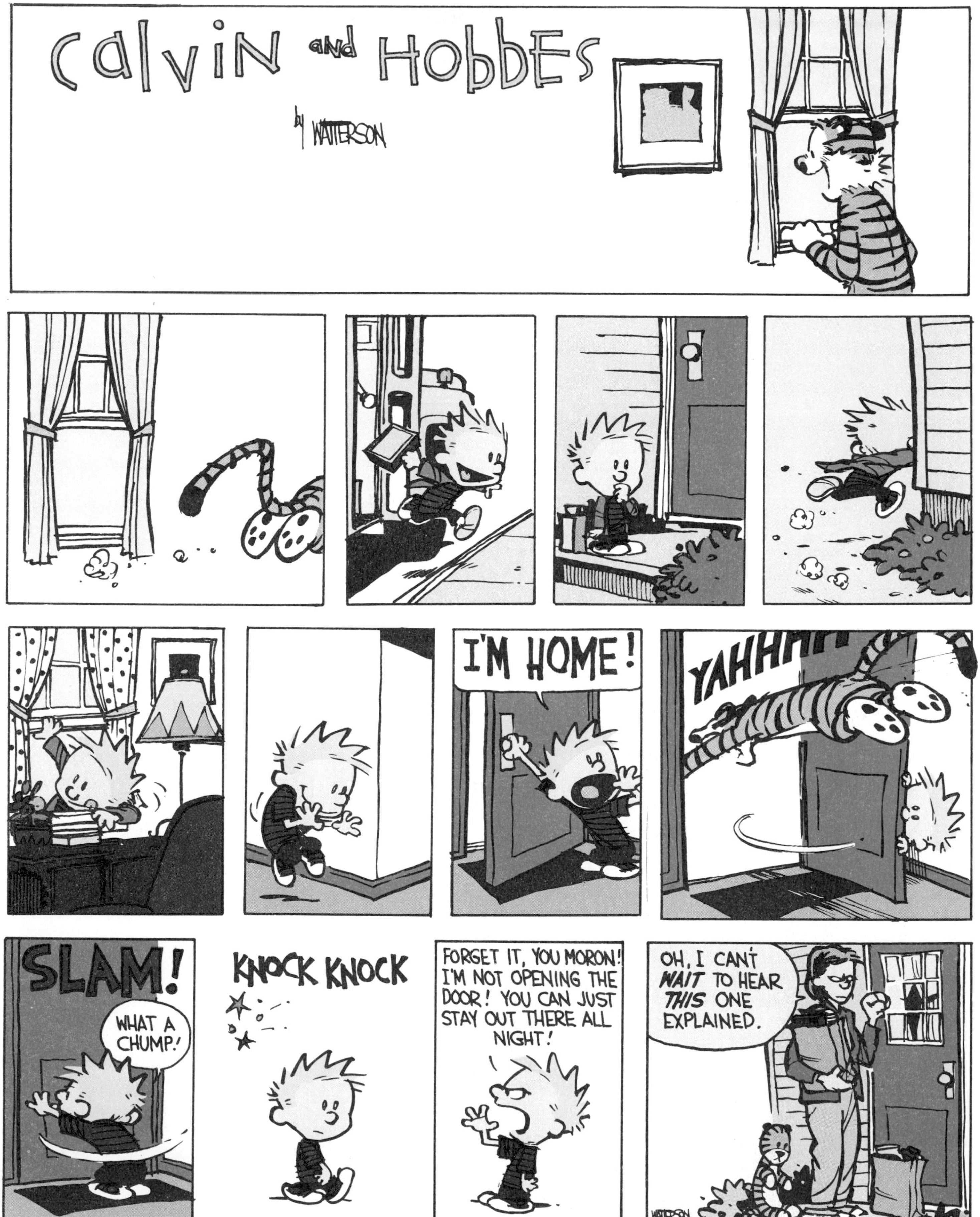
Calvin and Hobbes
by WATTERSON
I'M HOME!
YAHHHH
SLAM!
WHAT A CHUMP!
KNOCK KNOCK
FORGET IT, YOU MORON! I'M NOT OPENING THE DOOR! YOU CAN JUST STAY OUT THERE ALL NIGHT!
OH, I CAN'T WAIT TO HEAR THIS ONE EXPLAINED.
WATTERSON

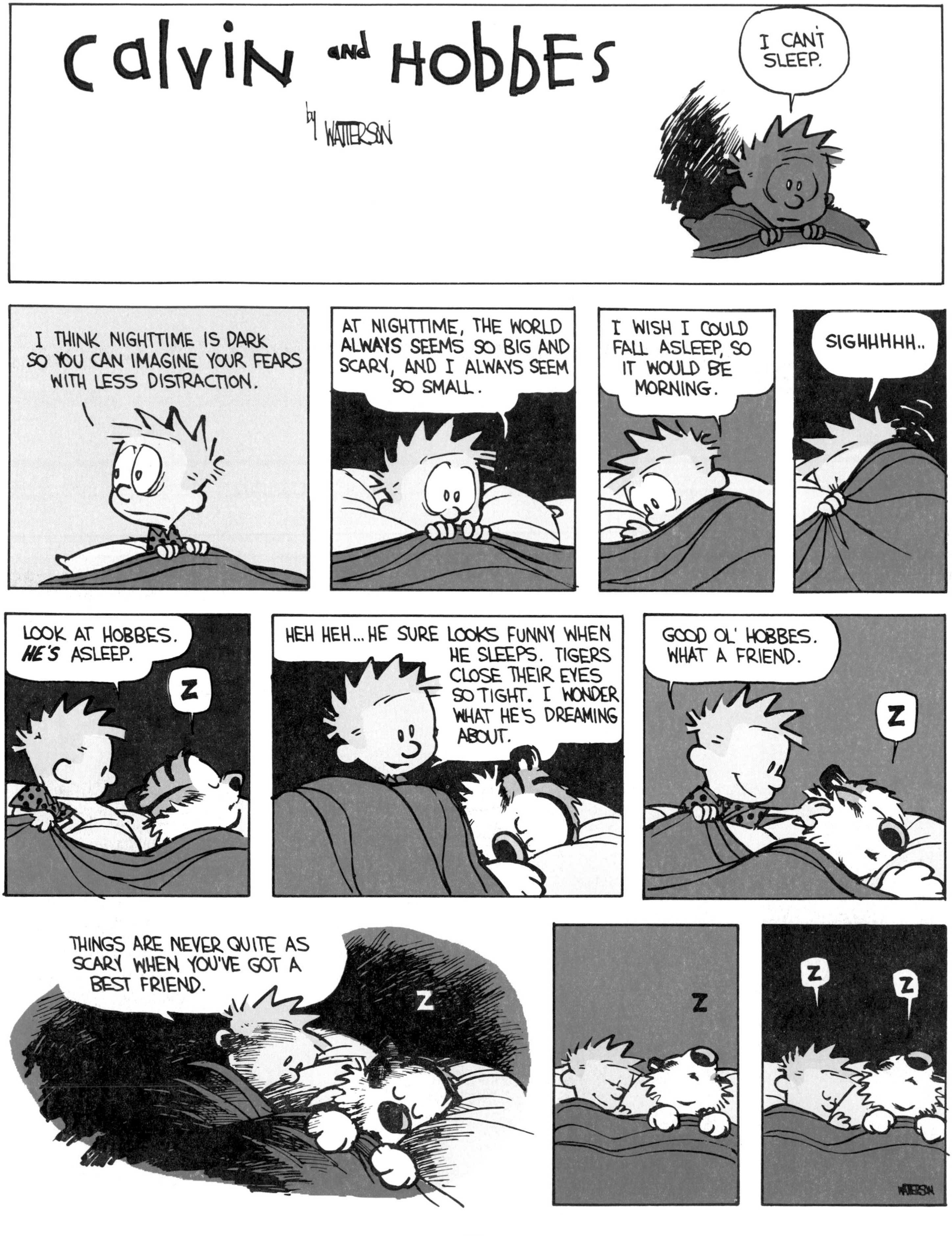
Calvin and HOBBES
by WATTERSON
I CAN'T SLEEP.
I THINK NIGHTTIME IS DARK SO YOU CAN IMAGINE YOUR FEARS WITH LESS DISTRACTION.
AT NIGHTTIME, THE WORLD ALWAYS SEEMS SO BIG AND SCARY, AND I ALWAYS SEEM SO SMALL.
I WISH I COULD FALL ASLEEP, SO IT WOULD BE MORNING.
SIGHHHHH..
LOOK AT HOBBES. HE'S ASLEEP.
Z
HEH HEH... HE SURE LOOKS FUNNY WHEN HE SLEEPS. TIGERS CLOSE THEIR EYES SO TIGHT. I WONDER WHAT HE'S DREAMING ABOUT.
GOOD OL' HOBBES. WHAT A FRIEND.
Z
THINGS ARE NEVER QUITE AS SCARY WHEN YOU'VE GOT A BEST FRIEND.
Z
Z
Z
Z
WATTERSON

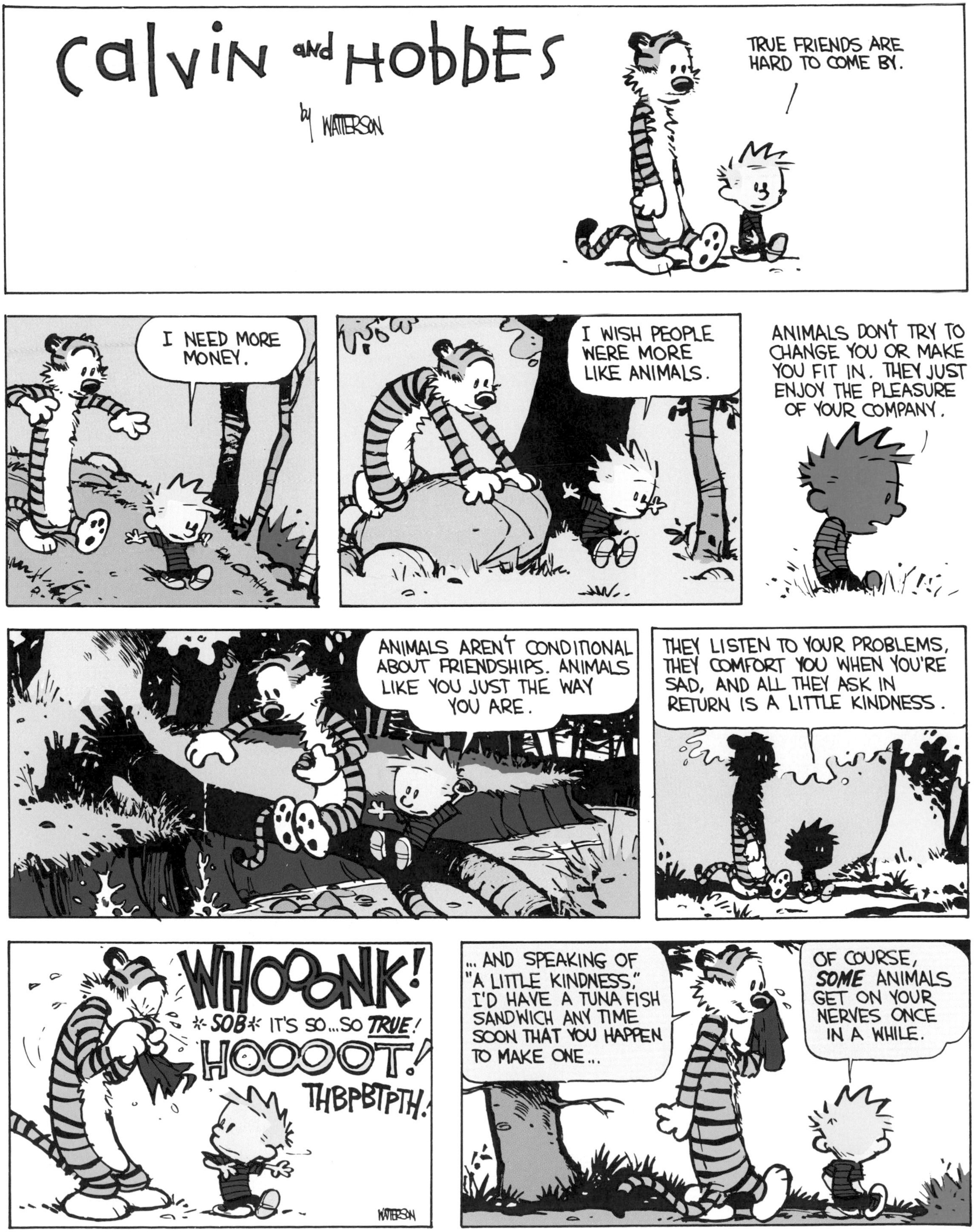
Calvin and HobbEs
by WATTERSON
TRUE FRIENDS ARE HARD TO COME BY.
I NEED MORE MONEY.
I WISH PEOPLE WERE MORE LIKE ANIMALS.
ANIMALS DON'T TRY TO CHANGE YOU OR MAKE YOU FIT IN. THEY JUST ENJOY THE PLEASURE OF YOUR COMPANY.
ANIMALS AREN'T CONDITIONAL ABOUT FRIENDSHIPS. ANIMALS LIKE YOU JUST THE WAY YOU ARE.
THEY LISTEN TO YOUR PROBLEMS, THEY COMFORT YOU WHEN YOU'RE SAD, AND ALL THEY ASK IN RETURN IS A LITTLE KINDNESS.
WHOOONK!
SOB IT'S SO...SO TRUE!
HOOOOT!
THBPBTPTH!
WATTERSON
...AND SPEAKING OF "A LITTLE KINDNESS," I'D HAVE A TUNA FISH SANDWICH ANY TIME SOON THAT YOU HAPPEN TO MAKE ONE...
OF COURSE, SOME ANIMALS GET ON YOUR NERVES ONCE IN A WHILE.

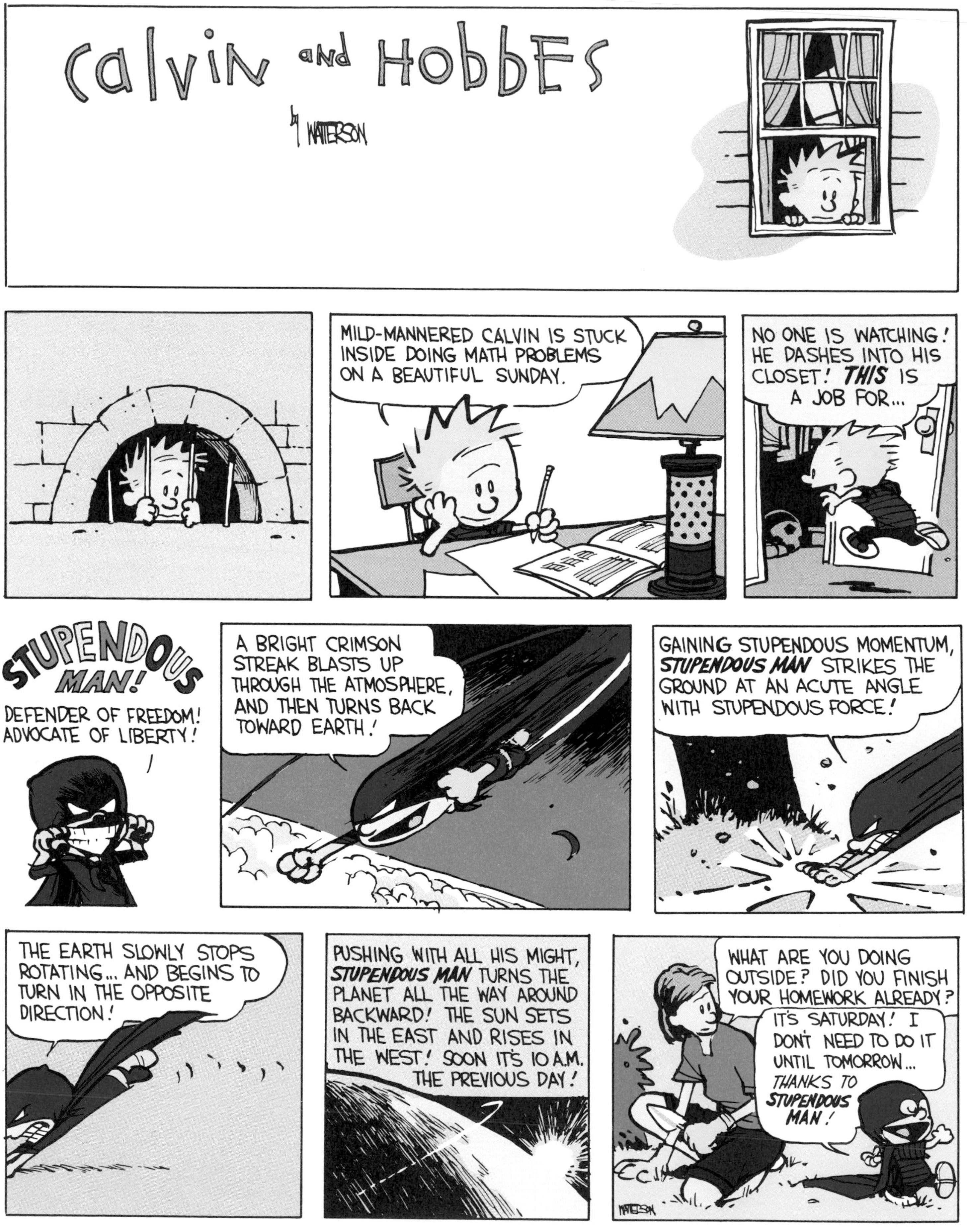
Calvin and HobbEs
by WATTERSON
MILD-MANNERED CALVIN IS STUCK INSIDE DOING MATH PROBLEMS ON A BEAUTIFUL SUNDAY.
NO ONE IS WATCHING! HE DASHES INTO HIS CLOSET! THIS IS A JOB FOR...
STUPENDOUS MAN!
DEFENDER OF FREEDOM! ADVOCATE OF LIBERTY!
A BRIGHT CRIMSON STREAK BLASTS UP THROUGH THE ATMOSPHERE, AND THEN TURNS BACK TOWARD EARTH!
GAINING STUPENDOUS MOMENTUM, STUPENDOUS MAN STRIKES THE GROUND AT AN ACUTE ANGLE WITH STUPENDOUS FORCE!
THE EARTH SLOWLY STOPS ROTATING... AND BEGINS TO TURN IN THE OPPOSITE DIRECTION!
PUSHING WITH ALL HIS MIGHT, STUPENDOUS MAN TURNS THE PLANET ALL THE WAY AROUND BACKWARD! THE SUN SETS IN THE EAST AND RISES IN THE WEST! SOON IT'S 10 A.M. THE PREVIOUS DAY!
WHAT ARE YOU DOING OUTSIDE? DID YOU FINISH YOUR HOMEWORK ALREADY?
IT'S SATURDAY! I DON'T NEED TO DO IT UNTIL TOMORROW... THANKS TO STUPENDOUS MAN!
WATTERSON

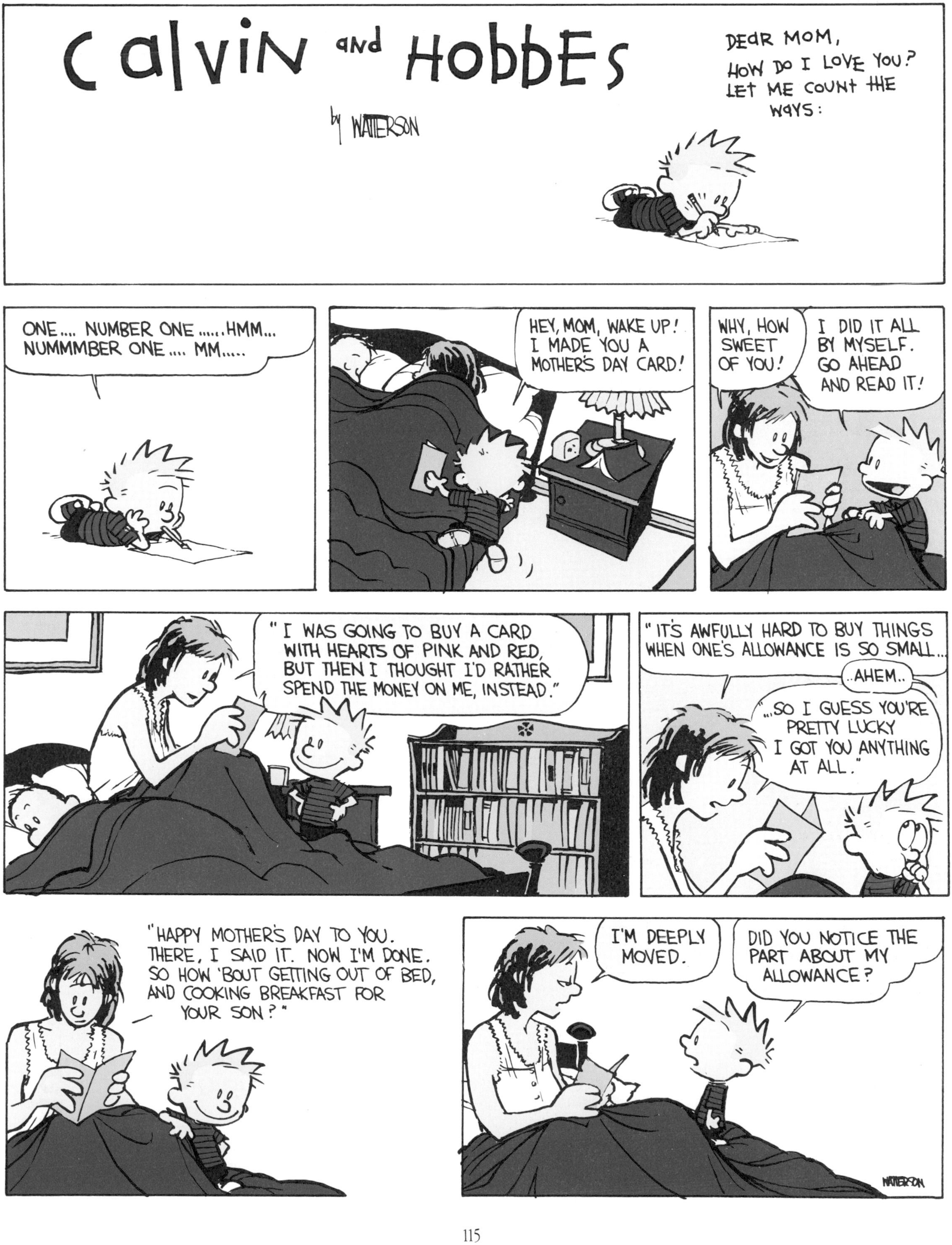
Calvin and HOBBES
by WATTERSON
DEAR MOM,
HOW DO I LOVE YOU? LET ME COUNT THE WAYS:
ONE.... NUMBER ONE......HMM... NUMMMBER ONE..... MM.....
HEY, MOM, WAKE UP! I MADE YOU A MOTHER'S DAY CARD!
WHY, HOW SWEET OF YOU!
I DID IT ALL BY MYSELF. GO AHEAD AND READ IT!
"I WAS GOING TO BUY A CARD WITH HEARTS OF PINK AND RED, BUT THEN I THOUGHT I'D RATHER SPEND THE MONEY ON ME, INSTEAD."
"IT'S AWFULLY HARD TO BUY THINGS WHEN ONE'S ALLOWANCE IS SO SMALL...
..AHEM..
...SO I GUESS YOU'RE PRETTY LUCKY I GOT YOU ANYTHING AT ALL."
"HAPPY MOTHER'S DAY TO YOU. THERE, I SAID IT. NOW I'M DONE. SO HOW 'BOUT GETTING OUT OF BED, AND COOKING BREAKFAST FOR YOUR SON?"
I'M DEEPLY MOVED.
DID YOU NOTICE THE PART ABOUT MY ALLOWANCE?
WATTERSON

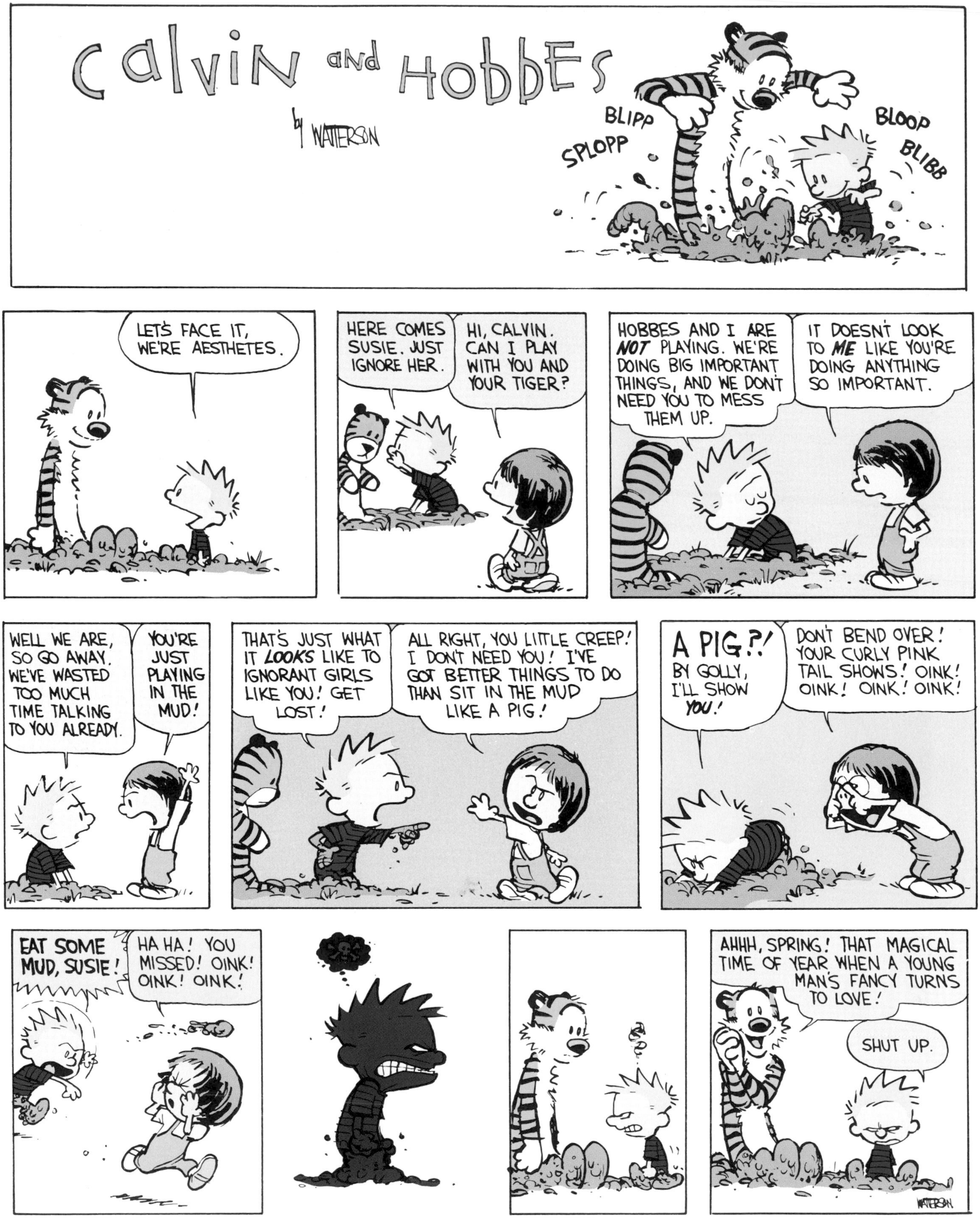
Calvin and HOBBES
by WATTERSON
BLIPP
SPLOPP
BLOOP
BLIBB
LET'S FACE IT, WE'RE AESTHETES.
HERE COMES SUSIE. JUST IGNORE HER.
HI, CALVIN. CAN I PLAY WITH YOU AND YOUR TIGER?
HOBBES AND I ARE NOT PLAYING. WE'RE DOING BIG IMPORTANT THINGS, AND WE DON'T NEED YOU TO MESS THEM UP.
IT DOESN'T LOOK TO ME LIKE YOU'RE DOING ANYTHING SO IMPORTANT.
WELL WE ARE, SO GO AWAY. WE'VE WASTED TOO MUCH TIME TALKING TO YOU ALREADY.
YOU'RE JUST PLAYING IN THE MUD!
THAT'S JUST WHAT IT LOOKS LIKE TO IGNORANT GIRLS LIKE YOU! GET LOST!
ALL RIGHT, YOU LITTLE CREEP! I DON'T NEED YOU! I'VE GOT BETTER THINGS TO DO THAN SIT IN THE MUD LIKE A PIG!
A PIG?! BY GOLLY, I'LL SHOW YOU!
DON'T BEND OVER! YOUR CURLY PINK TAIL SHOWS! OINK! OINK! OINK! OINK!
EAT SOME MUD, SUSIE!
HA HA! YOU MISSED! OINK! OINK! OINK!
AHHH, SPRING! THAT MAGICAL TIME OF YEAR WHEN A YOUNG MAN'S FANCY TURNS TO LOVE!
SHUT UP.
WATTERSON

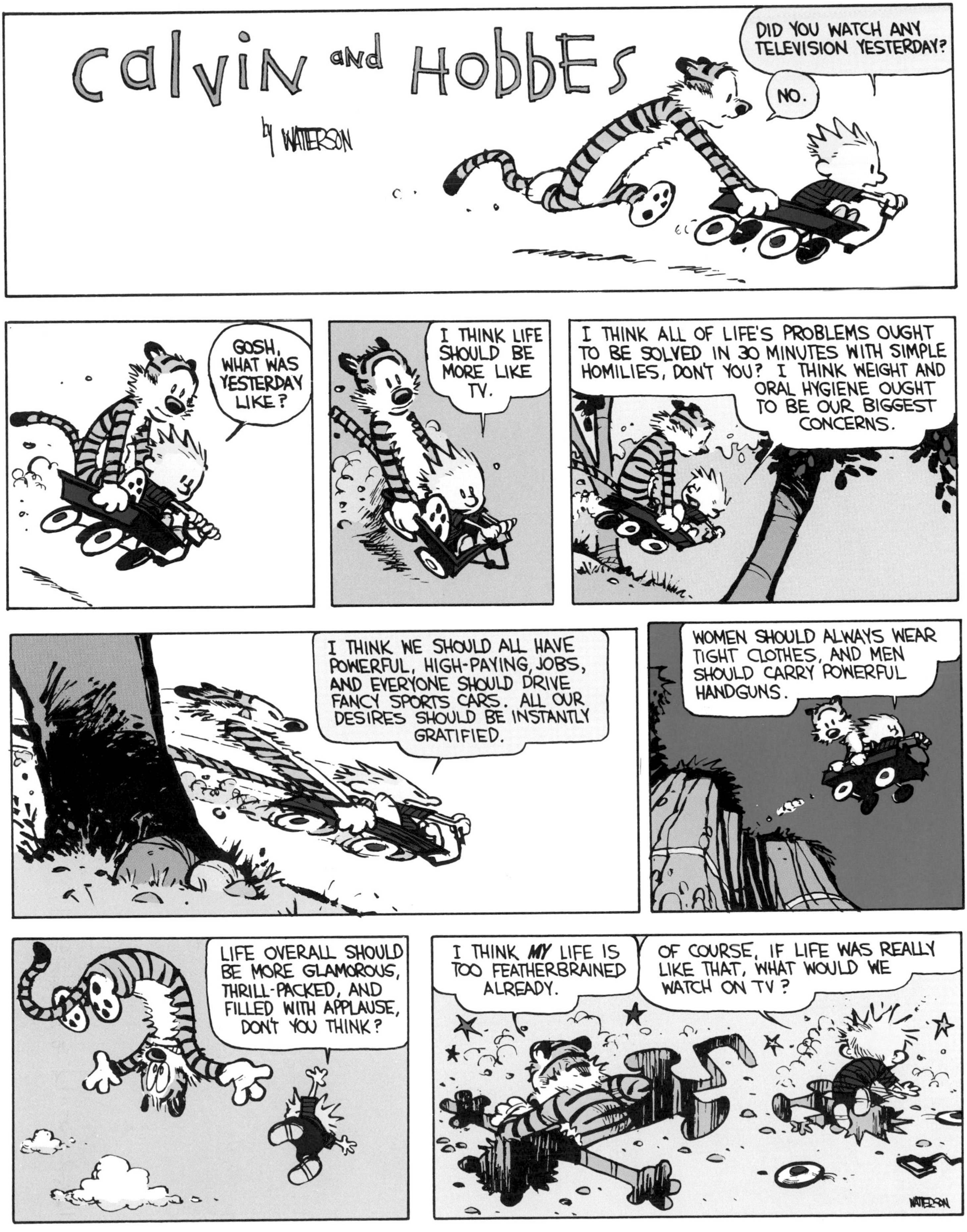
Calvin and HOBBES
by WATTERSON
DID YOU WATCH ANY TELEVISION YESTERDAY?
NO.
GOSH, WHAT WAS YESTERDAY LIKE?
I THINK LIFE SHOULD BE MORE LIKE TV.
I THINK ALL OF LIFE'S PROBLEMS OUGHT TO BE SOLVED IN 30 MINUTES WITH SIMPLE HOMILIES, DON'T YOU? I THINK WEIGHT AND ORAL HYGIENE OUGHT TO BE OUR BIGGEST CONCERNS.
I THINK WE SHOULD ALL HAVE POWERFUL, HIGH-PAYING JOBS, AND EVERYONE SHOULD DRIVE FANCY SPORTS CARS. ALL OUR DESIRES SHOULD BE INSTANTLY GRATIFIED.
WOMEN SHOULD ALWAYS WEAR TIGHT CLOTHES, AND MEN SHOULD CARRY POWERFUL HANDGUNS.
LIFE OVERALL SHOULD BE MORE GLAMOROUS, THRILL-PACKED, AND FILLED WITH APPLAUSE, DON'T YOU THINK?
I THINK *MY* LIFE IS TOO FEATHERBRAINED ALREADY.
OF COURSE, IF LIFE WAS REALLY LIKE THAT, WHAT WOULD WE WATCH ON TV?
WATTERSON

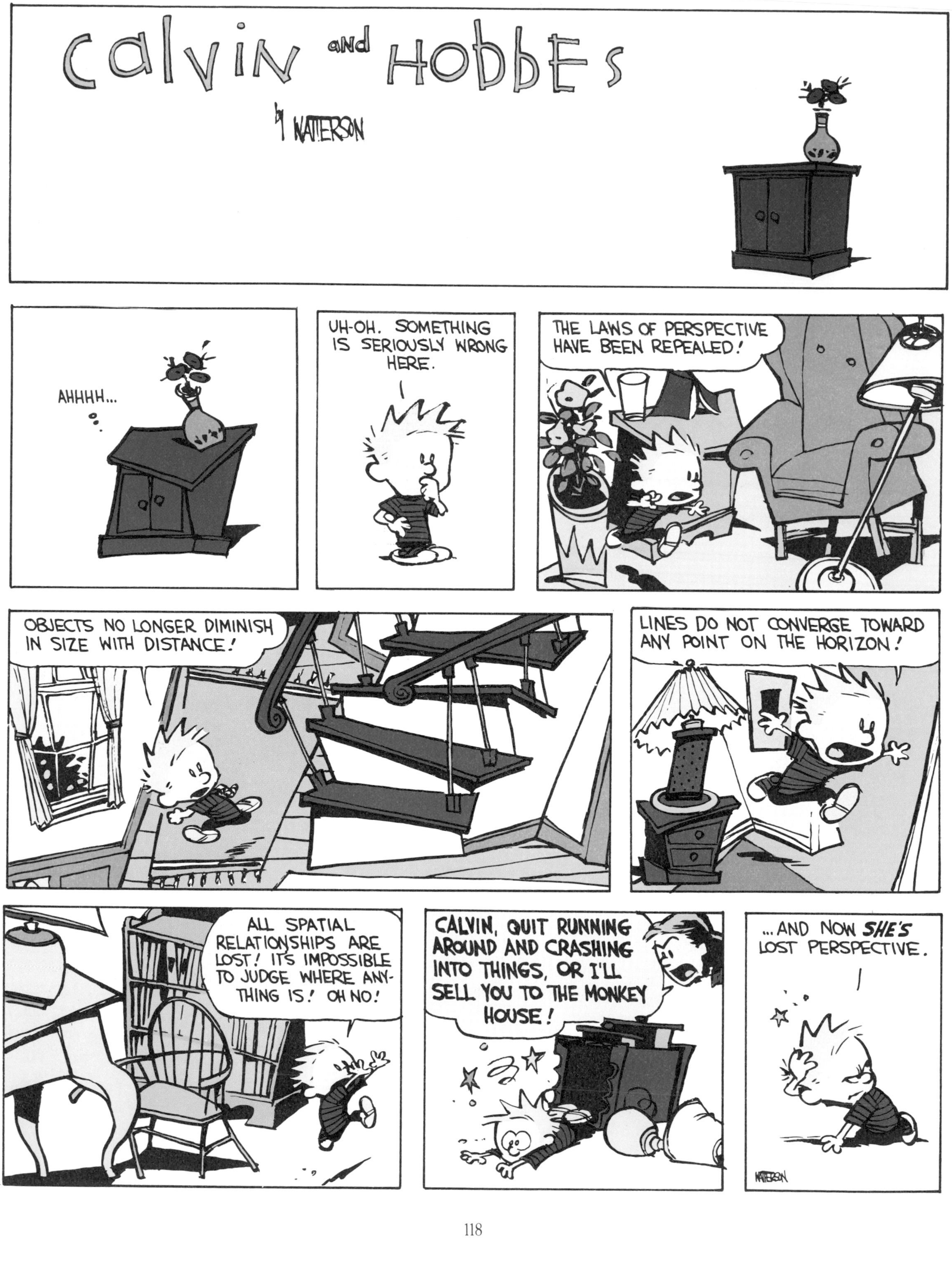
Calvin and HOBBES
by WATTERSON
AHHHH...
UH-OH. SOMETHING IS SERIOUSLY WRONG HERE.
THE LAWS OF PERSPECTIVE HAVE BEEN REPEALED!
OBJECTS NO LONGER DIMINISH IN SIZE WITH DISTANCE!
LINES DO NOT CONVERGE TOWARD ANY POINT ON THE HORIZON!
ALL SPATIAL RELATIONSHIPS ARE LOST! ITS IMPOSSIBLE TO JUDGE WHERE ANYTHING IS! OH NO!
CALVIN, QUIT RUNNING AROUND AND CRASHING INTO THINGS, OR I'LL SELL YOU TO THE MONKEY HOUSE!
...AND NOW SHE'S LOST PERSPECTIVE.
WATTERSON

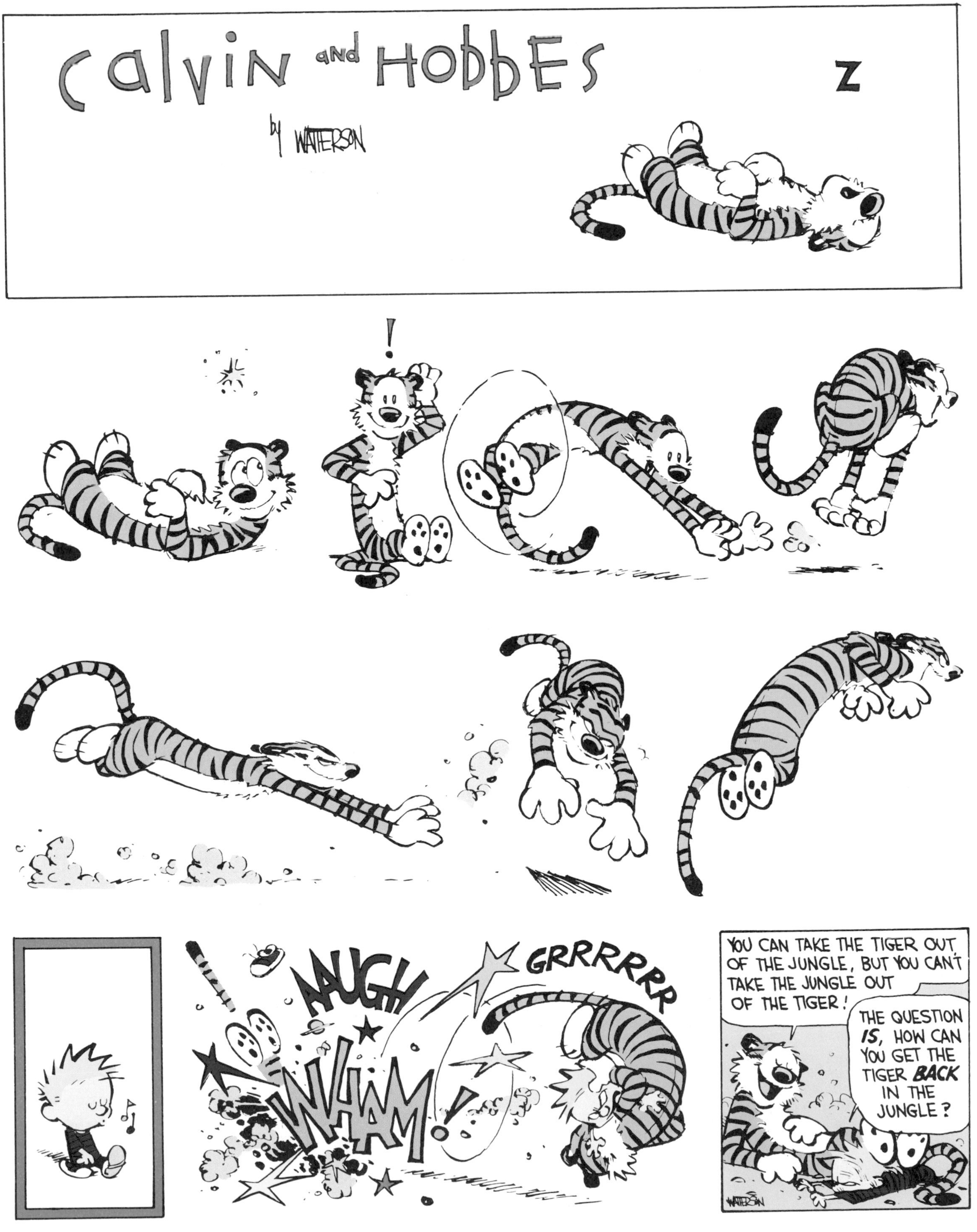
Calvin and HOBBES
by WATTERSON
Z
!
!
AAUGH
WHAM!
GRRRRRR
YOU CAN TAKE THE TIGER OUT OF THE JUNGLE, BUT YOU CAN'T TAKE THE JUNGLE OUT OF THE TIGER!
THE QUESTION *IS,* HOW CAN YOU GET THE TIGER *BACK* IN THE JUNGLE?
WATTERSON

CALVIN AND HOBBES

by WATTERSON

DO RE MI FA SO LA TI DO

A SPARROW ALIGHTS UPON A TREE BRANCH.

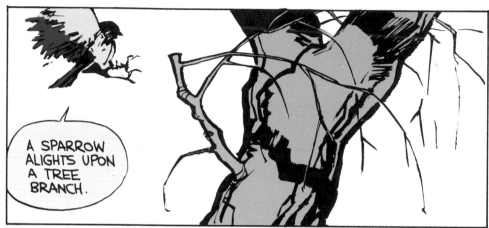

BUT THIS IS NO *ORDINARY* SPARROW! THIS IS A *SONG* SPARROW!

SWAYING GENTLY IN THE BREEZE, HE PREPARES TO BURST FORTH IN RAPTUROUS MELODY!

ON TOP OF SPA-GHETTI

ALL COVERED WITH CHEEEESE, I LOST MY POOR MEEEATBALLL, WHEN...

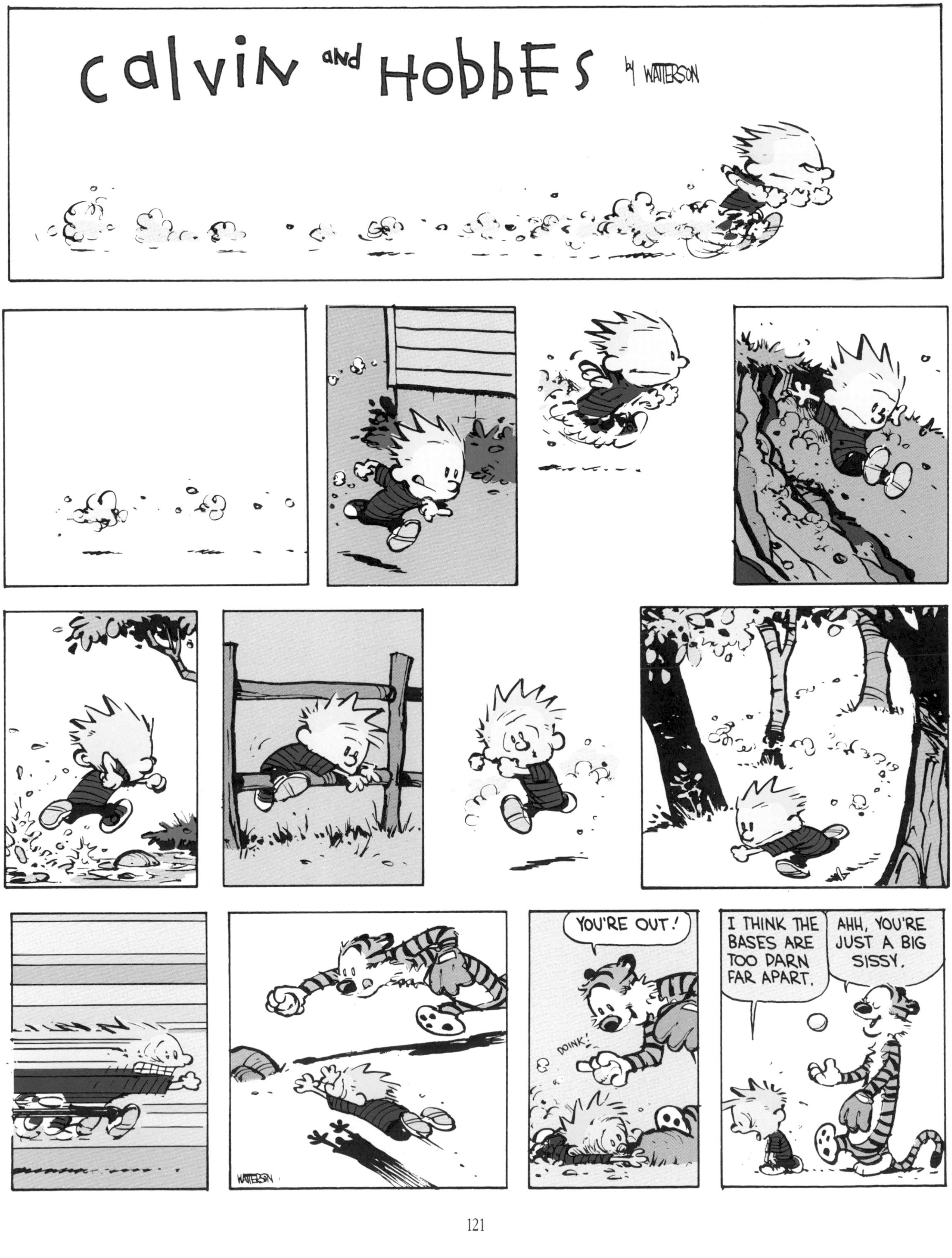

Calvin and Hobbes
by WATTERSON
DOINK!
YOU'RE OUT!
I THINK THE BASES ARE TOO DARN FAR APART.
AHH, YOU'RE JUST A BIG SISSY.
WATTERSON

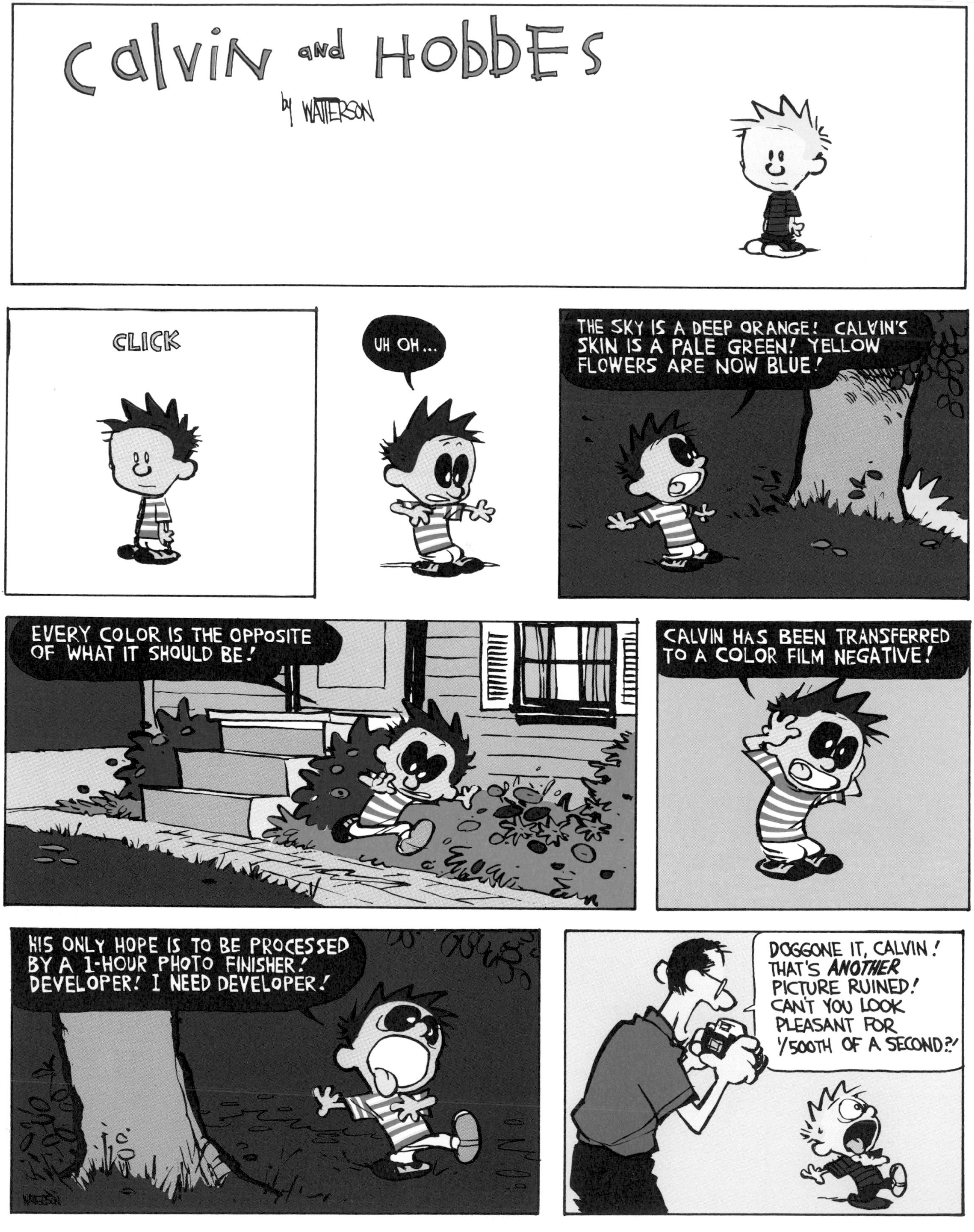
Calvin and HOBBES
by WATTERSON
CLICK
UH OH...
THE SKY IS A DEEP ORANGE! CALVIN'S SKIN IS A PALE GREEN! YELLOW FLOWERS ARE NOW BLUE!
EVERY COLOR IS THE OPPOSITE OF WHAT IT SHOULD BE!
CALVIN HAS BEEN TRANSFERRED TO A COLOR FILM NEGATIVE!
HIS ONLY HOPE IS TO BE PROCESSED BY A 1-HOUR PHOTO FINISHER! DEVELOPER! I NEED DEVELOPER!
DOGGONE IT, CALVIN! THAT'S ANOTHER PICTURE RUINED! CAN'T YOU LOOK PLEASANT FOR 1/500TH OF A SECOND?!

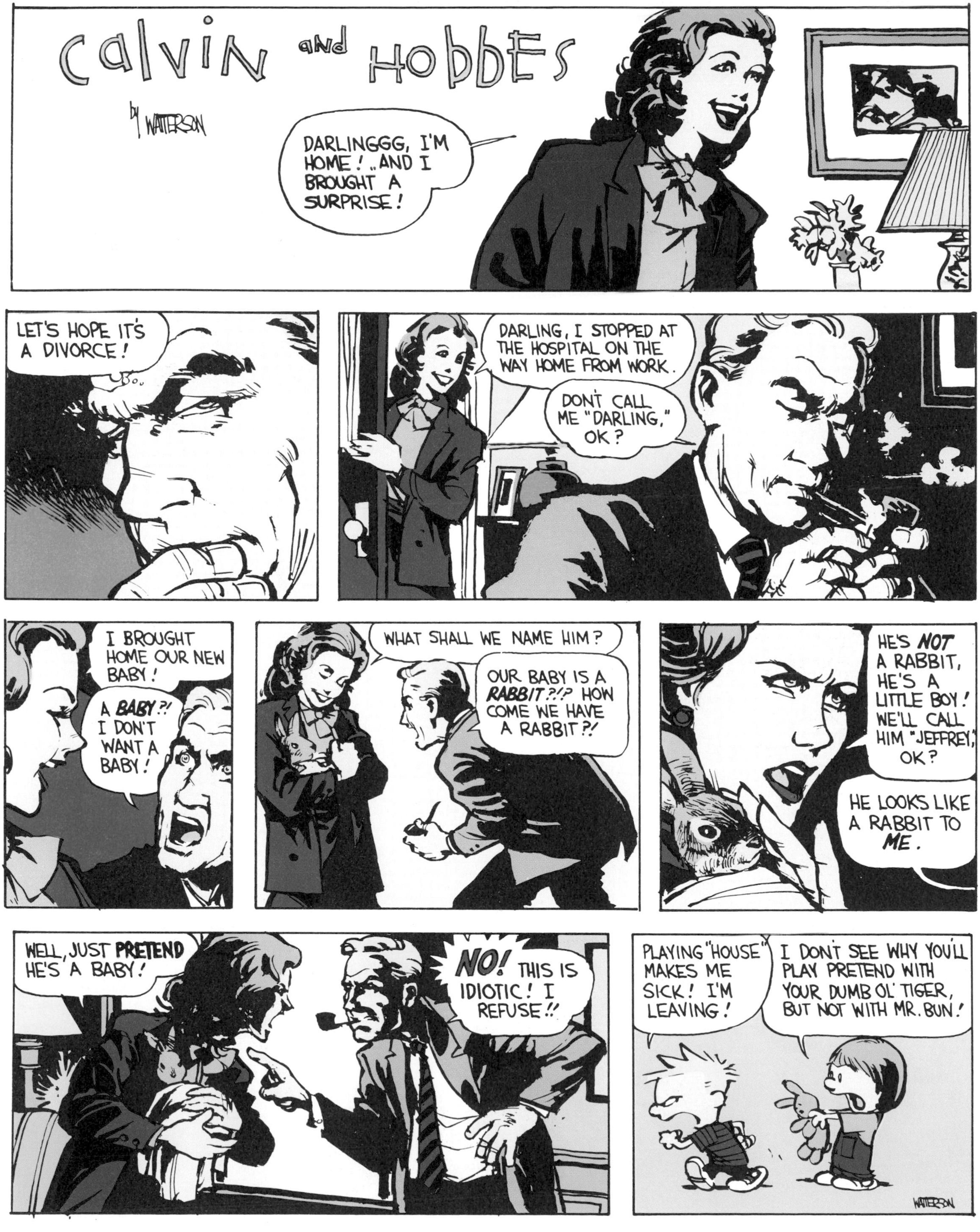
Calvin and Hobbes
by WATTERSON
DARLINGGG, I'M HOME! ..AND I BROUGHT A SURPRISE!
LET'S HOPE IT'S A DIVORCE!
DARLING, I STOPPED AT THE HOSPITAL ON THE WAY HOME FROM WORK.
DON'T CALL ME "DARLING," OK?
I BROUGHT HOME OUR NEW BABY!
A BABY?! I DON'T WANT A BABY!
WHAT SHALL WE NAME HIM?
OUR BABY IS A RABBIT?!? HOW COME WE HAVE A RABBIT?!
HE'S NOT A RABBIT, HE'S A LITTLE BOY! WE'LL CALL HIM "JEFFREY," OK?
HE LOOKS LIKE A RABBIT TO ME.
WELL, JUST PRETEND HE'S A BABY!
NO! THIS IS IDIOTIC! I REFUSE!!
PLAYING "HOUSE" MAKES ME SICK! I'M LEAVING!
I DON'T SEE WHY YOU'LL PLAY PRETEND WITH YOUR DUMB OL' TIGER, BUT NOT WITH MR. BUN!
WATTERSON

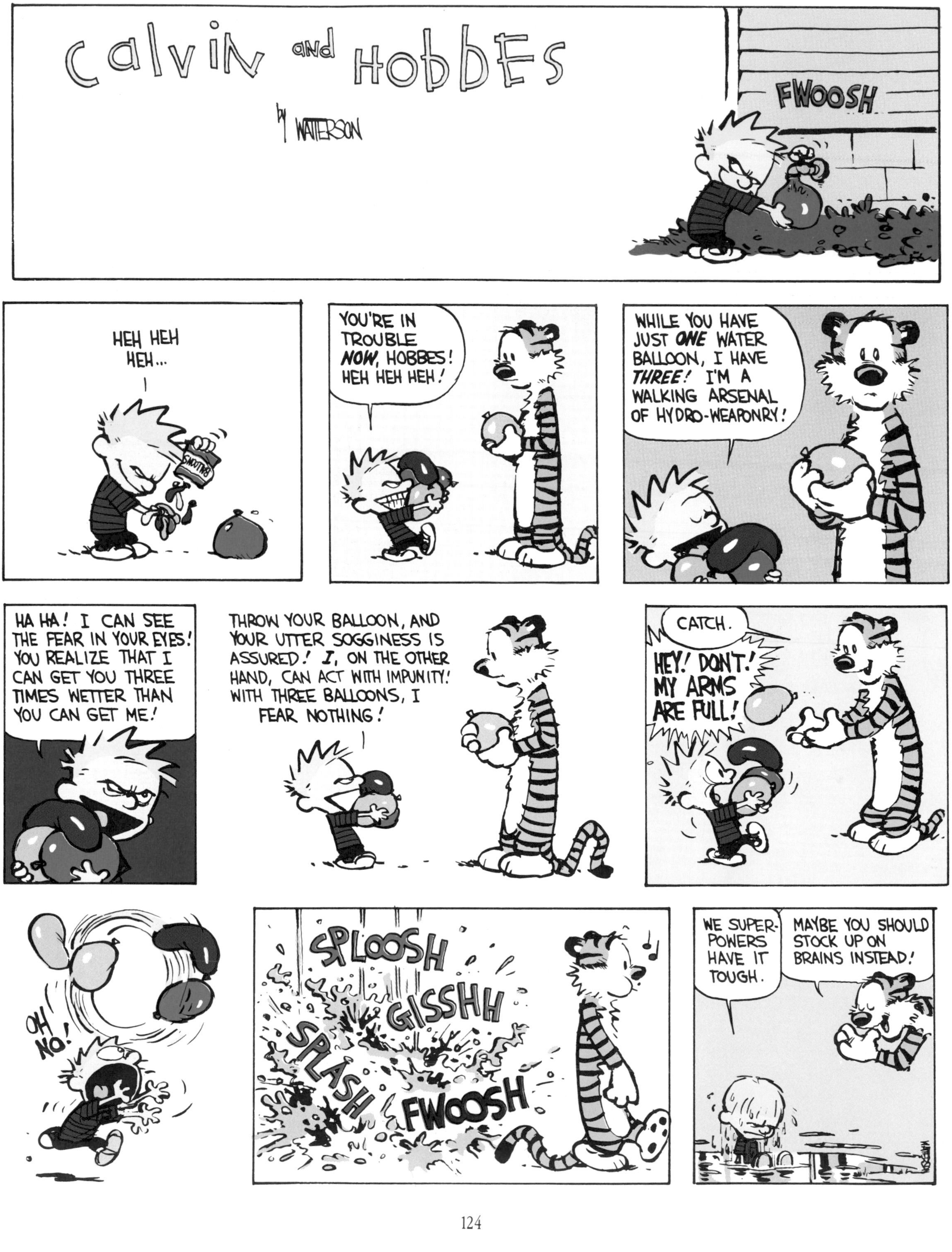

Calvin and HOBBES
by WATTERSON
FWOOSH
HEH HEH HEH...
YOU'RE IN TROUBLE NOW, HOBBES! HEH HEH HEH!
WHILE YOU HAVE JUST ONE WATER BALLOON, I HAVE THREE! I'M A WALKING ARSENAL OF HYDRO-WEAPONRY!
HA HA! I CAN SEE THE FEAR IN YOUR EYES! YOU REALIZE THAT I CAN GET YOU THREE TIMES WETTER THAN YOU CAN GET ME!
THROW YOUR BALLOON, AND YOUR UTTER SOGGINESS IS ASSURED! I, ON THE OTHER HAND, CAN ACT WITH IMPUNITY! WITH THREE BALLOONS, I FEAR NOTHING!
CATCH.
HEY! DON'T! MY ARMS ARE FULL!
OH NO!
SPLOOSH
GISSHH
SPLASH
FWOOSH
WE SUPER-POWERS HAVE IT TOUGH.
MAYBE YOU SHOULD STOCK UP ON BRAINS INSTEAD!

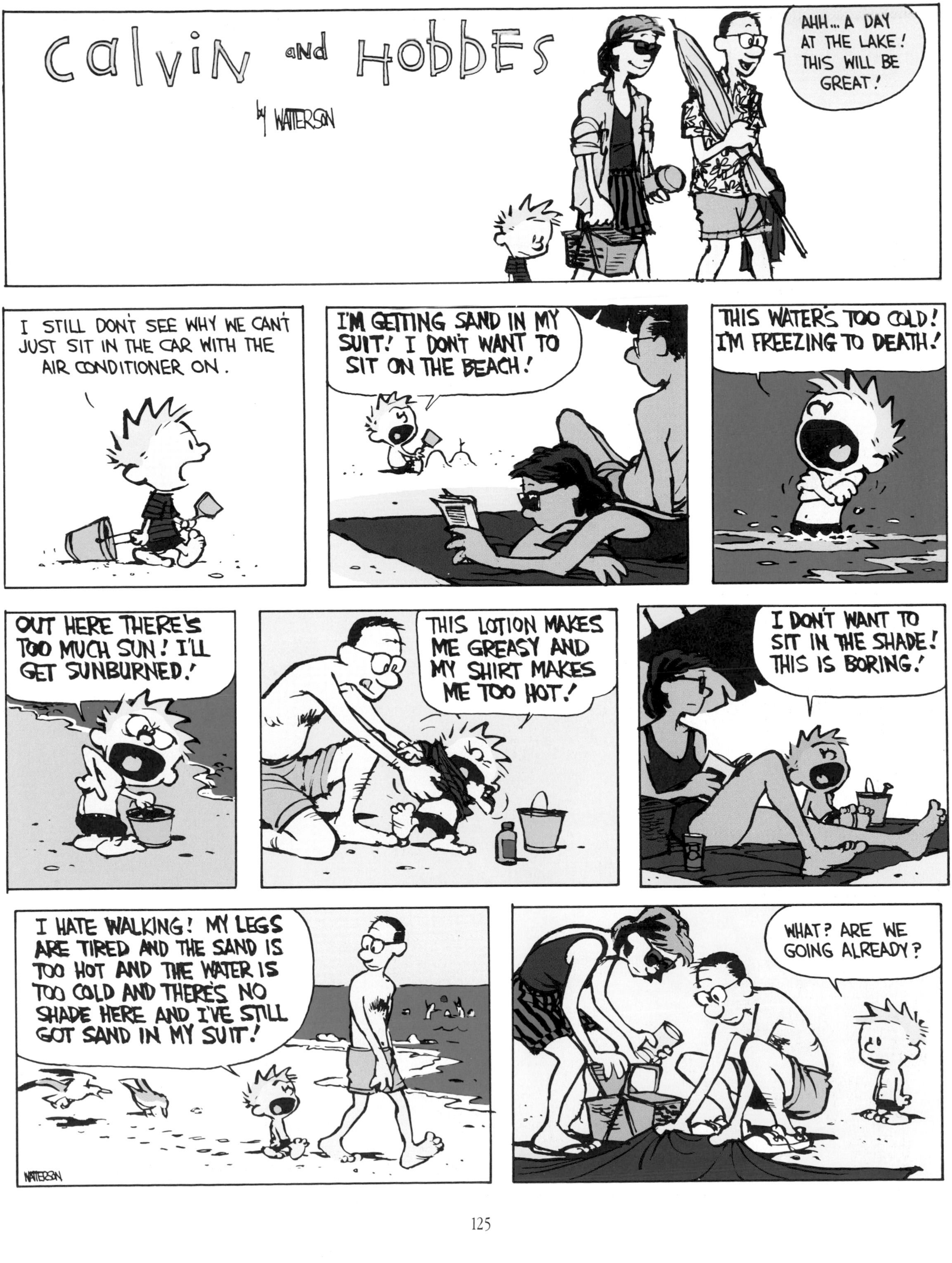
Calvin and Hobbes
by WATTERSON
AHH... A DAY AT THE LAKE! THIS WILL BE GREAT!
I STILL DON'T SEE WHY WE CAN'T JUST SIT IN THE CAR WITH THE AIR CONDITIONER ON.
I'M GETTING SAND IN MY SUIT! I DON'T WANT TO SIT ON THE BEACH!
THIS WATER'S TOO COLD! I'M FREEZING TO DEATH!
OUT HERE THERE'S TOO MUCH SUN! I'LL GET SUNBURNED!
THIS LOTION MAKES ME GREASY AND MY SHIRT MAKES ME TOO HOT!
I DON'T WANT TO SIT IN THE SHADE! THIS IS BORING!
I HATE WALKING! MY LEGS ARE TIRED AND THE SAND IS TOO HOT AND THE WATER IS TOO COLD AND THERE'S NO SHADE HERE AND I'VE STILL GOT SAND IN MY SUIT!
WATTERSON
WHAT? ARE WE GOING ALREADY?

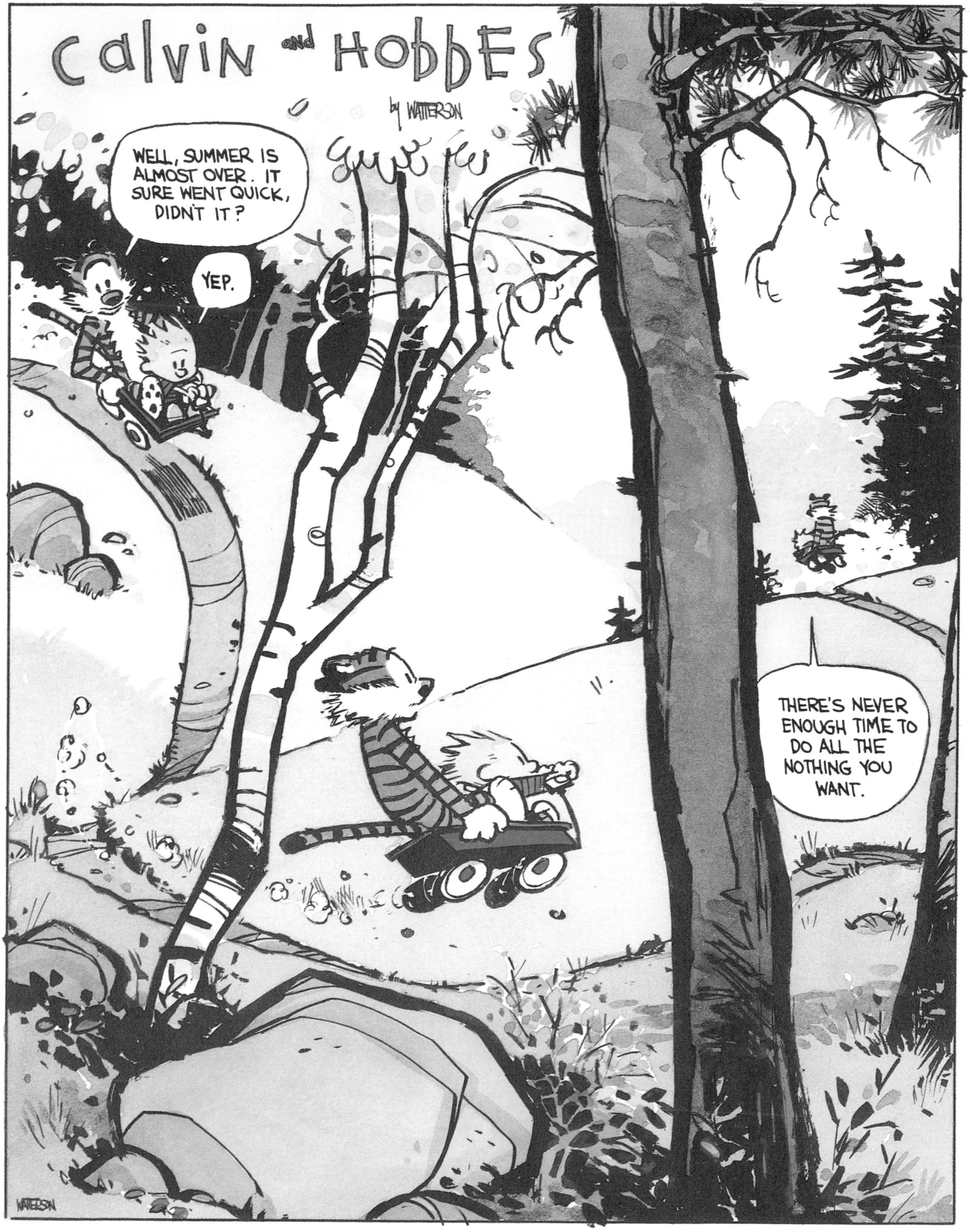
Calvin and HOBBES
by WATTERSON
WELL, SUMMER IS ALMOST OVER. IT SURE WENT QUICK, DIDN'T IT?
YEP.
THERE'S NEVER ENOUGH TIME TO DO ALL THE NOTHING YOU WANT.
WATTERSON

AFTERWORD

Long ago the Sunday comics were printed the size of an entire newspaper page. Each comic was like a color poster. Not surprisingly, with all that space to fill, cartoonists produced works of incredible beauty and power that we just don't see anymore, now that strips are a third or a quarter of their former size. Whereas Little Nemo could dream through 15 surreal panels back in the early part of the century, today it's rare to see a Sunday strip with more than six panels—especially if the characters move. All the things that make comics fun to read—the stories, the dialogue, the pictures—have gotten simpler and simpler in order to keep the work legible at smaller and smaller sizes. The art form has been in a process of retrograde evolution for decades. For those of us trying to return some of the childhood fun we had marveling at comic drawings, the opportunities today are discouraging.

Cartoons can be much more than we've been seeing lately. How much more will depend on what newspaper readers will demand. One thing, though, is certain: little boys, like tigers, will roam all the territory they can get.

—BILL WATTERSON

The End